ROBERT E. LEE'S CIVIL WAR

ROBERT E. LEE'S CIVIL WAR

BEVIN ALEXANDER

Adams Media Corporation
Avon, Massachusetts

Published by
Adams Media, an F+W Publications Company
57 Littlefield Street, Avon, MA 02322
www.adamsmedia.com

ISBN: 1-58062-135-X (paperback)

Printed in the United States of America.

J I H G F E D

Library of Congress Cataloging-in-Publication Data
Alexander, Bevin.
Robert E. Lee's Civil War / Bevin Alexander. — 1st ed.
p.   cm.
ISBN 1-58062-135-X (paperback)
1-55850-849-X (hardcover)
1. Lee, Robert E. (Robert Edward), 1807–1870—Military leadership. 2.
United States—History—Civil War, 1861–1865—Campaigns. 3.
Strategy—History—19th century. I. Title.
E457.1.L4A72   1998
973.7'3013—dc21   97–43148
                                    CIP

Maps by Jeffrey L. Ward.

*This book is available at quantity discounts for bulk purchases.
For information, call 1-800-872-5627.*

CONTENTS

(NATIONAL ARCHIVES)

Robert E. Lee

INTRODUCTION

Robert E. Lee occupies a special place in the American pantheon. He fought against the United States but is an American hero. Lee's fame comes from his actions as commander of the Confederate Army of Northern Virginia in the Civil War. His generalship permitted this army to hold off the main strength of the immensely more powerful Union from June 1, 1862, when he took command, until April 9, 1865, when he surrendered at Appomattox.

This record of leadership and the inspiration and determination to perform against incredible odds which he aroused in his men encouraged people everywhere, but especially in the South, to elevate Lee into a military genius. At the same time, Lee's personal attributes caused most Americans to see him as a beau ideal, incorporating practically all of the elements Americans value in human character—loyalty, integrity, compassion, charity, honor, dedication to a cause, sense of duty, and courage.

This book is concerned with Lee's actions as a military commander, and deals with Lee's magnificent human attributes only as they related to his generalship. However, the book does address briefly at its close another, less well-known, contribution of Robert E. Lee which commenced at Appomattox and guided the remainder of his life.

This contribution emerged from Lee's realization that the Civil War had convinced the Southern people that slavery was wrong. Lee told Union general Ulysses S. Grant at Appomattox that the South now was as opposed to human bondage as the North. Lee at once recognized that this removed the *only* fundamental issue dividing North and South. There was now no reason remaining for the South to want independence.

As a result, Lee urged his soldiers to be as good citizens of a united nation as they had been good soldiers in war. Coming from Lee, the most revered and admired man in the South in 1865, this admonition had immense and lasting power. It removed much of the rancor and animosity that affected many people, and caused them to think of cooperation with the North, not continued resistance to the North.

Lee, sooner than any other American leader, recognized that the people of the North and the South shared identical ideals and aspirations. He also saw that he, and perhaps he alone, had the trust of the Southern people to the degree that they would heed his calls to rejoin the nation as faithful, dedicated citizens.

From Appomattox until he died in 1870, Lee devoted himself to the reconciliation of the two sections of the country. He became president of Washington College in Lexington, Virginia, now Washington and Lee University, and commenced a conscious program of educating a new generation of Southerners to be patriotic, loyal citizens of a once-more-united nation.

Lee did more than any other American to make this reconciliation come about. For this, he should be honored by future generations.

However, Lee's place in history rests on his performance as a military leader. That is the principal subject of this book. It argues that Lee's high military reputation deserves a complete reappraisal.

Lee's soldiers revered him because of his personal attributes and his dedication, but also because the Confederacy held out so long against a Union with three times the population and eleven times the industrial strength of the South. It was apparent to his soldiers that Lee was superior to the Union commanders he faced.

However, it was only after the war that Lee was acclaimed as a general without fault. The defeated South desperately sought to find some purpose for the enormous losses in lives and treasure it had suffered. It was natural to rationalize the Confederacy's defeat as the inevitable result of overwhelming odds, and to conclude that Lee, who had held off the North for so long, had to have been a great general.

There are two errors in this reasoning. The years taken to defeat the South can just as well be ascribed to the missteps and blunders of Union commanders as to the genius of Robert E. Lee. And, most important, the North was not bound to win, whatever its strength. There is nothing preordained about military conquest. The size, power, and wealth of a state do not guarantee it success. Alexander the Great's Macedonia was poor and puny compared to the great Persian Empire it destroyed. Hannibal Barca's Carthaginian army was small and ill-supplied, yet defeated Rome's immensely larger, well-supported legions for seventeen years.

It was not the states Alexander and Hannibal represented or the armed men they led that made them great. It was the brilliance of the generals themselves that transformed their modest forces into conquering armies. These examples offer an argument that, if the Confederacy had indeed possessed a military genius in command of its principal army, it could have been victorious irrespective of the North's material superiority.

The key to understanding Lee as a commander is that he sought from first to last to fight an offensive war—that is, a war of battles and marches against the armies of the North. This offensive war, though it produced many spectacular clashes and campaigns which arouse fascination to this day, ultimately failed because Lee's methods and his strategy were insufficient to overcome the South's weakness in arms and manpower.

Lee endeavored to avoid the defensive war that President Jefferson Davis wanted to conduct. Davis was little interested in winning battlefield victories. His principal aim was to keep the Union from winning, in the hope that the Northern people would become weary and grant the South its independence.

Davis weakened his strategy by scattering military forces throughout the South to shield nonvital regions or protect against small-scale Union incursions from the sea. These attacks could not

(NATIONAL ARCHIVES)

Jefferson Davis

be decisive, but large numbers of Confederate troops were sent to contain the landings or to protect territory that was not essential. Davis refused to concentrate strength into two extremely powerful armies, one in Virginia and another northwest of Chattanooga, which could have prevented the penetration of Northern armies into the heart of the South.

Even without two huge armies guarding the portals, a defensive strategy would have exploited the South's advantages: its great size; its difficult mountains, forests, and swamps; and the practical inaccessibility of much of its territory owing to an inadequate railway system. These could have inhibited Northern movements into the South, and allowed the Confederacy to pursue a long war, preserving its other, more limited resources, especially its manpower. In time the North might have become weary of its inability to end the war and stop losses. Ironically, this is how the Communists defeated the United States in Vietnam. The American people at last became so disillusioned that they demanded the withdrawal of their forces.

Although Lee did not want to fight a defensive war, he was in fact far more gifted in conducting one than he was in fighting offensively. His 1864 campaign in Virginia was one of the most brilliant holding actions in military history. Though he commanded an army with only a shadow of its former power, Lee neutralized the attacks of Ulysses S. Grant, destroyed half of Grant's army, forced the Federals into a stalemate in front of Petersburg, and permitted the Confederacy to survive into 1865.

If Lee had embarked on such a defensive strategy from the outset, while he still had strength to make temporary strikes to keep

Federal armies from penetrating into Virginia, the North might have been stymied and might have agreed to a negotiated peace.

Although Lee thought in offensive terms, he did not truly understand offensive warfare. Like the majority of generals on both sides, Lee believed he could win by striking at the enemy directly in his path.

History had shown that this was not true, except in unusual cases. But the idea had gained doctrinal status because scholars studying Napoleon Bonaparte thought the great master had won his battles by bringing superior force against some decisive point of the enemy. While this was strictly true, it missed the subtleties of Napoleon's genius. Napoleon in fact had succeeded in his earlier campaigns by maneuver and surprise, and had won his later battles by breaking a hole in the enemy's line with canister—or a lethal cloud of metal balls or fragments—fired by massed batteries of artillery.

This latter solution was not available to the generals in the Civil War. Infantry now were armed with the Minié-ball rifle, which possessed a range greater than the effective range of canister. Cannons no longer could be rolled up close enough to shatter an enemy line, because sharpshooters could pick off gunners and horses before the guns could do much damage.

Since the Minié-ball rifle also had a range four times that of the infantry smoothbore musket used in Napoleon's day, direct attacks were almost certain to fail against resolute troops, and, in fact, did fail five out of six times.

Lee never understood the revolution that the Minié ball had brought to battle tactics. However, two of his senior lieutenants, Stonewall Jackson and James Longstreet, did. They came up with an antidote to direct assaults—a defensive posture—and urged this policy upon Lee.

Jackson saw in addition that, since Union forces were likely to fail with great losses if they attacked Confederate positions, the South should induce the Union commanders to make such attacks. Confederate forces then might swing around the flanks of the demoralized Union soldiers, cut off their retreat and line of supply, and force them to surrender.

Thomas J. "Stonewall" Jackson *James Longstreet*

Although Lee accepted Jackson's argument in principle, he failed to carry it out in a timely fashion at Second Manassas in August 1862, and lacked space on his flank to undertake it at Antietam the following month. On only one occasion did the strategy work in part—at Chancellorsville in May 1863—and there it failed to destroy the Union army, because Jackson was mortally wounded.

Thereafter, Lee returned to his earlier practice of frontal assaults into the heart of enemy resistance. In nearly all cases, they failed.

This tendency to move to the direct confrontation, regardless of the prospects or the losses that would be sustained, guaranteed Lee's failure as an offensive commander.

None of Lee's victories resulted in the destruction of a Federal army, and none caused so many losses that the North was induced to quit. Both Lee's victories and defeats produced such heavy casualties that the South was bled white in only a year of battle, from the Seven Days in June–July 1862 to Gettysburg in July 1863. These losses destroyed the offensive power of the Confederacy, and foreshadowed the South's defeat.

Nevertheless, Robert E. Lee was so superior as a military commander to the leaders of the North that the Confederacy's inherent weaknesses were not apparent until nearly the end of the war. Time after time—not by greater power but by aggressive action and movements forcefully and confidently carried out—Lee defeated or neutralized superior Union forces.

The North never actually conquered Lee. The Civil War is nearly unique in military history in that a single man, Lee, by determination and resolve, was able to stymie over a period of years the greatest efforts of an extremely powerful state, the Union.

The North wore down Lee's army only after grueling, agonizing, deadly marches and maneuvers, by desperate attacks, and by even more desperate defenses. The Northern Army of the Potomac never won a decisive, war-ending victory over Lee. It always limped away sorely wounded, battered, and depressed from every engagement, even the battles it won. Overall, it lost far more men than did Lee, and the seeming futility of overcoming Lee's Army of Northern Virginia led the North almost to despair more than once.

The North forced Lee to give up only when his forces had been reduced to a frail flicker of their former glory. The surrender at Appomattox was the moment when a great and splendid army, which had endured far more than most armies in history have had to endure, gave up its life and ascended into legend.

Yes, it could have been otherwise. The Confederacy made fatal mistakes. It scattered its forces, protected unnecessary places, and failed to fight a defensive war. Robert E. Lee himself made many errors. But these facts cannot take away from the remarkable, brilliant, extraordinary war that he fought over the hills and fields of Virginia, Maryland, and Pennsylvania over a century ago.

✴ 1 ✴

LEE TAKES COMMAND

On the late afternoon of May 31, 1862, a year into the Civil War, Joseph E. Johnston was struck twice while directing the Army of Northern Virginia in the Battle of Seven Pines, just east of the Confederate capital of Richmond.

The wounds were not fatal, but Johnston was to be out of action for six months. Major General Gustavus W. Smith, next senior in rank and former street commissioner of New York City, took over.

Confederate president Jefferson Davis and his military adviser, General Robert E. Lee, commiserated with Johnston and met with Smith. But they could learn little of Smith's plans. He was hesitant and indecisive. It became apparent that the burden of leading the army was too much for Smith. He was having what later generations would call a nervous breakdown. Within hours, the strain literally paralyzed him, although the affliction lasted only eighteen hours.

As Davis rode back to Richmond with Lee in the moonlight, he made a decision that saved the Confederacy for nearly three more years: he named Lee, at fifty-five years of age, with his beard already turning gray, to command the Army of Northern Virginia. Lee became the army's third and final chieftain.

Not long afterward, E. Porter Alexander, one day to become the artillery chief of the army's 1st Corps, was riding with Joseph Christmas Ives, who had served briefly on Lee's staff and who now worked for President Davis. Alexander asked Ives whether Lee had the audacity to meet the enormous odds the Federals were going to bring against the Confederacy. The North had a population of 22

E. Porter Alexander

million compared to the South's 9,500,000 (3,500,000 of them slaves), and 92 percent of the nation's industry.

Ives replied: "Alexander, if there is one man in either army, Federal or Confederate, who is, head and shoulders, far above every other one in either army in audacity that man is General Lee, and you will very soon have lived to see it. Lee is audacity personified. His name is audacity."[1]

The Battle of Seven Pines, or Fair Oaks, came to an inconclusive end the next day. It had been badly directed by Johnston, a Virginian who had commanded the army for nearly a year, since the Confederate victory in the Battle of Manassas, or Bull Run, on July 21, 1861. At Seven Pines, Johnston had planned a strike by James Longstreet's division around the right, or northern, flank of the two Union corps on the south side of the Chickahominy River. But Longstreet had come in behind D. H. Hill's division on Williamsburg Road (present-day U.S. Route 60) a couple miles south, and achieved nothing, and the northern envelopment never took place. D. H. Hill crashed headlong into the defending Federal troops on Williamsburg Road, drove them back, but also achieved nothing.

The Confederates suffered 6,100 killed, wounded, and captured, as against 5,700 Union casualties. In all, the Confederate commanders got about 24,000 men into the fight, but did not engage about 16,000 men who were on the field. The Federals, on the other hand, committed all 36,000 of their men, except for a single brigade.

It was thus apparent that the Army of Northern Virginia needed leadership, and President Davis, though reluctant to give up his right-hand man, realized that Lee was the most likely candidate. Davis made this decision despite the poor reputation that Lee

(NATIONAL ARCHIVES)

(NATIONAL ARCHIVES)

George B. McClellan   *Abraham Lincoln*

had established since offering his sword to his native Virginia on April 23, 1861.

Lee had not taken part in the Battle of Manassas, which had been won by Johnston and Pierre Beauregard of Louisiana against an inept Union commander, Irvin McDowell. Shortly after the battle, Davis had sent Lee to West Virginia to recover that rebellious anti-slavery region for the Confederacy. But the Confederate forces there were commanded by two former Virginia governors who spent more time trying to one-up each other than actually fighting Yankees, and Lee was unable to achieve any gains. With criticism of Lee rampant in the South's newspapers, Davis transferred him to the south Atlantic coast to build defenses against Union naval landings. In the spring of 1862, however, Davis brought Lee back to Richmond to serve as his adviser—a post that was the direct forerunner of today's chairman of the United States military's Joint Chiefs of Staff.

The Confederacy was fighting for its very existence. Beginning in mid-March 1862, the Union commander, George B. McClellan, had landed an army of well over 100,000 men at Fort Monroe on the tip of the peninsula between the York and James Rivers southeast of

Richmond. After delays, McClellan broke through a weak defensive line at Yorktown, and drove up to within four miles of Richmond.

Johnston's attack on May 31 had been designed to destroy the two Union corps south of the Chickahominy, and to either force the remaining three corps north of the river to surrender, or drive them back to Fort Monroe. Johnston's plan had been good, but its implementation bad. Moreover, Johnston was secretive with Confederate politicians, especially the president, fearing they would divulge military secrets to the enemy. He was also angry at Davis for not naming him the senior general in Confederate service. As a consequence, Davis and Johnston had been at odds for months, and his departure was a benefit to the Army of Northern Virginia.

Because of Lee's poor reputation, many officers of the army were doubtful whether his promotion would prove wise. Yet Lee had excellent credentials. He was scion of a distinguished Virginia family; he was married to Mary Randolph Custis, a great-granddaughter of Martha Custis Washington (wife of George Washington) and an heir to Arlington estate; and he was son of a Revolutionary War hero, General Henry "Light Horse Harry" Lee.

A highly regarded colonel in the U.S. Army, Lee was moderately tall, extremely handsome, unfailingly courteous to everyone high and low, an honor's graduate of West Point, a veteran of the Mexican War during which he served with distinction on the staff of General Winfield Scott, and superintendent of West Point from 1852 to 1855.

In mid-February 1861 General Scott, seventy-five years old and commander in chief of the U.S. Army, ordered Lee to leave his post in Texas and report to Washington, presumably to help force the seceded states back into the Union.

On April 18, 1861—four days after Fort Sumter in Charleston Harbor surrendered to Confederate forces, three days after Union president Abraham Lincoln called for 75,000 volunteers to quell the rebellion, and the morning after a convention in Richmond voted for Virginia to secede—Francis P. Blair Sr., a publisher and close associate of the president, met Lee in Washington and informed him that Lincoln and Secretary of War Simon Cameron had offered him command of the U.S. Army. Lee declined the offer, saying he could take no part in the invasion of the South. Though deeply distressed at the division of the nation, Lee felt he had to offer his sword to his native state. On April 20 he resigned his commission, took the train to Richmond, and accepted Governor John Letcher's appointment as major general of Virginia forces.

(NATIONAL ARCHIVES)

Fort Sumter in Charleston harbor under the Confederate flag, April 1861.

When Jefferson Davis placed Lee in command of the Army of Northern Virginia on June 1, 1862, he did so because Major General Gustavus Smith was clearly incapable and Lee was the best candidate available.

But Lee was an unknown quantity. His service in the West Virginia campaign had revealed little about his command capability. He had never held a major field command in the U.S. Army. After serving on General Scott's staff in the Mexican War, Lee had worked largely as an engineer, though he was the second-ranking officer of a cavalry regiment in Texas in the last year of peace.

President Davis was extremely pleased, therefore, to discover that Lee took control of the Army of Northern Virginia with confidence, established his authority firmly but without fanfare, got on well with his subordinate commanders though he never curried favor, and was objective in appraising his officers' abilities. Lee's success or failure would depend upon how well he led his army in battle, of course, but his swift and sure grasping of the reins of command was solid evidence that Lee was prepared for the heavy responsibility of high command, and relished the opportunity.

Lee also regularly told Davis what he was planning to do militarily, and asked Davis his opinions. General Johnston had never done this, and Lee's cordial attitude established a feeling of mutual confidence between the two men that permitted them to discuss most matters frankly. As time went on, Lee discovered that he and Davis saw the conduct of the war differently—Lee wanted to fight decisive battles, while Davis wanted the South only to hold on until the North got weary and quit. Lee found he could not divulge all of his aggressive plans or thoughts to Davis, but this did not affect the friendship that developed at once between them.

This friendly attitude permitted both men to let down their guards. Davis was so relaxed that he offered to lend Lee one of his own fine horses, after he noticed the rough gait of a gray horse Lee had acquired in the West Virginia mountains the previous winter, a horse Lee had named Traveller. Lee politely turned down the offer, and rode Traveller to the end of the war and beyond.

Confederate President Davis put his faith in the importance of King Cotton to the immense textile industries of Britain and the Continent. He believed the major European powers would intervene, force the North to accept Southern independence, and thereby save their economies. The South merely had to hold on until cotton stocks ran out at European mills. However, Europe learned quickly to do without Southern cotton, and Davis had to face the fact that he had staked the South's fortunes on a fiber, and had lost.

(LEIB IMAGE ARCHIVES)

Robert E. Lee on Traveller during the war.

To defeat the South, General Winfield Scott proposed the "Anaconda Plan": capture New Orleans and other Southern ports, seize the Mississippi River and cut off the Confederate states west of the river, and threaten Richmond, thereby containing Confederate forces east of the Allegheny Mountains. In this way, Scott believed, the South would be denied foreign arms, and its resistance would ultimately be squeezed to death, just as an anaconda snake squeezes its victims lifeless.

This was a good strategy, and Lincoln belatedly adopted it. However, it lacked a decisive offensive element to stamp out resistance in the event the Confederacy refused to quit. The answer was to seize Chattanooga, Tennessee, and Atlanta, Georgia, through which ran the main lateral railways of the Confederacy.

For his part, Davis should have recognized that the strategic frontier of the Confederacy ran from the Potomac River at Washington, along the Alleghenies to Chattanooga, then along the Tennessee River, crossing the Mississippi around Memphis, then to Little Rock on the Arkansas River. Kentucky, Missouri, and Tennessee were only advanced posts that could not be defended permanently.

The solution would therefore have been to base the South's main force on Chattanooga, with another strong army in Virginia. A vigorous defensive war in Tennessee would have protected the supplies of Mississippi, Alabama, and Georgia, kept open the railroads linking the entire strategical region with the Atlantic and Gulf ports, preserved crossings into Arkansas and Louisiana, and presented a constant threat to Kentucky and the main Union supply line leading back to Louisville. On the other hand, if Chattanooga and Atlanta were lost, the Confederacy in effect would be reduced to the Carolinas and Virginia.

Lincoln only insisted on the Chattanooga plan late in the war. Until then, both sides pursued vague, confused, and indecisive strategies west of the Appalachian Mountain chain. Davis also did not realize the importance of Chattanooga until it was too late, and he never insisted on positioning most Confederate strength to protect it.

Both sides instead riveted their attention and most of their strength on the Virginia theater and guarding their political capitals,

Washington and Richmond. Consequently, the Confederate victory at Manassas on July 21, 1861, froze Union activity until Lincoln could find some way to end the impasse and get Federal troops marching on Richmond again.

Lincoln called in George Brinton McClellan to command the Union army in the east. Thirty-four years old, auburn-haired, blue-eyed, handsome, and dashing, McClellan (1826–85) was a West Pointer, class of 1846, and, after excellent service in the Mexican War as an engineer, had become president of the Ohio and Mississippi Railroad.

He had received much publicity due to his success in driving several small, ill-led Confederate forces out of West Virginia in the spring. There had been little fighting, but McClellan had made the most of the campaign by issuing Bonaparte-like manifestoes. Dubbed the "Young Napoleon" by the press, McClellan caught the fancy of the Northern public, and impressed Lincoln, who on November 1, 1861, advanced him to command all the Union armies, replacing General Scott.

McClellan improved and extended a ring of forts along the hills around Washington to protect the city from attack. He did an exceptional job of organizing recruits into a well-trained, well-drilled, well-armed force of nearly 170,000 men with high morale, an ability to fire their weapons with some accuracy, and an almost worshipful admiration of the Young Napoleon.

But, as the months went by, his crippling weaknesses—reluctance to use his army, and a compulsion to overestimate the size of the enemy's army—became more and more apparent.

At the same time, President Davis emphasized his resolve for the South merely to stand on the defensive, hoping that the North would become weary of the war and grant the Confederacy its independence. On October 1, 1861, he had turned down a petition by Generals Johnston and Beauregard to draw 20,000 troops guarding the Southern coastline to join with their army of 40,000 men and invade the North and force the war to a victorious conclusion.

Davis feared the landings that joint Union army-navy expeditions were mounting around the coasts of the Confederacy. Their only strategic purpose was to establish bases to tighten the sea blockade of the South and prevent trade with Europe. But Davis and the governors of the affected states insisted on keeping large numbers of troops positioned as useless sentinels guarding hundreds of miles of unthreatened Confederate coastline. Davis could not see that the amphibious operations posed no immediate danger, and could strangle the South only in a long war of attrition.

With the war in danger of turning into a stalemate, President Lincoln finally demanded a direct attack toward Richmond along the Orange and Alexandria Railroad through central Virginia. This at last galvanized McClellan into transferring his army by ship through Chesapeake Bay to Fort Monroe and his slow march up the peninsula to the gates of Richmond. Part of his delay was caused by the appearance of the Confederate ironclad *Virginia* (generally known by people North and South by its original name, the *Merrimack*) in Chesapeake Bay. It sank or grounded three Union wooden ships and was threatening to drive the U.S. Navy from the bay when a Union ironclad, the *Monitor*, arrived and fought the *Merrimack* to a draw.

Confederate general Thomas J. "Stonewall" Jackson also helped to slow down McClellan's march by flashing down Virginia's Shenandoah Valley with a small army, routing a Union army under Nathaniel Banks, and making gestures threatening Washington. Lincoln, who realized that the center of the nation's concept of itself rested in Washington, withheld a 40,000-man corps under Irvin McDowell to help protect the capital.

As the Battle of Seven Pines ended, therefore, McClellan was still waiting hopefully for the arrival of McDowell's corps, standing at Fredericksburg, fifty miles north of Richmond. It never was going to arrive, however, because Lincoln feared Jackson might strike once more down the Shenandoah Valley at Washington. But Jackson already was moving his 18,000-man army in great secrecy by train and foot from the valley to Ashland, a few miles north of Richmond, to reinforce Lee.

✷ 2 ✷

THE SEVEN DAYS

In seven days and five battles from June 26 to July 2, 1862, Lee drove McClellan's army from the gates of Richmond to a defensive position around Harrison's Landing, on the James River, twenty-five miles from the capital.

To Southerners, Lee's campaign looked like deliverance from certain destruction, and Lee's fame and glory as a commander date from these battles. Yet the Seven Days was far from being either a Confederate triumph or an example of great generalship.

The South's strategic position actually declined. McClellan still had a huge Union army within striking distance of the Confederate capital, while the Army of Northern Virginia had lost one-fourth of its entire strength, 20,000 men. Since the North could easily replace its 9,800 killed and wounded, Lee's army was relatively weaker after the Seven Days than before.[*]

During the campaign Lee revealed his method of warfare. It consisted primarily of direct assaults by massed bodies of infantry against a waiting enemy. Although Lee's tactics improved over time, bloody frontal attacks into the rifles and cannons of the enemy remained his characteristic response when his more indirect methods failed, or were thought to have failed. This fixation produced the staggering casualties of the Seven Days, and similar losses from other frontal attacks in the campaigns ahead.

---

[*] The Confederates took more than 6,000 Union prisoners, plus 4,000 wounded and sick left behind, but prisoners on both sides were routinely exchanged on a one-for-one basis.

(NATIONAL ARCHIVES)

J.E.B. "Jeb" Stuart

The Seven Days also demonstrated that Lee had a weak sense of strategy, this being the art of applying military means to fulfill the ends of national policy. Lee built his campaign around the presumption that McClellan would defend his supply base at White House on the Pamunkey River, twenty miles northeast of his main defensive position just east of Richmond. In fact, McClellan was already planning to shift his base to the broader, deeper James River, and abandoned White House immediately after Lee attacked.

Lee fought the first two days of the campaign on a false premise, trying to drive Fitz John Porter's corps eastward down the north bank of the Chickahominy River, in order to uncover White House. Yet Porter plainly showed on the second day that he was not guarding White House, but had turned his defensive line ninety degrees to defend the main Union army south of the Chickahominy. Lee took another day to recognize this, giving McClellan such a huge head start that Lee was never able to catch him, let alone cut him off.

Lee could not have anticipated McClellan's decision to change his base, though he caused McClellan to do it. On June 12, Lee sent his cavalry chief, J.E.B. "Jeb" Stuart, on a reconnaissance to find out how far north of the Chickahominy Porter's corps extended, and whether White House remained the Union base. Lee could easily have sent spies or scouts on this mission. But the flamboyant Stuart used the opportunity to make a spectacular ride with 1,200 cavalrymen around McClellan's entire army, sweeping north of Porter, then coming back up River Road (present-day Virginia Route 5) on the James on June 15.

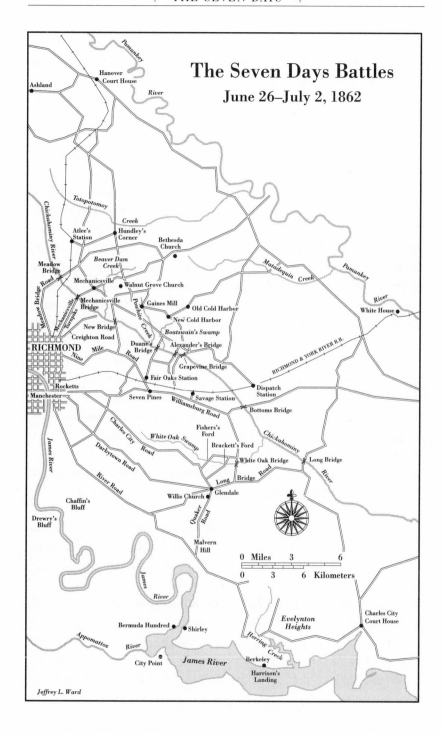

The Seven Days Battles
June 26–July 2, 1862

Jeffrey L. Ward

Stuart's ride around McClellan demonstrated the vulnerability of White House, and motivated McClellan to order supply ships to shift to the James. McClellan had located his base at White House in the first place because the *Merrimack* threatened Federal supply ships in the James. However, the Confederates had scuttled the *Merrimack* when General Johnston abandoned the lower peninsula and retreated to the outskirts of Richmond. The James was now safe for Federal ships.

McClellan had posted Porter's corps at Mechanicsville, north of the Chickahominy and four miles northwest of the main Union fortified line around Seven Pines. Porter was in this exposed position because McClellan expected Irvin McDowell's 40,000-man corps to march down from Fredericksburg, fifty miles north. This would have given McClellan about 145,000 men, against Lee's 80,000, and permitted him to wrap Porter's and McDowell's corps around Richmond from the north, while the main Union army attacked westward, forcing the Confederates to abandon the capital.

But McDowell was not coming, and Lee saw that Porter's corps might be destroyed before the rest of the Union army could rush to its aid. Then the Confederates might sweep down the north bank of the Chickahominy and seize Dispatch Station, eleven miles southeast of Mechanicsville and just north of the river. This would sever the rail line running from White House to Seven Pines that supplied the Union army, and force McClellan either to come out from behind his entrenchments and fight or to retreat down the peninsula to Fort Monroe.

Lee ordered Stonewall Jackson's 18,000-man force to move secretly to Ashland, about sixteen miles north of Richmond. Meanwhile he assembled three divisions south of the Chickahominy just opposite Mechanicsville—A.P. Hill's on the west around Meadow Bridge, and D.H. Hill's and James Longstreet's just south of Mechanicsville.

To guard against an attack straight into Richmond by McClellan's 75,000 men around Seven Pines, Lee ordered the 28,000 Confederates south of the river to demonstrate on June 26 as

A.P. Hill

D.H. Hill

if they were about to attack. The great Confederate military actor, General John Magruder, who earlier had confused McClellan on the Yorktown line with theatrical displays of power that disguised his pathetically small force, eagerly undertook new pretenses and false shows of strength. They were entirely successful, and McClellan's commanders south of the Chickahominy anxiously prepared for a Confederate attack all day.

All told, Lee had about 52,000 men against Porter's 30,000. But the key to victory was Jackson, who was to descend on Porter's right rear flank—that is, a point northeast of Mechanicsville—thereby imperiling Porter and forcing him to abandon a line of powerful entrenchments he had built along Beaver Dam Creek, a mile east of Mechanicsville. Once Porter realized that Jackson was on his rear, he would have to retreat. Thus, the initial purpose of Lee's movement was to prise Porter out of his strong defensive position without a battle.

Lee made no arrangements for Jackson to communicate with the Confederates south of the river, although Stuart's cavalry could have performed this job with ease. Instead, he sent Stuart to the east to guard against a surprise attack, though his ride had shown there was little danger. Lee also did not tell either of the two Hills or Longstreet when Jackson informed him by courier early on Thursday, June 26, that, because of rains and high water, he would be six hours late reaching his jump-off point six miles southeast of Ashland.

A six-hour delay would make no difference, for whenever Jackson arrived at his objective—Hundley's Corner, three miles northeast of Mechanicsville—Porter's flank would be turned, and he would be obliged to retreat without a battle. However, A. P. Hill could not stand waiting for Jackson on a hot afternoon. Hill did not have

(LEIB IMAGE ARCHIVES)

Young Confederate soldiers in the first days of the war.

the whole picture, and he was an extremely aggressive, impetuous, impatient officer. Consequently, he launched an attack across Meadow Bridge at Mechanicsville at 3 P.M. June 26, two hours before Jackson arrived at Hundley's Corner.

Porter at once withdrew to the Beaver Dam fortifications, and A. P. Hill moved up to attack. The whole purpose of Jackson's flanking movement had been to extricate Porter from Beaver Dam without a fight. Though Jackson had not yet arrived, Lee had every reason to believe he would reach Hundley's Corner before the day was out. Thus, an attack by A. P. Hill was unnecessary.

Yet, Lee did not wait for Jackson, agreed to A. P. Hill's attack, and detailed some of D. H. Hill's troops, who had arrived, to join in. At this moment Lee revealed his fundamental inadequacy as a commander. Showing little foresight, Lee behaved like most people, who focus on the obstacle directly before their eyes.* One of the factors that makes a general great, and therefore rare, is that he can withstand the normal human urge to rush headlong into direct challenges, and can instead see how to go around rather than through his opponent. What raises Lee's failure to an epic level is that he had *already* worked out a way to avoid Beaver Dam Creek, but, in the flush of emotion brought on by A. P. Hill's rash advance, abandoned his indirect plans and reverted to a direct confrontation.

---

* This is because humans have a strong urge to confront one another directly. We consider anybody who does otherwise to be underhanded, sly, shifty, as not fighting fair. Our language reflects how strongly we feel about this— "stab in the back," "backbiter," and "blindsiding" are all pejorative terms. Direct face-to-face dealing is deeply ingrained in the human psyche and is the normal response to conflict. Throughout his life, a human being is supported and reinforced when he deals with other people in a direct, straightforward manner, and is reviled and despised when he acts in backhanded, devious ways. Officers who are sneaky, false, and two-faced get bad reputations in every army, and seldom are promoted to general's rank. Most generals have always been direct-thinking, unsubtle warriors. Yet as the great Chinese strategist Sun Tzu wrote around 400 B.C.: "All warfare is based on deception. . . . The way to avoid what is strong is to strike what is weak. . . . Supreme excellence consists in breaking the enemy's resistance without fighting." To achieve this, Sun Tzu recommended that the successful general "march swiftly to places where he is not expected."

A. P. Hill ordered a frontal attack of three brigades against the creek on the north, sending the men against Union troops firing rifles from entrenchments behind abatis, or barriers made of felled trees, and against Union cannons pouring out canister shot, the metal balls and other chunks of metal designed to punch holes through flesh. Hill's attack failed, with staggering casualties. But A. P. Hill then ordered another attack on the southern end of the line. It, too, failed utterly.*

A. P. Hill's attack was one of the most terrible and useless slaughters in the Civil War. More than 1,400 Rebels fell. Porter lost only 360 men all day, mostly pickets retreating from Meadow Bridge and Mechanicsville. One North Carolina soldier remembered: "Nothing could be heard in the black darkness of that night save the ghastly moans of the wounded and dying."

D. H. Hill wrote afterward: "The blood shed by Southern troops there was wasted in vain, and worse than vain; for the fight had a most dispiriting effect on our troops. They could have halted at Mechanicsville until Jackson had turned the works on the creek, and all the waste of blood could have been avoided."[1]

Later in the evening, after reports of Jackson's position reached him, McClellan ordered Porter to withdraw from Beaver Dam Creek. It was Jackson's dangerous location, not A. P. Hill's attack, that prompted the decision. McClellan directed that White House be defended as long as possible, then the base transferred to the James River. Lee didn't know it, but his strategic position had changed essentially. He had not isolated Porter's corps, and McClellan no longer was trying to hold White House.

---

* Lee hesitated to give direct orders to subordinate commanders, preferring to suggest actions rather than to demand them. In the Mexican War, he had been influenced by Winfield Scott, who held it was the commanding general's job to devise the strategy and bring troops on the field at the proper time, but to leave actual movements or tactics to the division commanders. In addition, Lee was sensitive to the feelings of others, and was willing to leave many details to his subordinates. See Freeman, *R. E. Lee*, vol. 2, 239–40. This reluctance did not relieve Lee of responsibility for the actions of his army, however.

Here and in subsequent footnotes, some references to source works give only the last name(s) of the author(s) or editor(s). Works so referred to are cited in full in the Selected Bibliography. Numbers at the end of source citations refer to page numbers.

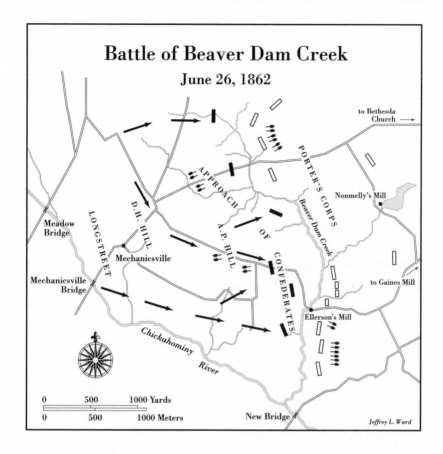

Battle of Beaver Dam Creek
June 26, 1862

On the morning of June 27, Lee, finding Porter gone, assumed that he had moved back to Powhite Creek, a south-flowing stream three and a half miles east of Beaver Dam Creek, and was facing westward, still protecting the railroad and White House. He ordered A. P. Hill and Longstreet to attack the line directly. This, Lee figured, would force Porter to abandon the Powhite line, and retreat toward Dispatch Station. Accordingly, he ordered Jackson, with D. H. Hill attached, to swing around to the northeast of Powhite Creek, and ambush Porter while he moved downriver.

Porter was not at Powhite Creek, but at Boatswain's Swamp, three-quarters of a mile east. And Porter's troops were facing *north* to protect the Chickahominy crossings, not west to guard Dispatch

Station, as Lee expected. McClellan ordered Porter to hold this position only long enough to cover the withdrawal of his supply train and heavy guns, and to give him time to set up a new supply base on the James.

Lee did not reconnoiter to find that Porter had oriented his corps facing north, and called the battle Gaines Mill, after a location on Powhite Creek, not Boatswain's Swamp, where it was fought. Without waiting for Longstreet to come up, he launched A. P. Hill into a direct attack against the swamp, where Porter had constructed three lines of defense. Hill lost 2,100 men, but his attacks failed and he accomplished nothing.

"Brigade after brigade seemed almost to melt away before the concentrated fire of our artillery and infantry," Porter noted. "Yet

Battle of Gaines Mill
June 27, 1862

others pressed on, followed by supports as dashing and as brave as their predecessors."[2]

Jackson and D. H. Hill, expecting Porter to move past them, did not get heavily into the fight until the afternoon. Then, Lee ordered a general assault by his whole force. It was also a frontal assault, and though it succeeded at nightfall, Lee lost 8,000 men to Porter's 4,000, and did not destroy the Union corps. Most of it retreated over the Chickahominy during the night.

Was there no alternative to this bloodbath? Indeed there was. If Lee had scouted out Porter's new position and found that Porter was protecting the bridges over the Chickahominy, he would have realized that Jackson's corps was already past Porter and could have marched unmolested to Dispatch Station, cut the railway to White House, crossed the Chickahominy, and placed his force on the rear of the entire Army of the Potomac. McClellan had forgotten to close the back door to his army! Jackson could have forced McClellan to fight on both his front and rear. This might have resulted in the surrender of the entire army.

McClellan ordered his army to retreat on June 28, 1862, to the James at Harrison's Landing, fourteen air miles southeast of Seven Pines and the closest point where transports could tie up safely. There was only one good road leading to it across the barrier of White Oak Swamp, three miles south of the Chickahominy. This road (now Virginia Route 156) led southeast about nine miles from Seven Pines to White Oak Bridge, then by the Quaker, or Willis Church, Road, which passed Glendale, a couple miles southwest, then ran due south four miles over Malvern Hill to River Road, which gave access to Harrison's Landing, five miles southeast.

Lee did not anticipate this retreat, believing McClellan would try to cover the railroad and White House, despite ample evidence to the contrary. Lee remained immobile for the whole day, although he got news early in the morning that Porter's corps had crossed the river and burned the bridges opposite Boatswain's Swamp. He also learned by noon from Jeb Stuart that the Federals had burned the railroad trestle over the Chickahominy at Dispatch Station, and that immense clouds of smoke were rising from White House, certain evidence that McClellan was abandoning the base.

During the morning ammunition magazines exploded south of the river and clouds of dust arose, signaling movement. And the retreat was not to be down the peninsula toward Fort Monroe, because Stuart's horsemen found no Federal troops marching toward the highway bridges in that direction. Shortly after noon on June 28 Lee had proof that the Federals were retreating and that their only possible destination was the James River. And the only possible route of the army was down the Quaker Road to Malvern Hill and River Road.

Despite this unequivocal knowledge, Lee did not move until Sunday morning, June 29.[*] This gave McClellan an invincible head start, and guaranteed that the Confederate army could only at best yap at the heels of the fleeing Federals.

Lee ordered a complex pursuit plan, sending Confederate columns down five separate routes. Only one of them, Theophilus H. Holmes's division, which was moving eastward down River Road, had even an outside chance of intercepting the Union army before it reached the James. But it was too small—6,000 men—to challenge McClellan's whole army. The other four columns moved behind the Federals. They faced violent, often superior opposition, since the Federals had ample time to prepare formidable rear guards.

Lee's orders for pursuit on June 29 were for Magruder, with 11,500 men, to move down Williamsburg Road and engage the

---

[*] The reason for his delay has never been satisfactorily explained. Lee's biographer, Douglas Southall Freeman, wrote that Lee didn't know whether McClellan was heading for Fort Monroe or the James, and was unwilling to move until he was certain. (See Freeman, *R. E. Lee*, vol. 2, 163.) But the absence of any troop movements toward Fort Monroe should have told him that the James was McClellan's destination.

Federals before they reached White Oak Bridge; for Benjamin Huger, with 9,000 men, to march eastward on the Charles City Road, south of White Oak Swamp, and take the Federals in flank the next day at Glendale on the Quaker Road; and for Longstreet (with A.P. Hill under his command), with 18,000 men, to march down to Darbytown Road, a couple miles south of Charles City Road, then turn eastward and also attack McClellan around Glendale on June 30.

Meanwhile, Holmes was to press eastward along River Road, and Jackson was to rebuild bridges over the Chickahominy, then move eastward to intercept McClellan if he turned toward Fort Monroe. However, it took Jackson's men nearly all day to rebuild two bridges, and they did not cross until after midnight.

None of the pursuits succeeded. Magruder was slow, and allowed himself to be stopped by a single Union brigade at Savage Station, three miles east of Seven Pines, permitting Union forces to get away under cover of night. Huger showed great hesitation, and got only six miles down Charles City Road before nightfall. Holmes likewise advanced only a short distance. Longstreet did better, reaching within three miles of Glendale by dark.

By Monday morning, June 30, the tail of the Union army had crossed White Oak Bridge, which it then destroyed, while the head of the army—with Erasmus D. Keyes's and most of Porter's corps— was nearing Malvern Hill, on the Quaker Road a mile north of River Road. McClellan ordered William B. Franklin with two divisions, 20,000 men, to hold the White Oak Swamp line until nightfall; Keyes and Porter to occupy Malvern Hill to shield the army's trains and the landing; and the remainder of the army, five divisions, about 40,000 men, to defend the area in between, focusing on Glendale.

McClellan had appeared on none of the battlefields. Now he departed Glendale as well, leaving no general in charge, riding down to the James, boarding the ironclad *Galena*, and having a good dinner with the skipper and the comte de Paris, a French nobleman.

Lee's plan for June 30 was to cut off and destroy the Federal rear around Glendale and White Oak Bridge. He ordered Longstreet to continue down Darbytown Road, and Huger down Charles City

Road, while Jackson crossed at White Oak Bridge, and drove the Union force there toward Huger and Longstreet, who should have been astride the Quaker Road or at least holding the Federals at bay. Since Magruder no longer served any purpose at Savage Station, Lee ordered him to march to Darbytown Road and come up behind Longstreet as a reserve.

If Jackson's, Huger's, and Longstreet's blows were coordinated, McClellan could lose his entire rear guard, almost two-thirds of his army. Porter Alexander wrote there were few times when "we were within reach of military successes so great that we might have hoped to end the war with our independence. . . . This chance of June 30th '62 impresses me as the best of all."[3]

Huger failed completely. When he started down Charles City Road, he was seized with the fear that Federal troops might attack him from White Oak Swamp, and sent a brigade to guard that flank, though there was no danger. His other two brigades continued toward Glendale, but found that Federal axemen had felled trees across the road. Instead of sending sharpshooters to evict the woodchoppers, and using teams of soldiers to lift the trees out of the road, Huger cut a new road through the woods! When he finally arrived a mile or so west of Glendale, Huger engaged in a minor artillery duel with Henry W. Slocum's division blocking him, having frittered away a day.

Jackson also achieved nothing. He faced a force nearly as large as his own at the broken White Oak Bridge. Intense shelling from Federal artillery as well as galling fire from Union sharpshooters in the heavy woods along the swamp prevented Jackson's engineers from repairing the bridge. Frustrated, Jackson made no effort to advance.

If Jackson had reconnoitered, he would have found that the Federals had only about 700 men and one cannon at Brackett's Ford, on a good road a mile upstream from the bridge. Jackson could have broken through at this ford, probably leading to Franklin's defeat, and possibly given the Confederates a great victory at Glendale.

Jackson's inaction has never been explained. He might have been exhausted from his long exertions, or possibly sick. But his failure to move doomed Lee's plan.

About noon, Longstreet approached Glendale, with A. P. Hill's division behind. At Frayser's Farm, just south of the crossroads, he encountered a large force of Federals in line of battle. Longstreet waited for Jackson and Huger to drive the Federals toward his position, but the day wore on and nothing happened.

Meanwhile, on River Road, Holmes reached the western face of Malvern Hill. He found only a few Union infantry on it, but Porter had thirty-six guns emplaced. Lee, informed of Holmes's arrival, went down to look. Seeing a chance to cut off the retreat of a large part of the Union army, Lee told Holmes to bring up his whole division and attack. If Lee had directed this move himself, he might have seized Malvern Hill and blocked Federal passage to Harrison's Landing. This would have forced McClellan to attack him on Malvern Hill, likely resulting in McClellan's defeat. But Lee ignored the opportunity, and returned to Glendale, where he ordered Magruder to march down and reinforce Holmes.

Holmes, fifty-seven years old and nearly deaf, proved incompetent as a combat commander. Though with Magruder he had 20,000 men, far more than Porter opposite him, Holmes moved his infantry into woods, brought up six 3-inch rifled guns, and opened fire. Porter promptly replied with his guns, reinforced by salvos from Federal gunboats in the James. The barrage produced a lot of noise and some damage, blowing up two caissons and sending some green Rebels scampering. This was not much loss, but Holmes withdrew, and refused to employ Magruder, who returned to the Darbytown Road, having marched all day to no avail.

At Malvern Hill, Lee had encountered cannons largely unprotected by infantry. Artillery could do great execution if shielded by infantry, but could not stand alone against enemy foot soldiers. Riflemen could shoot down gunners and horses, and sweep around the guns and capture them. Thus a great opportunity appeared at Malvern Hill. But back at Glendale the opposite was the case. A formidable enemy was arrayed in lines of battle and supported by well-protected cannons. Even so, Lee, around 5 P.M., realizing that neither Jackson, Huger, nor Holmes was going to move, ordered

Longstreet and A. P. Hill to launch a direct attack straight into the heart of the enemy position—just as he'd done at Beaver Dam Creek and Gaines Mill.

An attack now had little purpose, since it could not be decisive without a move by Jackson on the Federal rear. At best it would merely impel the rear guard faster toward Malvern Hill.

Longstreet sent an assault into the canister fire of much-superior Union artillery and the rifle fire of four Union divisions. Nowhere did the Rebels gain more than temporary advantage; nowhere did they crack the Union line. In large part the two sides stood opposite each other for hours, exchanging one volley after another, while artillery raked the lines of battle. Darkness ended the strife, but the Federals still held the Quaker Road. By morning, they and Franklin's force were gone, having moved during the night to Malvern Hill. In the battle, the Confederates lost 3,700 men, all but 220 killed or wounded, the Federals 3,800, half of them captured.

Since Lee had seen how strongly the Federals were defending Malvern Hill, he should have realized that they almost certainly were shielding Harrison's Landing, the most likely sanctuary for the Army of the Potomac. Upstream from the landing the James narrowed, offering ideal locations for Rebel batteries on the south bank to sink Union transports. Even if McClellan's destination were farther downriver, his army would have to pass by Harrison's Landing.

Therefore, Lee's proper course was not to press on the heels of McClellan, which guaranteed another direct assault, this time at Malvern Hill, where the Federal position was now incredibly strong. Rather, Lee should have kept a small covering force on the Quaker Road, and marched the bulk of the army straight for Harrison's Landing, on McClellan's rear, in hopes of finding a strongly defensible position blocking the Federals, and obligating them to attack the Confederates, not the other way around.*

There was such a position, so perfect for its purposes that it might have forced the surrender of the Union army. The place was Evelynton Heights, rising directly north of Harrison's Landing and River Road, and dominating everything roundabout. Harrison's Landing on the wide James was excellent for Union transports and gunboats, but otherwise badly sited. It was on a peninsula of low ground three miles long, with the river on the south and the wide tidal Herring Creek on the north. Every inch could be hit by guns from Evelynton Heights.

If Lee had occupied the heights, and brought up all his field pieces, Harrison's Landing would have been untenable. McClellan would have had to abandon Malvern Hill without a fight and, to preserve his army, assault the heights. This would have been a Herculean task, very likely to fail, because Herring Creek left only a narrow front exposed to attack. Porter Alexander, Lee's aide, Walter H. Taylor, and Jackson's biographer, G. F. R. Henderson, all thought occupation of Evelynton Heights was by far the best strategy for Lee, even four days later, after much Confederate bloodshed.[4]

Lee's attention, however, was focused on the retreating Union army, and his battle lust, already high as a result of Frayser's Farm, was getting higher. There is no evidence that Lee considered striking toward Evelynton Heights, though he knew the area well. His mother's girlhood home was Shirley Plantation, five miles west, and he'd visited often.

Malvern Hill was an open plateau, about 150 feet above the James, mostly open, planted in wheat, oats, and corn, three-fourths of a mile wide, and a mile and a half north to south. Just below it

---

* Napoleon Bonaparte always attempted to block the enemy's retreat and never made a frontal attack if he could do otherwise. He counted on the menace of a move on the rear, even if it failed, to shake enemy morale and force him into a mistake, which might give Napoleon an opportunity to strike. See Commandant J. Colin, *The Transformations of War* (London: Hugh Rees, 1912), 279–89.

River Road ran through low grounds next to the river. On the west a bluff faced River Road and a creek. The Quaker Road approached from the northeast.

Atop the bluff facing westward, Fitz John Porter had emplaced a powerful line of guns protected by an infantry division. Facing northward toward the Quaker Road, where he expected the Confederates to attack, Porter deployed two divisions, about 18,000 men, and thirty-seven cannons. Behind them were sixty more cannons, and ten heavy guns from the army's siege train.

Fearing that Lee might attempt to flank the Union position on the east, McClellan posted the remainder of the army on the right rear of Malvern Hill, near the river. McClellan rode around the hill early on Tuesday morning, July 1, 1862, but abandoned the field by 9:15 A.M., climbed back on the *Galena*, and steamed to Harrison's Landing. Again he made no provision for a commander, but Porter took over by default. McClellan returned about 3:30 P.M., but moved to the extreme right of the hill, far from the battle, and played no role in directing it.

As the Army of Northern Virginia followed the Federals down the Quaker Road on Tuesday morning, it was obvious to the senior commanders that Lee was planning to attack Malvern Hill. D.H. Hill was disturbed. He had been talking with the Reverend L.W. Allen, who had been reared in the neighborhood, and who told Hill of its commanding height, difficulty of approach, and ample area, which would permit Porter's field guns to sweep the terrain in all directions. "I became satisfied that an attack upon the concentrated Federal army so splendidly posted, and with such vast superiority in artillery, could only be fatal to us," Hill wrote.

D.H. Hill met Lee riding with Longstreet, and told Lee: "If General McClellan is there in force, we had better let him alone." Longstreet laughed, and said: "Don't get scared, now that we have got him whipped."[5]

The Confederate army arrived in front of Malvern Hill about noon on July 1. Jackson's corps deployed east of the Quaker Road, D.H. Hill's division just west of it, and Huger on the northwest.

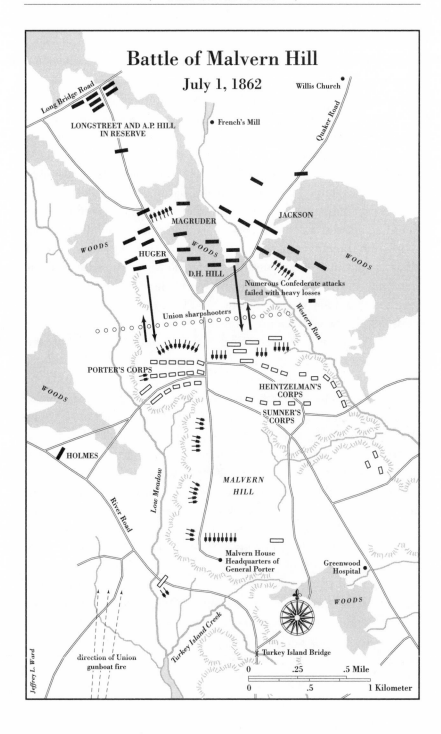

Battle of Malvern Hill
July 1, 1862

Willis Church

French's Mill

LONGSTREET AND A.P. HILL
IN RESERVE

Long Bridge Road

Quaker Road

MAGRUDER

JACKSON

WOODS

WOODS

HUGER

WOODS

D.H. HILL

Numerous Confederate attacks
failed with heavy losses

Union sharpshooters

Western Run

PORTER'S CORPS

HEINTZELMAN'S
CORPS

WOODS

SUMNER'S
CORPS

HOLMES

Low Meadow

MALVERN
HILL

River Road

Malvern House
Headquarters of
General Porter

Greenwood
Hospital

WOODS

direction of Union
gunboat fire

Turkey Island Creek

Turkey Island Bridge

Jeffrey L. Ward

0   .25   .5 Mile

0   .5   1 Kilometer

Magruder was to deploy next to Huger, but he took the wrong road and was hours late coming up. Longstreet's and A. P. Hill's divisions, which had suffered severely at Frayser's Farm, stayed in reserve. Holmes remained on River Road, doing nothing all day.

When Lee arrived, Jackson argued against a direct attack and proposed that Lee turn the Federal eastern flank. But Longstreet saw a good position for cannons on an open elevation about a mile west of the Quaker Road, and suggested that sixty field guns be mounted there. Lee examined the terrain east of the road where Jackson was emplaced, finding a high open field where a similar "grand battery" could be massed. Each gun position could hit the Federal guns from a different direction, possibly forcing them to withdraw. Lee ordered the plan put into effect, and designated Lewis A. Armistead, commanding a brigade in Huger's division in the center of the line, to give the signal for the grand assault—a bizarre arrangement, almost certain to cause confusion.

At best, an infantry assault could succeed only if the Confederates could emplace sufficient guns and force the Federal cannons to withdraw. Neither occurred.

Jackson got sixteen guns in place, and opened fire. This was the largest concentration of artillery the Confederates achieved all day. As soon as Jackson's cannons appeared, the Federal batteries poured deadly fire into them, shattering gun carriages, caissons, men, and horses, and forcing the guns to withdraw.

On the right the situation was worse. Only one of the twenty batteries of the army reserve was engaged, and this in spite of William N. Pendleton, chief of the reserve, who hid out all day, never approaching Lee. Lee made no effort to find Pendleton or his cannons, one-fourth of his army's entire stock of artillery, and virtually unused in the Seven Days, whereas the cannons attached to the divisions were nearly out of ammunition. Altogether just five more batteries went into action on the west, all from divisions. As each battery deployed, forty or fifty Union cannons turned on it, and it was crushed in a minute or two.

Since Lee had concluded that an attack against Malvern Hill required the Confederates to drive away the Union guns, his failure to locate Pendleton or call up his reserve cannons is inexplicable.

About 3 P.M. Lee recognized Confederate batteries could not break the Federal front, and reconnoitered on the east for a possible turning movement the next day. Coming back, however, he learned that Armistead had advanced and that Union troops were withdrawing from Malvern Hill. In fact, Armistead had sent his men only to drive back Union skirmishers, and the "withdrawal" was simply the movement of some Federal soldiers to get under the crest of the hill to avoid Rebel gunfire.

Lee, encouraged by the erroneous reports, allowed his attack order to stand. Magruder had arrived about 4 P.M., and sent in separate assaults by two Confederate brigades directly against the slope of Malvern Hill, 800 yards long, without any cover. This permitted the Union batteries to concentrate against each brigade as it advanced. General Porter, who saw the charges, wrote that the Confederate commanders showed "a reckless disregard for life."

D. H. Hill now ordered up his five brigades to assault. A few men got within two hundred yards of the Union batteries, but canister and rifle fire mowed most of them down, and the survivors rushed to the rear. Hill's brigades fell back, re-formed, and attacked again. Union fire stopped them once more. At seven o'clock Hill recognized his men were incapable of further exertion, and ordered them back.

Meanwhile, Magruder continued to feed in one brigade after another. "As each brigade emerged from the woods," D. H. Hill reported, "from fifty to one-hundred guns opened upon it, tearing great gaps in its ranks; but the heroes reeled on and were shot down by the reserves at the guns. . . . It was not war—it was murder."[6]

Porter Alexander wrote: "Next morning the enemy was gone and the melancholy field was ours, to collect our wounded and bury our dead." The cost was staggering, nearly 5,600 Confederates killed or wounded, about 2,000 Federal casualties, most left on the field. On that morning, a third of the bodies on the field were dead.

But a Federal officer who was there said, "Enough were alive and moving to give the field a singular crawling effect."[7]

Both armies were exhausted and demoralized, conditions not improved by a heavy rain that fell much of the day. When the Federals reached Harrison's Landing, they collapsed, making no effort to defend the position. The Confederates were little interested in pursuing, and scarcely budged.

Early on July 3 Jeb Stuart with a few horsemen evicted a small Federal outpost on Evelynton Heights, pulled up a single howitzer, and began shelling the Union camps at Harrison's Landing. The Federals, after recovering from shock, sent up a division that drove off Stuart. Thus, McClellan at last, and with ease, captured the very hill that under strong Confederate occupation could have spelled his destruction.

In this fashion the Seven Days ended. McClellan had been driven from the gates of Richmond. But his army remained powerful, and the cost to the South was staggering: 20,000 men lost.

Robert E. Lee's audacity might win battles, but the cost in blood was going to be more than the South could bear.

THE REVOLUTION IN WARFARE

Robert E. Lee was no different from many other commanders on both sides who did not recognize that a new weapon, the Minié-ball rifle musket, had revolutionized the battlefield and made traditional military tactics obsolete.

The Minié bullet, or Minié ball, was invented in 1849 by a French army officer named Claude-Étienne Minié. It had an effective range of 400 yards, four times that of the existing infantry weapon, the smoothbore musket, and was lethal and somewhat controllable out to a thousand yards.*

By quadrupling the killing zone through which attacking soldiers had to march, the Minié-ball rifle—combined with a growing emphasis on defensive fortifications—made the orthodox methods of conducting battle so costly that attacks were becoming exercises in murder and mayhem. Both commanders North and South were

---

* Rifles, which had been around for centuries before Minié's invention, were more accurate and longer ranged than muskets, but had not become standard military weapons because the rifling in the barrel quickly became fouled by products of combustions of gunpowder. Minié produced a bullet with a hollow base. When the rifle was fired, the explosion expanded the base to fit snugly against the rifling grooves, scouring the fouling of the previous shot from the grooves. A Minié-ball rifle could fire many rounds before the barrel had to be cleaned. By the Seven Days, most soldiers on both sides were armed with the rifle, though the Confederates had difficulty acquiring it, and many of their troops still carried the musket.

following outdated battle tactics that had been built around military forces armed with the smoothbore musket.

These tactics called for troops to march up shoulder to shoulder to about a hundred yards from an opponent's position in a long line of battle two men deep. In an era of single-shot weapons, the only way firepower could be multiplied was to increase the number of men carrying weapons and to get them close enough to hit the enemy. For soldiers, the saving grace of the line of battle was that, provided they were shielded from artillery fire, they were relatively safe until they got within range of enemy muskets. Since it took twenty to thirty seconds to reload a musket, a defending force usually could get off only two or three shots before the attacking enemy was upon it.

Although sometimes defenders shattered an attack with well-aimed fire, attackers were successful more often than not. This became all the more the case in the early years of the nineteenth century. Napoleon Bonaparte wheeled smoothbore cannons to within a couple hundred yards of the enemy and knocked a hole in his line with canister. Since muskets were effective for only a hundred yards, the enemy could do little about it, and Napoleon won most of his later battles in this way.

The Minié ball alone would have changed everything, but its effect was greatly intensified by experiments with field fortifications. These included abatis to slow the advance of attackers, entrenchments to shield defending soldiers, and cleared spaces in front of breastworks to expose attackers to defenders' fire.

During the Seven Days the Union generals, being on the defensive, paid some attention to field fortifications. Confederate commanders, being on the offensive, ignored them. The varying views reflected the contradictory teachings of West Point, from where most senior commanders on both sides had graduated.

Dennis Hart Mahan had been professor of military tactics at West Point since 1832 (he retired in 1871), and preached the strength of the tactical defense and the defensive value of field entrenchments. But he also was a disciple of the Swiss Antoine-Henri Jomini (1779–1869), who had set himself up as interpreter of

Napoleon's method of warfare, and whose ideas permeated military teaching at West Point during Mahan's career.

Jomini virtually ignored field emplacements, and preached offensive warfare. He taught that the key to victory was to bring superior force against a numerically weaker enemy at some decisive point. Napoleon had maneuvered and fought brilliant battles on largely unfortified fields. To commanders who wanted to emulate the great Napoleon, it seemed an incongruity to fight behind static fortifications. Many commanders

Henry Halleck

(LIBRARY OF CONGRESS)

also felt that, if soldiers built safe barricades, they would be reluctant to leave them and advance in the open against the enemy.

Though General Lee had been an engineer officer in the U.S. Army and was an expert on fortifications, he gave little attention to them at this stage, and remained dedicated to offensive warfare. However, several Confederate generals, notably Stonewall Jackson and James Longstreet, were questioning Jomini's or Napoleon's offensive tactics in light of the dismaying losses suffered in the Seven Days attacks.

No one wanted to go as far as Union general Henry Halleck, who advanced only a mile or so a day to Corinth, Mississippi, after the Battle of Shiloh, ordering his men to throw up embankments and dig foxholes, or "ditches," as they called them, even for a night's stop. Nevertheless, a number of officers were coming to the judgment of Union general Jacob D. Cox, who said that "one rifle in the trench is worth five in front of it."[1]

Although the combination of field fortifications and the Minié ball immensely increased the power of the defense, commanders had no method to reach a decision except with the line of battle, and they continued to employ it, though attacks failed five times out of six.

Just one assault in the Seven Days succeeded—at Gaines Mill— and this only because the Confederates possessed overwhelming strength, and even then casualties were twice as high for the attackers as the defenders. Four attacks failed, most with gruesome losses.

Civil War artillerymen could not employ Napoleon's solution. The Minié-ball rifle had an effective range longer than the effective range of canister. When artillery tried to move up close to the enemy, sharpshooters shot down both gunners and horses and usually sent the batteries hurrying to the rear. Thus, in the Civil War, the infantry tended to dominate the artillery, despite the first widespread use of rifled cannons in warfare.[*]

Rifled guns were long-range, high-velocity pieces used for direct fire. But gunpowder, the only explosive available, was not strong enough to shatter shells into enough pieces to be efficient destroyers of men and matériel, while the inaccurate fuzes of the period could not guarantee that shells would explode on target. Rifled guns also tended to spin out the balls and pellets of canister into a doughnut pattern, with nothing in the center. Finally, rifled pieces buried projectiles in sloping ground. Rifled artillery was useful, but not decisive.

Nor did cavalry offer an alternative. In Napoleon's day, cavalry was sometimes able to achieve a victory because charging horses might crack an opposing infantry line with shock. The best defense against a cavalry charge was for the infantry to form a square, with musketeers facing outward on four sides. But infantry armed with

---

[*] Cannons normally fired straight at their targets. Civil War gunners usually had to see what they were aiming at and to have an open "field of fire" to it. They needed fairly level places to locate, since the guns had no recoil mechanisms, and absorbed the shock of recoil by rolling backward. Before being fired again, the guns had to be rolled back "into battery," or the original firing positions. The work-horse canister cannon on both sides was the 12-pound Napoleon smoothbore (named after Napoleon III, not Napoleon Bonaparte), a light, highly maneuverable weapon. Its maximum range was about 1,000 yards, but it was usually fired at much closer ranges.

the Minié-ball rifle could usually stop a cavalry charge long before the horses got close enough to break a line. In the Civil War the result was that cavalry lost its decisive role, and fell to screening advances and retreats, guarding flanks, exploiting routs, reconnoitering, and hit-and-run raids.

Some way out of the impasse had to be found. The Confederacy was inevitably going to lose if it continued to rely on headlong offensive attacks. The cost in manpower was too great. After the Seven Days, both Jackson and Longstreet began to advocate that Lee not initiate attacks but stand on the defensive. Jackson carried the idea further, developing the concept of maneuvering the enemy into such a position that he was either induced or obliged to attack.

Jackson came to this theory only after he had failed to convince President Davis to strike at the North's weakness, not its strength, and thereby achieve victory with few battles and little loss of life. In October 1861 he proposed that the Confederates attack into Maryland, bypass Washington's formidable defenses, seize Baltimore and Philadelphia, destroy Northern railroads, factories, and other property, and bring the cost of the war home to the Northern people. In this way, he said, the North would give up the war and grant the South independence.[*]

Davis had already rejected a similar proposal from Generals Joseph E. Johnston and Pierre Beauregard, and rejected Jackson's

---

[*] Jackson did not want to strike directly at Washington, but to cut the capital's food supply by severing its railway connections with the rest of the North. This would force Lincoln and his government to evacuate. It is doubtful whether Jackson had read the treatise *On War* by the Prussian theorist Carl von Clausewitz (1780–1831). However, Jackson advocated precisely what Clausewitz preached regarding a country involved in an insurrection or torn by internal dissension. In such a case, Clausewitz wrote, the capital, the chief leader, and public opinion constitute the "center of gravity," where collapse has the greatest chance of occurring. Jackson saw that the Confederacy's opportunity lay in isolating or capturing Washington, evicting Lincoln, and influencing Northern public opinion by damaging Northern industry and railroads—not attacking the Northern field army. See Carl von Clausewitz, *On War*, book 2, chapter 1 (Harmondsworth, England: Penguin Books, 1968), 173 (reprinted in New York by Dorset Press, 1991); Raymond Aron, *Clausewitz, Philosopher of War* (Englewood Cliffs, N.J.: Prentice-Hall, 1985), 108–09, 158–59, 213.

as well. Jackson renewed the proposal three more times, but Davis rejected them all. The president was convinced that, if the South merely stood on the defensive, the North would become weary and give up the war.

Lee believed in attacking the enemy—as he had demonstrated in the Seven Days—but he endorsed Davis's refusal to take the war to the Northern people. Lee was not interested in distant prospects, and he opposed threatening the enemy's civilian population. He always focused on the Union army directly in front of him.

Shortly before the Seven Days, for example, Jackson had asked that his army be raised to 40,000 men so that he could strike into the North, causing Abraham Lincoln to bring McClellan's army back to deal with the invasion, and relieving the siege of Richmond without a shot being fired. Lee told Jackson's emissary, Alexander R. Boteler: "Colonel, don't you think General Jackson had better come down here first and help me drive these troublesome people away from before Richmond?"[2]

With the final rejection of his invasion plan, Jackson turned to a more direct method of overcoming the effects of the Minié ball. His aim from now on was to defeat the North by destroying one or more of its armies.

Jackson probably reached this judgment in the Seven Days, but it was not officially recorded until the Battle of Fredericksburg, five months later. By that time he had distilled it into a maxim. Heros von Borcke, a Prussian officer on Jeb Stuart's staff, looking at the vast Federal army arrayed in front, turned to Jackson and wondered aloud whether the Rebels could stop so powerful an assault. Jackson replied: "Major, my men have sometimes failed to take a position, but to defend one, never!"[3]

At some time Jackson took the next logical step and arrived at a theory: place one's troops in a preselected, strong defensive position anchored by cannons, with at least one open flank, and maneuver the enemy into a situation where he is obligated to attack. The Seven Days had proved such an attack would fail, causing enormous casualties and demoralizing the survivors, as Confederates had been disheartened at Malvern Hill. Then one's army could move swiftly on the open flank of the unnerved enemy, surround his army, and destroy it.

No one wrote down Jackson's theory until after he was wounded at Chancellorsville in May 1863. Then he told his medical officer, Hunter McGuire, "that he intended, after breaking into [the Federal commander] Hooker's rear, to take and fortify a suitable position, cutting him off from the [Rappahannock] river and so hold him until, between himself and General Lee, the great Federal host should be broken to pieces."[4]

Since Lee commanded the army, Jackson had to convince him to undertake what essentially was a defensive strategy, but interwoven with maneuvers and deceptions to entice or force the enemy to attack. Jackson was devoted to the idea that a commander must "mystify, mislead, and surprise the enemy."[5] Though accepting in principle Jackson's concept of guile and indirect approach, Lee found it counter to his nature. Lee was a bellicose, direct soldier, as the Seven Days had demonstrated. He remained predominately focused on striking at the force before his eyes. Lee worked either to defeat this force, or to maneuver it out of position.

✶ 4 ✶

"POPE MUST BE SUPPRESSED"

Immediately after the Seven Days Lee faced a new threat northwest of Richmond. Abraham Lincoln had placed all Union field forces in the theater that were not in McClellan's army in a new, 50,000-man Army of Virginia under General John Pope.

As Lee pulled his army back from Harrison's Landing, leaving Jeb Stuart's cavalry on guard, Pope began consolidating his widely separated forces between Sperryville, on the eastern slopes of the Blue Ridge, and the Rappahannock River, about thirty miles west of Manassas. His aim was to drive down the Orange and Alexandria Railroad to Gordonsville, about fifty miles northwest of Richmond, and attack the capital through the back door.

Lincoln also named a new general-in-chief of the army, Henry Wager Halleck (1815–72). Both Halleck and Pope had gained some notoriety in the West, yet both were dismal choices. Though Halleck had graduated third in his class at West Point (1839), and bore the nickname "Old Brains" for having written scholarly works on war, he was slow, hesitant, envious of the success of others, had little strategic sense, and saw dangers at every turn.

John Pope was inadequate in different directions. A forty-year-old West Pointer (1842), he was puffed up with pride and confidence, and an ardent antislavery Republican wanting to punish the South. Pope made an excellent impression on Lincoln, Secretary of War Edwin M. Stanton, and the abolitionist congressional Committee on the Conduct of the War, but he was incautious, ridiculed generals who thought strategy was more important than headlong fighting, and unable to see danger until it hit him in the face.

Pope also brought in a new level of horror to the war by instructing his army to live off the country and reimburse only citizens loyal to the United States, and to hold local citizens hostage for actions of guerrillas, without distinguishing between partisans and ordinary Confederate cavalry. He went as far as to treat a mother who wrote her soldier son as a traitor, subject to being shot as a spy.

Pope's orders so incensed Lee that he wrote twice that Pope must be suppressed. Pope was the only adversary whom Lee regarded with undisguised contempt. With the approval of President Davis, Lee notified Halleck that the Confederacy would be compelled to retaliate if Pope's orders were enforced. Halleck modified Pope's orders materially, but did not suppress them entirely.

Lee felt himself caught between two fires. As Pope's army slowly gathered in northern Virginia, McClellan did nothing at Harrison's Landing, but remained formidable. Lee had replaced some of his losses in the Seven Days, and had about 72,000 men, whereas McClellan commanded 90,000, Pope would have 50,000 when his forces concentrated, and Ambrose E. Burnside's 13,000-man corps, brought up from New Bern, North Carolina, was sitting in transports in Chesapeake Bay off Fort Monroe, capable of reinforcing either McClellan or Pope.

Not knowing which direction to turn, Lee remained immobile until July 12, 1862, when Pope occupied Culpeper, only twenty-seven miles north of Gordonsville. If he seized the "Gordonsville loop" of the east-west Virginia Central Railroad, he could break connections with the Shenandoah Valley, the granary of the Confederacy, and endanger the food supply of Richmond and the army.

The prospect of this maneuver was too much. Despite the potential for disaster by dividing his army, Lee ordered Stonewall Jackson, commanding two divisions, Charles S. Winder's and Richard S. Ewell's, a little more than 12,000 men, to move to Gordonsville. Jackson's corps arrived on July 19.

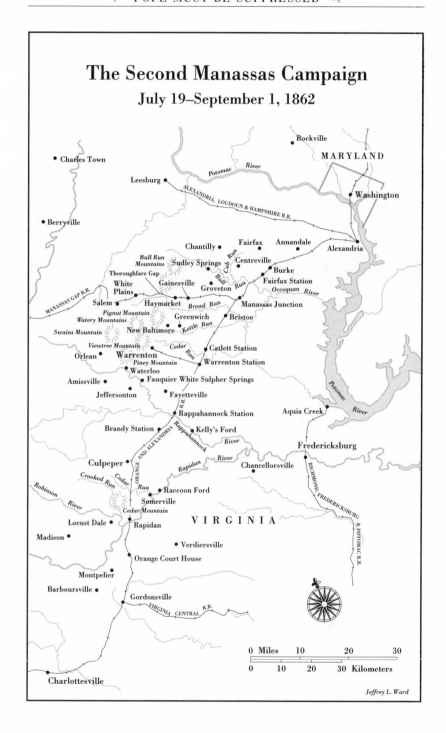

The Second Manassas Campaign
July 19–September 1, 1862

John Pope

Ambrose E. Burnside

Jackson saw a great opportunity at Gordonsville. With McClellan idle on the James, the largest Union army was, for the moment, neutralized. If Jackson could get sufficient troops, he might destroy a part of Pope's forces before he could consolidate his whole army. Jackson asked Lee for reinforcements, but Lee hesitated, still not certain what McClellan would do.

Lee didn't know it, but Lincoln had lost confidence in McClellan, and wanted to bring his army back toward Washington. He visited McClellan on July 8 at Harrison's Landing for the sole purpose of determining whether the army could be withdrawn. He concluded that it could be.

Lincoln was intent on moving the war in a revolutionary new direction. The Union losses at Shiloh* and in the Seven Days had cast a pall over the North, and caused many people to wonder whether preservation of the Union was worth such a terrible cost.

---

* On April 6–7, 1862, Confederates and Federals fought a gruesome, inconclusive battle at Shiloh, Tennessee, that cost the North 13,000 casualties and the South 10,700.

Lincoln concluded that he must arouse the Northern people to a moral crusade. To do this, he had to promise to free the slaves, and planned to issue an Emancipation Proclamation, but applicable only to the seceding states, keeping slavery intact in the four slave states—Delaware, Maryland, Kentucky, and Missouri—that remained in the Union.

On July 22, 1862, when Lincoln read a proposed proclamation to his cabinet, Secretary of State William H. Seward objected. Coming on the heels of the humiliation of the Seven Days, he said, "it may be viewed as . . . our last shriek on the retreat." The proclamation should be postponed until the Union attained a military success. Lincoln agreed, pocketed the paper, and waited for a victory.

Richard S. Ewell

(US MILITARY HISTORY INSTITUTE)

On July 24 Halleck went to Harrison's Landing and told McClellan it was imprudent to keep two Union armies divided with Lee between them, able to strike at one before the other could come to its aid. McClellan protested, pointing out that his army was in the heart of the Confederacy, only a score of miles from the capital. But Halleck concluded that McClellan would never take the offensive, wrote that he did "not understand strategy and should never plan a campaign," but didn't tell McClellan to evacuate the James River until August 3.[1]

Consequently, as Porter Alexander wrote, the Federal army "began the evacuation of the only position from which it could have forced the evacuation of Richmond. They were only to find it again after two more years' fighting, and the loss of over 100,000 men; and they would find it then only by being defeated upon every other possible line of advance."[2]

To prevent Confederate interference with McClellan's retreat, Halleck ordered Pope to make demonstrations toward Gordonsville to occupy Jackson. Accordingly, Pope dispatched his cavalry to the Robinson River, a tributary of the Rapidan River, only sixteen miles north of Gordonsville.

Lee now concluded that Pope's movements were getting too threatening, and sent A. P. Hill's division of 12,000 men to reinforce Jackson at Gordonsville. It arrived July 29.

On July 30, Halleck ordered Ambrose Burnside's corps, still in ships off Fort Monroe, to proceed to Aquia Creek, near Fredericksburg, and for McClellan to send his sick northward by boat. These moves got back to Lee through spies and nearly convinced him that McClellan would soon evacuate the peninsula. But he could not take the chance on moving until McClellan actually was gone.

Meanwhile, Jackson was preparing to advance, though he had only half the men Pope was assembling. Gathering reports from spies, Jackson saw a narrow window of opportunity. Burnside hadn't arrived, and Pope's troops were still spread out. If he could catch a part of Pope's army and defeat it, he might throw Pope on the defensive until Lee could come up with the whole army. Then, if McClellan's forces hadn't yet redeployed alongside Pope, the Army of Northern Virginia would be about equal to Pope's force, and might maneuver him into a corner where he would have to attack or surrender.

Pope was concentrating at Culpeper, but only a part of his army had arrived. Jackson hoped to defeat this advanced force, then turn on the remaining parts as they came up. It was a long shot, but he set his army in motion northward on August 7 on the Gordonsville–Culpeper road (present-day U.S. Route 15).

Because of traffic tie-ups at a ford over the Rapidan, Jackson got only eight miles north of Orange Court House on August 8. Meanwhile, Pope sent Nathaniel P. Banks's corps, just arrived, to reinforce a picket of Federal cavalry at Cedar Mountain, six miles south of Culpeper.

Jackson had failed to catch a separated part of Pope's army. But Pope conveniently did the job for him, isolating Banks at Cedar Mountain. Banks was an impulsive, injudicious general, and attacked Jackson when he came up on August 9, 1862. Jackson routed the whole force, costing the Federals 2,400 men out of 9,000 committed. Jackson lost about 1,250.

Jackson rendered Banks's corps combat-ineffective. Pope relegated the remaining men to guard the trains during the campaign coming up. The wider significance of Jackson's victory was to throw Pope onto the strategic defensive, giving Lee more than a week to concentrate the Army of Northern Virginia.[3]

On the morning after the Battle of Cedar Mountain, Jackson realized he no longer had the strength to confront Pope alone. Three additional Federal divisions had arrived, and a fourth was a day's march away, while Burnside's corps would likely be coming up soon from Aquia Creek.

Jackson was glad to accept a Federal proposal on August 11 for an armistice for both sides to remove the wounded. This gave him the opportunity to steal back across the Rapidan that night, leaving burning campfires as a cover.

Pope interpreted Jackson's retreat as a victory, and wired Halleck he was pursuing. This was what Jackson was hoping for, thinking Pope might once more expose a part of his army. "Beware of the snare," Halleck wired back. "Feigned retreats are 'Secesh' tactics."[4] Pope took the advice, and concentrated nearly his whole army between Cedar Mountain and the Rapidan, about seven miles south.

Despite strong hints, Lee still could acquire no positive evidence that McClellan was abandoning Harrison's Landing. But Jackson's position was getting perilous, and on August 13, he ordered Longstreet's corps to Gordonsville. The next day, D. H. Hill, guarding the south bank of the James, reported that Fitz John Porter's corps was marching to Fort Monroe, final proof that McClellan was abandoning the peninsula. His whole army got away on August 17.

If Lee could concentrate most of his troops at Gordonsville, he might deal Pope a blow before the Army of the Potomac could complete its roundabout journey by water and land to reinforce Pope. But no time could be lost. Lee ordered Huger's old division, now under Richard H. Anderson of South Carolina, to move to Gordonsville, leaving as Richmond's protection three divisions under a refreshed Gustavus W. Smith. A Confederate force of about 55,000 men began to assemble at Gordonsville.

Lee himself arrived on August 15, and sat down with Jackson and Longstreet. Jackson had been studying Pope's dispositions, and believed he had found a potentially fatal flaw. Pope now had about 50,000 men just north of the Rapidan, but had allowed his left, or eastern, flank to remain weak and virtually unguarded. The Confederates could sweep around Pope's left, block reinforcements coming from Aquia Creek, and cut the Orange and Alexandria Railroad, thereby severing Pope's supply line. Pope then could be pressed against the Rapidan and the Blue Ridge to the west, forcing his army to surrender or to attack the Confederates, with the possibility that it might be destroyed.

Lee, however, did not aspire to destroy Pope's army. Despite the rapid transfer of the bulk of his forces to Gordonsville, his aim was only to evict Pope from Virginia. He expressly stated this to President Davis in a letter on August 30, 1862: "My desire has been to avoid a general engagement, being the weaker force, and by maneuvering to relieve the portion of the country referred to [central and northern Virginia]."[5]

The lesson Lee had drawn from the Seven Days was to shun battle when possible. This aversion was only a temporary aberration, brought on by the losses he'd suffered, but it did govern the campaign against Pope. However, Lee did not convey this plan to his senior lieutenants, and only hinted at it in the way he conducted the campaign.

It has never been satisfactorily explained why Lee adopted a maneuver strategy against Pope. In following it, Lee reverted to the system prevalent in Europe for a century and a half prior to

Napoleon. In this period armies maneuvered to cut off the enemy's access to fortresses, where their food and ammunition were stored. Once an army severed this connection, the enemy was obliged to retreat. Wars often had few battles or none, and consisted primarily of marches on the enemy's rear. Lee saw that the same effect could be achieved by maneuvering on the railroad that delivered supplies to Pope's army. If this line could be cut, Pope would be obliged to withdraw without battle.

Lee never again adopted a maneuver-only offensive plan, and he never commented on why he took it up and why he then abandoned it. Perhaps he recognized after the campaign that maneuver strategy has three crippling faults: it is indecisive; it inflicts little permanent harm on the enemy; and it can't force the enemy to make peace.

In the upcoming campaign, Lee tried to avoid a general battle. It was Jackson, not Lee, who brought it on, while Lee, finding battle thrust upon him, was slow to exploit it. These two facts explain why Second Manassas was not the decisive Confederate victory that Stonewall Jackson planned for.

Accordingly, Lee and Jackson went into the campaign with vastly different goals. Jackson wanted to annihilate Pope's army. Lee wanted to maneuver Pope back to Washington. Lee adopted in general terms Jackson's plan, but refused to accept Jackson's timetable, thereby guaranteeing its failure. Jackson wanted to strike fast, because he believed the moment Pope realized he was going to be attacked, he would run for the protection of the Rappahannock River, some twenty-five miles north.

Lee often kept vital facts to himself, and did not share the reality of a situation with Jackson and his other senior generals. Lee realized that in the Seven Days he had left too much to the judgment of his lieutenants; several had made wrong decisions. He wanted to change this, and take more control into his own hands. However, Lee had always shied away from confronting other people, shrinking from "scenes" in which he was compelled to assert rank or authority. Instead, he sought harmony, preferring to suggest and depend upon others to recognize the wisdom of his suggestions.[6] This had not worked in the Seven Days. In the upcoming campaign Lee did not tell his senior generals everything he was thinking. This prevented them from going too far beyond his purposes, but Lee's reticence to level with Jackson caused the junior officer to anticipate that Lee intended to give battle, when in fact he did not.

To prevent Pope from evacuating the Rapidan line, Jackson urged the army to move into position the next day, August 16, and strike on the early morning of August 17. Longstreet objected. He hadn't gotten his commissary organized and wanted time to bake bread. Jackson said he'd give Longstreet enough biscuits for the march, but this didn't suit Longstreet.

Since Lee's purpose was to maneuver Pope off the Rapidan, speed was not his primary consideration. Also, he put emphasis on a cavalry strike by Jeb Stuart to burn the railroad bridge at Rappahannock Station (now Remington), about twenty-five miles northeast of Pope's main position, thereby cutting Pope's supply line. Jackson was not much interested, because a movement on Pope's eastern flank would inevitably reach the railroad, and halt Pope's supplies just as readily as burning the railroad bridge.

To give Stuart time to move, however, Lee ordered infantry to approach the eastern Rapidan fords, at Somerville (where U.S. Route 522 now crosses) and Raccoon (two miles east), on August 17 and attack August 18. As things worked out, it took even longer, and Jackson's hopes to destroy Pope's army vanished.

One cause of the delay was Stuart. He ordered Fitzhugh Lee's cavalry brigade to move on August 17 from Beaver Dam Station, thirty-five miles southeast, to Raccoon Ford, where Stuart planned to cross. But Fitz Lee, not alerted to a need for haste, marched roundabout to Louisa Court House, where he drew ammunition and rations from a supply base, and did not arrive on time.

Meanwhile, Stuart and his aides rode to Verdiersville, eleven miles east of Orange, on the evening of the 17th. Finding no Fitz Lee, Stuart sent his adjutant, Major Norman Fitzhugh, down the road to locate the missing brigade. Federal cavalry captured Fitzhugh, and found on his person a copy of a letter from Lee outlining the movement against Pope.

This letter alone might have sent Pope flying, and Lee had already decided to delay the attack until the 19th because Anderson's division had not arrived from Richmond, and Longstreet's commissary still hadn't baked enough biscuits. When he got word from Fitz Lee that his horses were worn from the long march, General Lee deferred the Confederate advance until August 20.

For Lee, the delay was not vital, since Pope would retreat as soon as the Confederates moved. Accordingly, he overruled a request by Jackson for the attack to go forward without Stuart's cavalry.

Pope indeed had become alarmed, and set his troops in motion on the afternoon of August 18. By nightfall on August 19 he had them safely behind the Rappahannock.

Thus, when the Confederates rushed across the Rapidan on August 20, all they found were rear guards and a few stragglers. One of the great opportunities for a crowning Confederate victory had been lost. Union general George H. Gordon, present during the campaign, wrote: "It was then most fortunate that Jackson was not in command of the Confederate forces on the night of the 18th of August; for the superior force of the enemy must have overwhelmed us, if we could not have escaped, and escape on that night was impossible."[7]

On August 20, 1862, the Army of Northern Virginia came up on General Pope's army along the river from Rappahannock Station to Kelly's Ford, four miles downstream. When Rebels tested the fords they found them fiercely defended.

Lee, knowing that McClellan's army was beginning to come ashore at Aquia Creek, feared that part of Pope's army would join McClellan and march directly on Richmond.

Lee sent 17,000 men in two divisions—D.H. Hill's and Lafayette McLaws's—to the North Anna River above Hanover Junction to stand guard, and hoped to maneuver the rest of Pope's army off the Rappahannock before turning back toward Aquia Creek and Fredericksburg.

But as Jackson's corps moved upstream on Pope's right, and Longstreet's corps took over the places vacated by Jackson, Pope's men marched up the opposite bank. In this way, both armies, clashing along the way, moved their western flanks to Waterloo, thirteen miles upriver from Rappahannock Station.

Lee, still confident Pope's troops would retreat if his rail connection were broken, approved a strike to be conducted by Stuart's cavalry on the night of August 22 against Catlett Station on the railroad, twelve miles north of Rappahannock Station. The raid began during a raging thunderstorm, and the railroad bridge was too wet to burn. However, Pope's headquarters was there, and Stuart found Pope's dispatch book, containing his orders.

The book revealed that Pope had not detached any troops to Fredericksburg after all, but planned for McClellan to join him along the Rappahannock. Many Federal troops were already on the way. Lee had only a few days before Pope's army would be entirely too large to deal with.[*]

Lee ordered the divisions of D.H. Hill and McLaws to join him, but he could not wait for them. He still relied on another strike at the railroad, but this time it would be with infantry, and Jackson would lead them. On August 24, Lee told an astonished and delighted Jackson to take his whole corps, 23,000 men, get on Pope's rear, and cut his communications with Washington. Lee would be left with 32,000 men until D.H. Hill's and McLaws's

---

[*] Jesse L. Reno's corps, 8,000 men, from Burnside's force had already arrived. Fitz John Porter's and Samuel P. Heintzelman's corps from McClellan's army, plus John F. Reynolds's Pennsylvania division—in all, 25,000 men—were within two days' juncture with Pope, while Jacob D. Cox, with 7,000 men from West Virginia, Samuel D. Sturgis, with 10,000 from Washington, and the remainder of McClellan's army were not more than five to eight days away. Pope soon would possess more than 120,000 men.

troops arrived. Lee knew that one of the basic tenets of warfare is to keep an army concentrated in the face of the enemy. But to remain idle on the Rappahannock would invite destruction.

Since Fitz John Porter's corps was approaching from the east, it was obvious that the flanking move should be to the west. But Lee did not specify where Jackson should strike, and his expectations were modest. As his biographer, Douglas Freeman, wrote, the reason for Lee's division of force was "that an attack on Pope's line of communications seemed to be the only means of maneuvering into a retreat an opponent whom he did not feel strong enough to fight. Had he any intention to give battle, it is unlikely that Lee would have adopted such a dangerous course."[8]

Thus, a remarkable process began to unroll. Lee did not want a battle, and Jackson, given Lee's delay in crossing the Rapidan, surely suspected as much. However, Lee and Jackson both knew that if Jackson stayed on Pope's line of communications long enough to ensure a Federal retreat, Pope would almost be bound to attack him. Jackson based his actions on this probability, and Lee must have expected it as well, because he did not intend for Longstreet to be separated from Jackson longer than necessary to mask Jackson's advance. So knowingly, Lee reconciled this contradiction, and marched toward an inevitable battle, yet didn't seek one.

But Jackson had no doubts: he wanted to provoke an attack by Pope. Immediately after leaving Lee, Jackson summoned his engineer, Captain J. Keith Boswell, and told him to select "the most direct and covered route to Manassas," on the railroad twenty-five miles in Pope's rear, and only eighteen miles from Alexandria.*

---

* Jackson's plan was almost identical to the deadliest of Napoleon Bonaparte's strategic moves, the *manoeuvre sur les derrières*, which led, among others, to victories in the Italian campaign of 1796, the Marengo campaign of 1800, and the opening stage of the Austerlitz campaign of 1805. Napoleon committed a strong force to hold the enemy in place on his main line by a fierce attack or threat, then sent a powerful column around the enemy's flank deep into his rear, and there established a strategic barrage or barrier across his line of supply and retreat. This forced the enemy to withdraw from his main line and, if the barrage were set in place in time to block the enemy, could result in his defeat or destruction.

Possession of Manassas Junction not only would sever Pope's umbilical cord, but was so close to Washington as to threaten Pope's passage to it. Moreover, Jackson would be isolated in the heart of enemy country, presenting Pope an almost irresistible impulse to attack.

Jackson assembled his corps, three divisions commanded by A.P. Hill, Richard S. Ewell, and William B. Taliaferro. (Taliaferro had taken over from General Winder, mortally wounded at Cedar Mountain.) Jackson ordered his men to cook rations for three days, and to put into the column only ambulances and ammunition wagons. The haste was so great that some men didn't get their biscuits cooked, and had to rely on green corn and apples grabbed from fields and orchards they passed.

Just before dawn on August 25, Jackson's corps moved to Amissville, then north across the Rappahannock to Salem (now named Marshall) behind the Bull Run Mountains, a hard march of twenty-six miles. Meantime, Longstreet remained on the Rappahannock, keeping up an active skirmish with the Federals.

Federal soldiers on a mountain near Warrenton discovered Jackson's movement and calculated its approximate size. But Pope was not worried, figuring Jackson was headed to the Shenandoah Valley, and the rest of Lee's army might be moving behind him. But Pope did nothing to confirm this judgment, failing to send even a cavalry force to find out where Jackson was going.

Consequently, after dropping down at Salem on the night of August 25, Jackson's corps rose on the 26th and had an unobstructed passage into the rear of Pope's army through Thoroughfare Gap in the Bull Run Mountains. About 4 P.M. on August 26, the corps marched into Gainesville at the junction with the Warrenton– Alexandria turnpike (now U.S. Route 29), where Jeb Stuart's cavalry joined it. The horsemen had arrived via back roads through the Bull Run Mountains. Despite the clouds of dust raised by soldiers and horses, Pope had no idea the Confederates were in his rear.

Eight miles beyond Gainesville lay Manassas Junction.

Meanwhile, along the Rappahannock, Irvin McDowell, commanding a corps under Pope, became convinced that the bulk of the Rebel army was somewhere north of Waterloo. Suddenly seeing danger, Pope broke his 75,000-man army away from the river in the afternoon, directing it to concentrate the next day, August 27, around Warrenton, six miles east.

Lee, who had been watching Pope's movements closely, feared that Pope might have discovered Jackson's whereabouts and was going to block him. Lee immediately disengaged, and Longstreet moved his corps off on the path Jackson had taken.

Thus, on the evening of August 26, both hostile armies drew away from one another, Longstreet and Lee moving northward behind the Bull Run Mountains, Pope turning eastward to Warrenton. But despite Lee's anxiety, Pope still had not discovered the whereabouts of Jackson.

When Jackson arrived at Gainesville, he did not march for Manassas Junction, but to Bristoe Station, four miles below Manassas, where he cut the telegraph and blocked the railroad, but not before a locomotive coming north with a string of empty cars broke through and rushed on to Manassas to warn authorities. A small Confederate force then moved north and seized Manassas during the night.

Morning at Manassas revealed a vast treasure of food and supplies, enough to refurnish Jackson's whole corps several times over. Jackson sent forward Taliaferro's and A. P. Hill's divisions, leaving Ewell to guard Bristoe Station. At Manassas the Rebels scattered a Union cavalry regiment and the 1st New Jersey Brigade, sent by Halleck. Fitz Lee's horsemen pursued the survivors all the way to Burke's Station, twelve miles from Alexandria.

Pope, when he got word of the strike, thought it was only a small cavalry raid, and told Samuel P. Heintzelman at Warrenton Junction (now called Calverton), ten miles south of Warrenton, to send a regiment by railway to repair the wires, replace the track, and protect the line. Early on August 27, however, the regiment returned with the news that the enemy was in force at Bristoe Station. Now

(NATIONAL ARCHIVES)

Joseph Hooker

alarmed, Pope ordered Joseph Hooker to march his division from Warrenton Junction to deal with the enemy force. And, realizing his army was in jeopardy, he directed most of it to move back to Gainesville, twelve miles east of Warrenton, the remainder to close in around Warrenton Junction.

Thus Jackson achieved Lee's principal aim: by cutting off his supplies, Pope, without a fight, had run for the third time.

Hooker came up on Ewell, but the Confederate commander, in a series of adroit movements, destroyed the railway bridges at Kettle Run, two miles south of Bristoe Station, and at Broad Run, just north, and moved to Manassas Junction. Hooker stopped at Broad Run.

On the evening of August 27 Pope arrived at Broad Run and learned for the first time that he faced Stonewall Jackson's entire corps. Until this moment, Pope had clung to the idea that the railroad had been cut by a small force, and that Jackson's corps was just east of Thoroughfare Gap and could be blocked at Gainesville. Now Pope jumped to another false conclusion: that Jackson was planning to move around the eastern flank of Hooker's division at Bristoe, so as to get back south and rejoin Lee! Pope should have known this was absurd, since he had received reports that Lee had marched northwest the day before.

Now Pope became absorbed in trying to "bag" Jackson at Manassas Junction. He ordered Porter's two-division corps to move from Warrenton Junction, and Philip Kearny's division of Heintzelman's corps to come from Greenwich, six miles to the northwest, giving him, with Hooker, four divisions at Bristoe. He also ordered Nathaniel Banks's corps to move on August 28 with the army trains to Kettle Run, and repair the railway bridge there.

If Pope had stopped with this, he would have been admirably situated to deal with Jackson, who was at Manassas, and Longstreet, who was approaching through Thoroughfare Gap. For Pope had three divisions of McDowell's corps and two of Franz Sigel's at Gainesville or nearby, while Jesse L. Reno's 8,000-man corps was at Greenwich, about equidistant between Gainesville and Bristoe. Pope had unwittingly landed in Napoleon's "central position," between Lee and Jackson, and could destroy one wing of the Confederate army before the other could come up to assist. At best, the Rebels would have to attack if they were to reunite.

But Pope entirely disregarded Longstreet's wing of the Confederate army—although Federal cavalry had encountered Longstreet's troops at Salem, proving that they were just west of Thoroughfare Gap on the night of August 27.

Pope never grasped his spectacular strategic advantage, and made a devastating error. Assuming that Jackson would remain quietly at Manassas Junction, he ordered Reno, McDowell, and Sigel to march to Manassas at daylight the next day, August 28. He thereby planned to abandon Gainesville, give up his central position, and make it possible for the two wings of the Rebel army to rejoin.

Jackson was not aware of Pope's efforts to encircle him at Manassas, but knew he could not remain exposed there. He had already worked out where he was going, and Pope would find his trap at Manassas empty the next morning.

But before departing, Jackson loaded his wagons with all the supplies they could hold, then threw the depot open to his soldiers. It was a wonderful revel, remembered long afterward. They refitted themselves with Union shoes and clothing, and ate every delicacy they could hold: one ragged private indulged in Union canned lobster and Rhine wine. The men marched away with whatever luxuries or tradable goods they could carry. One soldier bore twenty boxes of cigars, another canned fruits, a third a larder of coffee, a fourth a string of shoes hung around his neck, and yet another a haversackful of French mustard. The mustard turned out to be the best of the booty. He traded it for meat and bread, and it lasted him into the next campaign.[9] As the corps departed Manassas that night, August 27, 1862, the rear guard set fire to the vast supply of goods they had to leave behind.

✴ 5 ✴

SECOND MANASSAS

Stonewall Jackson didn't know Pope was trying to concentrate at Manassas on August 28, 1862. The evidence seemed to point, rather, to Pope's intention to occupy Gainesville, and thereby prevent the junction of the two wings of the Confederate army.

However, Pope already had a reputation for running as soon as he encountered moves against him. Therefore, the forced marches along the Warrenton–Alexandria turnpike on the 27th might just as well indicate Pope was withdrawing behind Bull Run, a bold stream three miles north of Manassas. There, he could reestablish the supply line Jackson had cut, and have almost unlimited reserves to draw upon. If Pope got behind Bull Run, he would be invincible.

Though Lee wanted merely to evict Pope from northern Virginia, Jackson knew no damage would be done to the Federal war effort unless Pope was severely defeated. His principal aim, therefore, was to prevent Pope from retreating behind Bull Run, and to induce him to attack.

Jackson had two pressing obligations, however: to get his corps to a place of safety, and to find a way to reunite with Lee without going through Gainesville.

Jackson knew the landscape from the year before, when his brigade had occupied the neighborhood after First Manassas. At the time Jackson had found a tree-covered ridgeline above Groveton, three miles east of Gainesville and about a mile north of the Warrenton–Alexandria turnpike. From it, if need be, Jackson could rejoin Lee by way of two passes through the Bull Run Mountains a few miles north of Thoroughfare Gap. But the primary attraction of Groveton Heights was its suitability for defense, having an unfinished railroad line running just under it, with deep cuts that could serve partially as defensive emplacements.

Three other elements made it an admirable site to test Jackson's new theory about defensive battles. It had an open western flank at Gainesville, around which an enveloping force might strike. It commanded the turnpike, the best retreat route for the Northern army back to Washington. And the Stone Bridge over which the Federals had fled at First Manassas the year before offered the only adequate crossing of Bull Run in the vicinity.

If the Union army could be enticed into attacking Jackson along Groveton Heights, it could be defeated, and the Confederates might then sweep around the western flank, pin the Union army against Bull Run, and destroy it.

As his corps marched away from Manassas Junction on the night of August 27, Jackson covered both of his obligations. He sent Taliaferro straight up the Sudley Springs Road (present-day Virginia Route 234) to secure Groveton Heights. And he sent A. P. Hill across Bull Run to Centreville on the turnpike, and ordered Ewell to cross the stream and follow along the north bank to the Stone Bridge. If Pope tried to get over Bull Run during the night or early morning, Ewell and A. P. Hill could stop him until Longstreet and Taliaferro could come up on his rear. If not, they could join Taliaferro on Groveton Heights.

On the morning of August 28, none of Pope's forces had tried to cross Bull Run, and both Ewell and A. P. Hill marched to Groveton Heights.

On this same morning, Irvin McDowell's and Franz Sigel's corps proceeded down the pike to Gainesville, then turned toward Manassas, hoping to "bag" Jackson, whom the two Federal corps were actually leaving in their rear. During the day, Jackson moved Ewell's and Taliaferro's divisions off Groveton Heights to within a few yards of the turnpike.

Around noontime, Pope and the forces from Bristoe arrived at Manassas Junction, and found nothing but the charred remains of the Federal depot. Pope was thoroughly nonplussed. Where had Jackson gone? About 4 P.M. he got word that Fitz Lee's cavalry had been raiding Fairfax Station and Burke's Station on the railroad, and also learned that A. P. Hill had marched to Centreville the night before. This news threw Pope entirely off the track, and at 4:15 P.M., thinking Jackson was over Bull Run blocking his access to Washington, he ordered all his forces to march on Centreville.

Thus in mid-afternoon the Federal soldiers started out on a new wild-goose chase. Only Phil Kearny got to the village by nightfall, finding no Rebels, while most of the remainder of Pope's exhausted army dropped down in a wide arc to the south.

Jackson's corps had lain undetected all day just north of the Warrenton–Alexandria pike, but Jackson himself had gotten more and more anxious as the day wore on. At first he was confident that Pope was converging on Manassas, where he could do no damage. Then reports by Stuart's scouts told him that the Federals were trying to get across Bull Run. Did that mean that Pope was retreating behind the stream after all? If so, there would be no possibility of getting Pope to attack. Jackson searched for some means to draw Pope's attention to his corps.

Almost at nightfall, scouts reported that a large Federal force was marching right down the turnpike straight for Centreville. Here was the chance Jackson was seeking. As Jackson's biographer, G. F. R. Henderson, wrote, Jackson concluded that "if Pope was to be fought in the open field before he could be reinforced by McClellan, he must be induced to retrace his steps."[1]

The force Jackson encountered was Rufus King's division of 10,000 men. It had managed to march only a few miles toward Manassas before it got word to strike for Centreville. King returned to Gainesville, then started down the turnpike, marching in column formation, oblivious to the presence of a Confederate corps only yards away on the north side of the road.

Jackson ordered Taliaferro's division and two brigades of Ewell's division to attack. Confederate cannons opened up as the middle of King's column came past. The Rebel infantry went forward with a rush, but quickly came to a halt as the Federals wheeled into line of battle and returned fire. The Rebels were facing primarily a New York and a Pennsylvania regiment of Abner Doubleday's brigade, and John Gibbon's "black hat" Indiana and Wisconsin brigade (wearing nonregulation black slouch hats).

Federal guns unlimbered, caught the Rebel cannons in enfilade, and forced them to withdraw. The battle degenerated into a gruesome bloodletting.

As General Taliaferro expressed it: "A farm house, an orchard, a few stacks of hay, and a rotten 'worm' fence were the only cover afforded the opposing lines of infantry; it was a stand-up combat, dogged and unflinching, in a field almost bare. There were no wounds from spent balls; the confronting lines looked into each other's faces at deadly range, less than one hundred yards apart, and they stood as immovable as the painted heroes in a battle-piece."[2]

The opponents drew away only with nightfall. The battle was fought largely by brigadiers, who brought less than half of their forces into action. King was still in Gainesville and both Taliaferro and Ewell were wounded early, Ewell losing a leg. The Federals lost about 1,500 men, the Confederates more than a thousand. Command of Taliaferro's division passed to William E. Starke, Ewell's division to Alexander R. Lawton.

The Battle of Groveton, as it was called, was precisely the kind of engagement Jackson was trying to avoid. And if Pope was determined to retreat across Bull Run, assaulting a single one of his divisions had no chance of stopping it. But the battle served Jackson's purposes, for it showed Pope where Jackson was, and deliberately challenged him to a battle.

The clash at Groveton caused Sigel's corps and John F. Reynolds's Pennsylvania division to turn abruptly away from their march on Centreville, and rush toward the sound of the guns. Sigel pushed his two divisions up the Sudley Springs Road, reaching the turnpike at darkness. Reynolds got his division about a mile west of Sigel. They were in excellent position to confront Jackson on Friday, August 29.

While the Groveton fight was going on, another engagement was being fought at Thoroughfare Gap, six miles west of Gainesville. McDowell had told one of his division commanders, James B. Ricketts, to watch for Longstreet, and only turn toward Manassas if Longstreet hadn't appeared. Ricketts got word that Rebel advance parties had arrived at Thoroughfare Gap that morning. Ricketts accordingly marched to the gap, arriving just as Longstreet's corps came up in mid-afternoon.

Lee took no chances. To be blocked here could bring disaster. He had Longstreet press David R. Jones's division forward on the main road, but also sent a strong flanking force, John B. Hood's division, by a narrow path above Hopewell Pass, three miles north. Ricketts deployed one brigade forward into the gap, but Jones's men seized the heights on either side, and drove Ricketts back to the eastern foot of the pass. After nightfall, Ricketts began withdrawing to Gainesville on reports that Hood was advancing on his flank.

A courier from Longstreet informed Jackson of his proximity. Jackson now knew that if Pope attacked the next day, Longstreet's corps would be on his right.

On August 28, Longstreet's corps was bivouacked on both sides of Thoroughfare Gap; Jackson's corps was near the turnpike at Groveton facing King. The Federal army was scattered over the map: King's division was at Groveton, Reynolds and Sigel were within supporting distance on King's east, Ricketts was nearing Gainesville, Kearny's division and Jesse Reno's corps were around Centreville, Joseph Hooker's division was just north of Manassas, Fitz John Porter's corps was at Bristoe Station, and Banks's corps was with the army trains at Kettle Run, about two miles south of Bristoe.

When Pope heard of the clash at Groveton, he drew the wrong conclusion. Earlier he had misconstrued A. P. Hill's presence at Centreville. He thought Jackson's whole corps had been there, and that Kearny's march on the village had forced Jackson to retreat, leaving A. P. Hill as the rear guard. Pope entirely missed the fact that A. P. Hill had left Centreville in the morning, not in the late afternoon when Kearny arrived, and could not have been retreating from Kearny. This error led Pope to believe that King and Ricketts were blocking Jackson's effort to rejoin Lee and Longstreet west of the Bull Run Mountains.

Pope was now seized with the desire to stop Jackson before he could make good his escape. Pope had gotten the whole situation wrong, but he still took Jackson's bait.

The most remarkable aspect of Pope's decision to attack was that he entirely ignored Longstreet's corps at Thoroughfare Gap, and the virtual certainty that it would march on Gainesville early on August 29. Pope believed he would have to deal only with Jackson, and assumed that King and Ricketts were firmly blocking Jackson from rejoining Lee.

However, King and Ricketts were about to remove themselves entirely from the scene. As the night wore on, King got increasingly nervous. He couldn't confer with McDowell, who had gone to Manassas to see Pope (but got lost). Around 11 P.M. King learned that Ricketts was falling back from Thoroughfare Gap. That was the last straw. King decided he was in an exposed position, and at 1 A.M. set his division marching to Manassas! Ricketts, certain Lee would march eastward the next morning and feeling alone at Gainesville, also ordered retreat at dawn to Bristoe.

Having no idea that King and Ricketts were abandoning their splendid position between the two wings of the Confederate army, Pope ordered his corps commanders to converge on the supposedly fleeing Jackson around Groveton early the next morning.

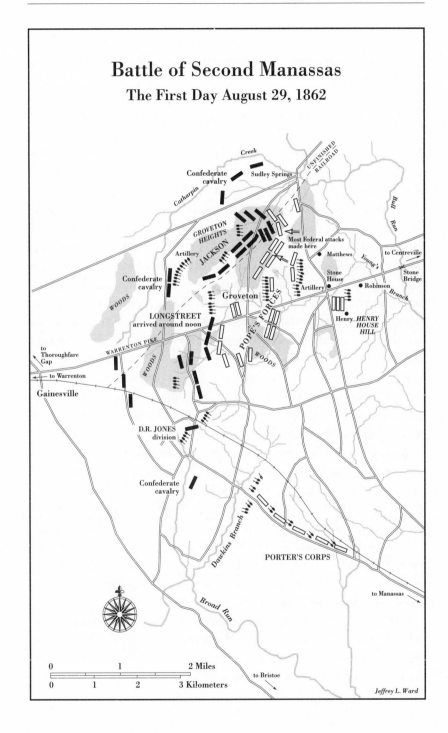

Battle of Second Manassas
The First Day August 29, 1862

Creek

UNFINISHED RAILROAD

Confederate cavalry

Sudley Springs

Catharpin

Bull Run

GROVETON HEIGHTS

JACKSON

Most Federal attacks made here

to Centreville

Artillery

Matthews

Young's

Stone Bridge

Confederate cavalry

Stone House

Robinson

Branch

Groveton

Artillery

WOODS

POPE'S FORCES

Henry

HENRY HOUSE HILL

LONGSTREET
arrived around noon

to Thoroughfare Gap

WARRENTON PIKE

WOODS

WOODS

to Warrenton

Gainesville

D.R. JONES
division

Confederate cavalry

Dawkins Branch

PORTER'S CORPS

to Manassas

Broad Run

| 0 | | 1 | | 2 Miles |
| 0 | 1 | 2 | | 3 Kilometers |

to Bristoe

Jeffrey L. Ward

Before dawn, however, Pope learned of the defection of King and Ricketts, and around daylight on August 29 sent a directive to Sigel to attack Jackson directly, supported by Reynolds.

Pope didn't know where Ricketts had gone, but he sent orders to Porter, who had moved to Manassas, to "push forward with your corps and King's division, which you will take with you, upon Gainesville. I am [with Kearny, Hooker, and Reno] following the enemy down [west on] the Warrenton Turnpike. Be expeditious, or we will lose much."[3]

During the night Jackson had pulled his corps up to Groveton Heights. He was occupying a short line two miles long on elevated land suitable for artillery, running along cuts of the unfinished railway from Sudley Springs on the east to a point above the turnpike a half mile west of Groveton. It was shielded on both flanks by Jeb Stuart's cavalry. The position was one and a quarter miles distant from the turnpike on the east and a quarter of a mile from it on the west. Thus the line faced southeast, at an angle to the Union forces lining up along the east-west turnpike. A. P. Hill was on the left, or northeast, Lawton in the middle, and Starke on the right. The troops were largely positioned in woods. In front of them, however, the ground was open, except for woods, four hundred to six hundred yards wide, mostly along Hill's front, but also extending into Lawton's.

Jackson disposed his troops to exploit the superiority of the rifle as a defensive weapon. The shortness of the line gave him five rifles or muskets to the yard, and allowed him to concentrate five artillery batteries on the heights. In addition, Jackson gave each local commander authority to bring up reinforcements on his own authority to any point he saw threatened. Each brigadier commanded his own reserves in a second line directly behind the first. He also gave to each division commander half of his entire force to form a third line to be thrown forward wherever danger appeared.

The Federal attacks struck almost entirely Hill's division on the left, though it was farthest from the turnpike. The principal reason was that the approach to Hill's position could be made through woods, giving a degree of protection.

On the Federal left, or west, the Union troops largely contented themselves with skirmishing and artillery duels, and accomplished nothing.

On the extreme east some skirmishers of Carl Schurz's division got around Hill's flank near Sudley Springs, but Stuart's cavalry drove them away. A greater threat appeared in front of Maxcy Gregg's South Carolina brigade. There Schurz's main body advanced through the woods; Gregg's men rushed into the timber, flanked the "Dutchmen," as the Rebels called Schurz's Germans, and, in a violent clash, split two Federal brigades apart and broke the division's center. Schurz's men rallied, but again Gregg's brigade drove the Federals out of the woods in disorder.

Schurz's division tried again, reinforced by other foreign soldiers from Adolph von Steinwehr's brigade, striking Gregg again and Edward L. Thomas's Georgia brigade, just west of Gregg, with Lawrence O'B. Branch's North Carolina brigade coming up to help. Here a violent battle raged in the railway cut, the "Dutchmen" making a small penetration, but falling back in disorder when two Rebel regiments struck their flanks. Schurz's division pulled away about noon, exhausted and demoralized.

While these bitter fights were going on, Lee and Longstreet marched down from Thoroughfare Gap, the main body arriving at Gainesville about 11:30 A.M. Longstreet turned east along the turnpike and drew up on either side of it, facing approximately east and at a near right angle to Jackson's line.

At about the same time, Porter arrived at Dawkins Branch, about four and a half miles south of Gainesville, with his two divisions and King's, about 17,000 men. McDowell joined him there at noon. They heard from Federal cavalrymen that Longstreet's van had passed through Gainesville, and they could see dust clouds, indicating the whole corps was marching to the aid of Jackson.

Here was a chance to strike a telling blow before Longstreet could get into position, using the 17,000 men in place, and bringing up Ricketts's 7,000 men and Banks's 10,000 at Kettle Run. But neither Porter nor McDowell suggested an attack. They thought only of making contact with the rest of the Union army on the turnpike. But, deciding the terrain was too rough, both agreed that Porter should stay where he was, and McDowell should move King's division up the Sudley Springs Road toward the turnpike, with Ricketts to follow. That is, McDowell would march two divisions from the flank of the Confederate army in order to attack that army directly in front! And the two remaining divisions would remain idle at Dawkins Branch!

Meanwhile along the turnpike Pope spent much of the day preparing for a massive blow against Jackson's position, to go in as soon as he heard from McDowell and Porter on the left wing. Pope had received no word of the arrival of Longstreet, McDowell and Porter having failed to inform him. Nor had they told him that McDowell was moving away from Dawkins Branch. Pope therefore expected McDowell and Porter to strike Gainesville.

To support this advance, Pope planned two simultaneous attacks on the turnpike, one by Hooker, the other by Kearny's and Isaac I. Stevens's divisions. Hooker selected only one brigade, Cuvier Grover's Massachusetts, New York, New Hampshire, Pennsylvania outfit, to conduct the attack. Grover ordered his soldiers to load their pieces, fix bayonets, and move slowly until they felt the enemy's fire, then to deliver a volley, charge, and carry the position by main force, relying on the bayonet.

Grover's men went up against Thomas's and Gregg's now-exhausted forces, marching up to the railway cut, delivering the volley, and rushing forward, driving the stunned Rebels beyond the railway. But Confederate artillery staggered the Federals, and Rebel reserves hurried down and broke the valiant force. Over a quarter of Grover's 2,000 men were killed, wounded, or captured.

Kearny's and Stevens's attack did not go in at the same time as Grover's, as ordered; the two commanders waited until Grover had failed, then lined up at 5 P.M. and prepared to assault Gregg's brigade, which had already lost a third of its 1,500 men, and was sagging with fatigue. When the Federal storm burst against Gregg, the South Carolinians fell back to a last-ditch stand on the hill behind the railway cut.

But Hill was not relying on the valor of Gregg's men. He had in reserve Jubal A. Early's Virginia brigade, plus the 13th Georgia and the 8th Louisiana, and sent them in. Early struck the Federal center with a single, powerful blow. The line crumpled; the Rebels rushed through; and the two Union divisions broke and ran back over the railroad cut and beyond, pursued by Early's frenzied soldiers.

Jubal A. Early

(US MILITARY HISTORY INSTITUTE)

At 4:30 P.M., just as the final assault against Jackson's line was about to go in, Pope sent a peremptory order to Porter to attack the Confederate flank and rear. Porter didn't get the order until 6:30 P.M., and decided correctly not to launch it, since Longstreet had more than 32,000 men, and Porter had only 10,000.*

While Pope was wholly absorbed in assaulting Jackson's line, Longstreet, on Pope's left flank, remained idle all day. Longstreet reasoned to Lee that Porter at Dawkins Branch might attack, although the Federals were no threat and remained in column formation on the road. Lee asked Longstreet three times whether he was ready to attack, and three times Longstreet said no. Though Lee ascertained by his own observation that the Federal force at Dawkins Branch numbered only about 10,000 men, he accepted Longstreet's decision, indicating that he was still unwilling to fight a general engagement with Pope.

---

* Pope court-martialed Porter after the battle. When the court finished its deliberations months later, it cashiered Porter, and it was not until 1882, after a board had largely vindicated Porter, that President Chester Arthur remitted Porter's sentence.

The result was that more than half of the Confederate army remained idle on August 29, while Jackson stood alone, absorbing assault after assault.

Yet an attack by even half of Longstreet's corps might have caused Pope's army to collapse, and, if launched early enough, could have resulted in seizure before darkness of Henry House Hill just south of the Stone Bridge, thereby cutting off Federal retreat across the bridge. This might have forced the bulk of Pope's army to surrender.

The first day of Second Manassas, known in the North as Second Bull Run, ended. Pope had assembled 60,000 of his 75,000 men, and had to deal only with Jackson's 23,000 men. Jackson's new-model defensive system shattered Pope's attacks, but Pope himself contributed to the failure by launching one disconnected assault after another. Jackson was able to concentrate more men than Pope could at every critical point. Jackson had used the railroad embankment as a defensive line, which showed that he was moving toward field fortifications. But he did not follow this idea to its logical conclusion, and order his men to build and use entrenchments and breastworks. In the partially stand-up fights and the counterassaults that his troops accordingly carried out, Jackson sustained heavy casualties, but only a quarter of the 6,000 suffered by Pope, and his force was never in danger.

The next day, Saturday, August 30, 1862, General Lee entertained no plans to attack Pope, and soon concluded that the Federals would retreat. But John Pope had decided to attack again.

Napoleon Bonaparte once remarked that the general ignorant of his enemy's strength and dispositions is ignorant of his trade. Pope is proof of this dictum. For he believed he had won the first day's battle, and thought Jackson was retreating, and *still* ignored Longstreet's corps sitting on his left flank! From these misjudgments arose an immense opportunity for the Confederacy.

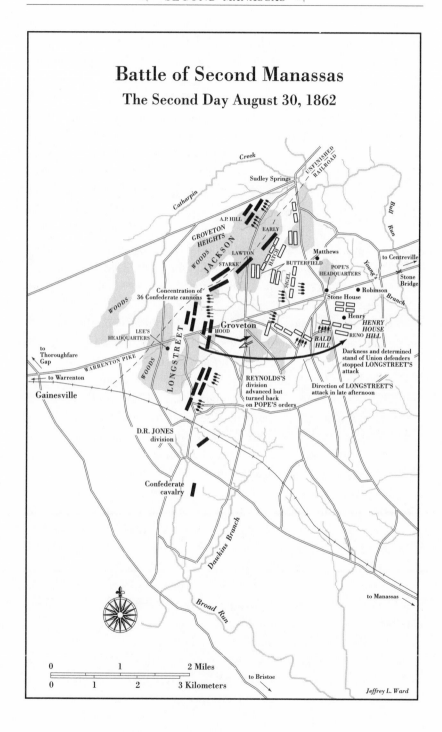

Battle of Second Manassas

The Second Day August 30, 1862

Pope convinced himself that he had won because he fell for an almost transparent deception: Jackson had pulled his men off the unfinished railway line back into the woods on the crest of Groveton Heights to rest them and to mystify the Federals.

Pope endangered his position by removing the one element that had given Longstreet an excuse not to attack on the 29th: he ordered Porter's corps to join the main army on the Warrenton–Alexandria turnpike.

Pope resolved to attack the "retreating" Jackson, ordering Rickett's division toward Sudley Springs on Jackson's extreme northeastern flank, and Porter to push his corps westward along the turnpike toward Gainesville and around Jackson's right flank.

The sweep around Jackson's left flank collapsed the moment Ricketts discovered that Jackson was still in force along the unfinished railway.

Porter did not march along the turnpike, falsely concluding that no pursuit was possible until Jackson had been defeated along his front. He proposed instead to attack head-on into the right of Jackson's line. Then, Porter felt, he could wheel around Jackson's left. Porter, like Pope, ignored Longstreet, and, moreover, revealed he did not know the purpose of a turning movement, which is to avoid having to break an enemy's front by direct attack.

McDowell, charged with tactical command that day, approved Porter's plan, and Pope backed him.

Greatly accentuating this tactical blunder were thirty-six Confederate cannons on an elevation just off the turnpike at the juncture of Jackson's and Longstreet's corps. These cannons generally faced east over open fields across the center and right of Jackson's line, and could fire into the flank of Union infantry attacking Jackson. The guns' only barrier was the belt of trees about 1,300 yards away in front of Jackson's left wing—the same woods that had sheltered the attacks on the 29th.

North of Groveton and behind the belt of woods, Porter lined up almost 20,000 men, facing west: John P. Hatch's division on the right, and two brigades of George W. Morell's division on the left under Daniel Butterfield. General Morell had mistakenly gone off to Centreville with the division's other brigade. Since Porter aligned the divisions to attack west, they would strike Jackson's line, running northeast-southwest, at an acute angle, Hatch being much closer to the Rebels than Butterfield.

The two divisions gave Porter a superiority of force of only 30 percent, not enough to ensure success. Yet half of Pope's army remained idle.

The woods would protect Hatch's troops' advance to the railroad. On Butterfield's front, the few woods quickly gave way to open fields stretching about half a mile that were open to the Confederate cannons near the turnpike.

Jackson had changed his tactical positions from the day before. He divided his corps into two lines of battle. One moved to the railroad cut as the attack materialized; the other waited as a reserve two hundred yards in the rear in the woods.

Before Porter launched his attack, Pope sent Reynolds's division westward south of the pike. At about 3 P.M., McDowell sent two brigades of Ricketts's division to Henry House Hill, and Pope sent Nathaniel C. McLean's Ohio brigade of Robert C. Schenck's division to Bald Hill, immediately west of Henry House Hill and in Reynolds's rear.

These moves seemed to indicate that Pope and McDowell had finally become aware of the exposure of the Union army's left, and were taking steps to correct it. However, as Porter's assault got under way and Jackson's first line rushed out of the woods to man the railroad line, Pope directed Reynolds to move north of the pike to the rear of Porter! He thereby abandoned the shield Reynolds had formed on the left flank. Reynolds began to withdraw at once, and two brigades got north of the turnpike.

Hatch's division struck mainly the left sector of Lawton's division. Here the fighting was severe, but the Confederates repulsed the Federal attack, though Lawton had to bring up his second line and call in troops from A. P. Hill's division on his left.

Butterfield had deployed his two brigades in three lines of battle. As the first line emerged into the open fields, it received severe fire but still crashed into Lawton's and Starke's divisions. The battle raged at close range and with great fury for thirty minutes, neither side giving way. The Union soldiers attempted assault after assault, but were halted every time. Some Rebels ran out of ammunition and grabbed cartridges from wounded and dead comrades, or resorted to throwing rocks.

Butterfield's first line was now ready to collapse. As the second and third lines emerged behind them into the open, the Confederate cannons posted in enfilade directed merciless fire on them. This bombardment was the final straw. In ten minutes, all three of Butterfield's lines broke and ran in panic for the rear.

Lee at last recognized his opportunity, and ordered a general attack. At about 4:30 P.M. Longstreet's corps sprang forward in a spectacular advance on the left flank of the Union army, followed by Jackson's corps.

(LIBRARY OF CONGRESS)

Damaged rolling stock caused by Stonewall Jackson's burning of the Federal stores at Manassas Junction.

The great enemy of the Confederates now was not the Union army, but time. Only a few hours of daylight remained to press the five miles to Henry House Hill. Most of the Federal army would be obliged to surrender if the Rebels could capture the hill, and block passage across the Stone Bridge a mile away.

John B. Hood's division led off the attack, bowled over Reynolds's third brigade still south of the turnpike, and a few other isolated Federal units, but was checked at Bald Hill, now

John B. Hood

(NATIONAL ARCHIVES)

defended by McLean's brigade and the two brigades of Rickett's division that had rushed over from Henry House Hill. Hood's drooping soldiers, supported by Nathan George "Shanks" Evans's South Carolina brigade, were unable to carry the hill on the first assault, and this delay foretold the doom of the Confederates' effort to destroy the Union army.

As the Rebels regrouped and struck Bald Hill from three sides, driving the Federals onto Henry House Hill, McDowell barely had enough time to rush Union troops in front of the Stone Bridge. Just as night was falling, the Confederates collided with a division from Reno's corps, drawn up in a line of battle only moments before. The fighting ceased. The Confederates dropped down exhausted. Soon a heavy rain began to fall and continued all night.

Federals elsewhere on the field withdrew rapidly. Thousands surrendered, but most got away over the Stone Bridge, some across Sudley Springs and other fords to the north. Pope's surviving units formed a shaky defensive line just beyond Bull Run around a part of William B. Franklin's corps, which had marched up in late afternoon.

Darkness had prevented a decisive Confederate victory. Lee had sent in the flank attack too late. He had only driven Pope back. He had not improved the South's strategic position. The whole campaign cost the North 10,200 men killed and wounded, and about 7,000 captured. Confederate losses were almost 9,100 killed and wounded, but only 81 missing or prisoners. Thus, real Confederate losses were not much fewer than Federal.

The next day, August 31, Jackson crossed Sudley Springs Ford and marched northwest to the Little River Turnpike (now U.S. Route 50), in an attempt to turn the Federal right and evict Pope from Centreville. The following day he struck the Federal flank guard at Ox Hill, about three miles east of Chantilly, and fought a hard battle in driving rain. The Federals lost two division commanders: Isaac I. Stevens, shot down, and Philip Kearny, killed when he rode by mistake into Confederate skirmishers. Lee sent Kearny's body back under a flag of truce.*

The fight at Ox Hill was enough for Pope. He withdrew into the Washington defenses. Lincoln, deeply depressed, relieved Pope, and sent him to Minnesota to fight Indians. Lincoln also relieved McDowell, who never held another field command. With no other general available, he reinstated George B. McClellan.

---

* When Kearny's widow applied for Kearny's mount and horse furnishings captured when he fell, Lee had them appraised, paid for them himself, and sent them to Mrs. Kearny. See Freeman, *R.E. Lee*, vol. 2, 420–21; *Official Records*, vol. 19, pt. 2, 645, 654–55.

⋆ 6 ⋆

THE LOST ORDER

The Federal army, demoralized and broken, had pulled under cover of the fortifications around Washington. Both General Halleck and President Lincoln doubted the capital could be saved, but told McClellan to do what he could to protect it.

"I repeated my firm conviction," McClellan wrote, "that I could and would save it."[1] McClellan, of course, knew that Robert E. Lee had no intention of battering the Army of Northern Virginia to pieces against the impregnable fortresses circling Washington. The danger lay elsewhere: a Confederate strike into Maryland or Pennsylvania.

Such a campaign seemed on the surface to offer immense opportunities. Lee's army was in the flood tide of its success. In three weeks of campaigning, it had driven out of central and northern Virginia an army greatly superior to it in numbers and armament, and had forced McClellan's army to withdraw from the peninsula.

Yet appearances were deceiving. In the spring, when Stonewall Jackson had called for an invasion of Maryland, the vast bulk of Federal strength was locked up on the peninsula. There would have been little to stop a Confederate thrust into the North. Now the situation was reversed. Pope's old army was consolidated into McClellan's Army of the Potomac and outnumbered Lee's almost three to one.

Nevertheless, Lee decided to invade. He had a broad, political purpose. He wanted to establish an army on Northern soil, and then offer the Northern people peace, provided they recognized Southern independence. "Such a proposition," he wrote President Davis, "coming from us at this time, could in no way be regarded as suing for peace; but being made when it is in our power to inflict injury upon our adversary. . . . The rejection of this offer would prove to the country that the responsibility for the continuance of the war does not rest upon us but that the party in power in the United States elect to prosecute it for purposes of their own."[2]

Lee intended to show the Northern people that only Lincoln and the Republicans were still striving to subjugate the South. Many Northerners now looked upon the war more as a party issue, less as a national issue. Lee knew Lincoln and the Republicans would never accept Southern independence. But if the North suffered another military setback—and it occurred on Northern soil—many voters might turn against the Republicans in the November congressional elections. Northern governors were meeting at Altoona, Pennsylvania, in late September to challenge Lincoln's war leadership. In Britain, Foreign Secretary Lord Russell had asked Prime Minister Lord Palmerston for the cabinet to debate recognition of the Confederacy in October, a proposal designed to lead to concerted action by European powers.

Nevertheless, Lee wrote Davis, "the army is not properly equipped for an invasion of an enemy's territory. It lacks much of the material of war, is feeble in transportation, the animals being much reduced, and the men are poorly provided with clothes, and in thousands of instances are destitute of shoes. Still, we cannot afford to be idle, and though weaker than our opponents in men and military equipments, must endeavor to harass if we cannot destroy them."[3]

Lee turned his columns toward Leesburg and the fords over the Potomac on the morning of September 3, 1862, as soon as he was satisfied that Pope had withdrawn to Washington. Not only were there no shoes, but three weeks of hard marching and inadequate food had taken a toll on the men. Straggling from the line of march soon began, and quickly worsened. Thousands of men dropped along the way. A few were genuinely deterred by the thought of invading another country, and fell back for this reason. But bare feet, stony roads, diarrhea,

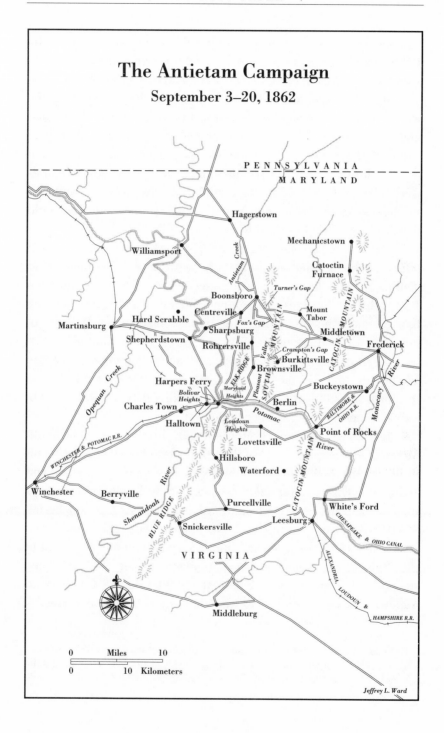

The Antietam Campaign
September 3–20, 1862

PENNSYLVANIA
MARYLAND

Hagerstown

Mechanicstown

Catoctin
Furnace

Williamsport

Antietam Creek

Turner's Gap

Boonsboro

Mount
Tabor

Centreville

Hard Scrabble

Fox's Gap

Middletown

Martinsburg

Sharpsburg

Shepherdstown

Rohrersville

Frederick

Crampton's Gap

Burkittsville

Brownsville

Harpers Ferry

Maryland
Heights

Buckeystown

Bolivar
Heights

Charles Town

Berlin

Potomac

Halltown

Loudoun
Heights

Point of Rocks

Lovettsville

Hillsboro

Waterford

Winchester

Berryville

Purcellville

White's Ford

Snickersville

Leesburg

VIRGINIA

Middleburg

0   Miles   10

0   10   Kilometers

Opequan Creek

Shenandoah River

WINCHESTER & POTOMAC R.R.

BLUE RIDGE

SOUTH MOUNTAIN

ELK RIDGE

Pleasant Valley

CATOCTIN MOUNTAIN

CATOCTIN MOUNTAIN

Monocacy River

BALTIMORE & OHIO R.R.

CHESAPEAKE & OHIO CANAL

ALEXANDRIA, LOUDOUN & HAMPSHIRE R.R.

Jeffrey L. Ward

and sheer exhaustion were the principal reasons why much of the Rebel army melted away as it crossed the river and marched to Frederick, Maryland, eleven miles north of White's Ford.

Mary Bedinger Mitchell, who lived at Shepherdstown, Virginia, wrote: "I saw the troops march past us every summer for four years, and I know something of the appearance of a marching army, both Union and Southern. There are always stragglers, of course, but never before or after did I see anything comparable to the demoralized state of the Confederates at this time. Never were want and exhaustion more visibly put before my eyes, and that they could march or fight at all seemed incredible."[4]

McClellan, commanding an army of 85,000 men, slowly moved after Lee on a twenty-five-mile arc, with seven divisions under Ambrose Burnside on the north protecting the Baltimore and Ohio Railroad, five divisions in the center under Edwin V. Sumner, and four divisions on the south near the Potomac under William B. Franklin. McClellan's uncertainty as to Lee's position, plus his natural hesitation, induced him to advance cautiously, keeping Washington and Baltimore covered. He also had to contend with the irrational fears of Halleck, who kept thinking that Lee was about to swing around and attack the capital.

Lee hoped to deceive McClellan by his move east of South Mountain, the extension of the Blue Ridge into Maryland. McClellan would regard occupation of Frederick as a threat to Washington and Baltimore. This, Lee reasoned, would pull the Union army north of the Potomac, and force Halleck to withdraw garrisons at Winchester, Harpers Ferry, and Martinsburg. The Shenandoah Valley would then be opened as a more protected line of supply than the roads east of the Blue Ridge. Once his communications were secured, Lee intended to move west of South Mountain into the Cumberland Valley to draw the Union army away from its main supply points.[*]

---

[*] In a campaign in the North, the Southern army did not need to worry about food. This was harvest time, and the men could get plenty of sustenance throughout the region. Longstreet told Lee that, if all else failed, the soldiers could find ample "roasting ears" in the ripening cornfields. See Johnson and Buel, vol. 2, 663. Lee

Lee may have hoped McClellan would attack him in the Cumberland Valley, but his main purpose was to press on into Pennsylvania and destroy the Pennsylvania Railroad's long bridge over the Susquehanna River at Harrisburg. This was the plan he explained on September 8 to division commander John G. Walker. Since the B&O Railroad would be cut by the army's movement north, Lee said, "there will remain to the enemy but one route of communication with the west, and that very circuitous, by way of the [railroads near the Great] Lakes. After that, I can turn my attention to Philadelphia, Baltimore, or Washington, as may seem best for our interests."[5]

Lee never attempted this strategic strike at the Northern railway system because of two unexpected developments. The first was the obstinate refusal of Halleck to withdraw the Union garrison at Harpers Ferry, thereby endangering the Confederate supply route through the Shenandoah Valley. The second was the mysterious disappearance of a copy of an order sent by Lee to respond to Halleck's decision.

Union general Julius White withdrew the 2,500-man garrison he commanded at Winchester on September 2, marched to Martinsburg, and took charge of a little Federal force there.

McClellan urged Halleck to evacuate the 10,000-man garrison at Harpers Ferry under Colonel Dixon S. Miles. But Halleck was unwilling to sacrifice the supplies stored at Harpers Ferry or give up, even temporarily, the B&O Railroad bridge there.

When Lee got to Frederick, he issued a proclamation to the people of Maryland, inviting them to join the Confederacy. Few responded. While there, Lee learned that the Union garrisons at Martinsburg and Harpers Ferry were still in place, now cut off from any hope of immediate relief. This offered a compelling attraction.

---

did not wish to take chances, however, and wrote President Davis on September 9 that he was moving into the Cumberland Valley toward Hagerstown, Maryland, and Chambersburg, Pennsylvania, "for the purpose of opening our line of communication through the [Shenandoah] valley, in order to procure sufficient supplies of flour." His aim, also, was to guarantee supplies of ammunition and gunpowder. See *Official Records*, vol. 19, pt. 2, 602–03.

McClellan was notorious for moving slowly; Lee figured he could send part of the army to seize these garrisons, and still reconcentrate within a few days in Maryland.

Perhaps because of the Harpers Ferry opportunity, or perhaps because of a more realistic appraisal of the political situation, Lee radically altered his strategy. Later, in 1868 at Lexington, Virginia, Lee told historian William Allan that "had McClellan continued his cautious policy for two or three days longer, I would have had all my troops reconcentrated on the Maryland side, stragglers up, men rested and intended then to attack McClellan, hoping the best results from the state of my troops and those of the enemy."[6]

As his plan to cut the railroad bridge at Harrisburg indicated, Lee had gone into Maryland hoping to avoid a battle, hoping that the presence of the Confederate army in the North would affect the November elections and Lincoln's control of the country. However, he must have soon realized that such hopes were illusions. For Lincoln was intensely aware of the consequences of an election defeat, and would not allow the Southern army to roam unhindered through the North. Lincoln was certain to demand that McClellan attack at the first opportunity. Lee could not secure a political victory without also securing a military victory.

Lee accordingly girded himself for battle. Yet it is astonishing that he planned to attack. He was reversing the strategy of avoiding battle he had just employed against John Pope. This time his army was weaker, while the Federal army was much stronger. He had not absorbed the lesson Stonewall Jackson had taught on Groveton Heights about the strength of the defense. And he made this decision despite strong opposition from Longstreet, who said: "General, I wish we could stand still and let the damned Yankees come to us!"[7]

Jackson shared Longstreet's feeling that the Confederates should not attack. Jackson also opposed the army's withdrawal into the Cumberland Valley, and wanted to stay east of South Mountain.[8] Jackson knew that if the Confederate army maneuvered north of Washington, McClellan would face an insoluble problem.

Lincoln would insist on keeping the Federal army between Lee and Washington. McClellan might then be able simultaneously to cover Baltimore, but he would have to leave the road to Philadelphia wide open.

If the Confederate army made its way to Philadelphia, McClellan would be forced to attack on ground and terms favorable to the Confederates. Lee could choose a readily defensible position, with an open flank, as Jackson had done on Groveton Heights. Jackson was sure the Federal attack would fail, and the Rebels could then sweep around McClellan's flank and possibly destroy his army. At the least, the Southern army could remain in the North and gravely damage the Republicans in the November elections. Lee, however, rejected the advice of both his senior commanders.

Deciding to pick the plum of Harpers Ferry, Lee ordered the army to split up, and to reassemble when finished west of South Mountain, in Maryland. Once his army reconnected, Lee planned to attack McClellan. On September 9, 1862, over Longstreet's objections but with Jackson's support, Lee issued Special Orders No. 191, which scattered the army into three segments detailed to seize Harpers Ferry and Martinsburg, and a fourth segment to proceed west over South Mountain to Boonsboro.

Jackson's corps, with divisions under Alexander R. Lawton, A.P. Hill, and John R. Jones (replacing William E. Starke), was to move west, cross the Potomac, destroy or capture any enemy at Martinsburg, and come up on the rear of Harpers Ferry.

Lafayette McLaws, with his division and that of Richard H. Anderson, was to go through South Mountain and descend on Maryland Heights, on the Potomac directly north of Harpers Ferry. John G. Walker's division meanwhile was to cross the Potomac, and take possession of Loudoun Heights, on the eastern side of the Shenandoah River opposite Harpers Ferry.

Longstreet was to stop at Boonsboro at the western foot of South Mountain. There, or at Hagerstown, eleven miles northwest, the army would reunite once Harpers Ferry was captured.

Altogether, about 28,000 Confederates moved to invest Harpers Ferry, leaving fewer than 17,000 men with Lee and Longstreet around Boonsboro.[9]

The bulk of Jeb Stuart's cavalry was to remain about seven miles east of South Mountain on and around Catoctin Mountain, the extension into Maryland of the Bull Run Mountains. Stuart was to observe the enemy and retard his advance.

As three parts of the army marched off on September 10 to capture Harpers Ferry, Lee changed Longstreet's orders and sent two divisions to Hagerstown to secure supplies stored there, and to block an enemy force reportedly coming from Chambersburg, Pennsylvania, though the report's veracity should have first been confirmed by dispatching cavalry. Lee accompanied Longstreet. There was no Union force moving on Hagerstown, and only D.H. Hill's division remained at Boonsboro to guard Turner's Gap on the Frederick–Boonsboro turnpike over South Mountain, as well as a northward escape route that the Union Harpers Ferry garrison might take.

Jackson moved fast, crossing the Potomac at Williamsport on September 11. General Julius White abandoned Martinsburg and retreated to Harpers Ferry. By midday on Saturday, September 13, Jackson came up on Colonel Miles's force drawn up behind entrenchments on Bolivar Heights, just west of Harpers Ferry.

Meanwhile, General Walker seized Loudoun Heights and got five artillery pieces in position on September 14, where they dominated Harpers Ferry several hundred feet below. McLaws passed through South Mountain, captured Maryland Heights, and dragged four cannons on top the same day.

Thus, McLaws and Walker could seal off retreat of the Union garrison north or east, while Jackson was opposite Bolivar Heights in position to sweep down on the town.

Confederate guns quickly silenced the Federal artillery on Bolivar Heights, permitting Jackson to push around both flanks. Jackson's gunners mounted batteries able to fire into Colonel Miles's entrenchments. This placed the Federal garrison in a hopeless position. It could be hit from the rear by Walker's and McLaws's guns and from the sides by Jackson's guns. The question was, when would Colonel Miles recognize his situation?

Meanwhile, McClellan marched into Frederick on September 13. Union infantry camped in the same meadow D.H. Hill's division had occupied the day before. A soldier found three cigars wrapped with a copy of Special Orders No. 191, addressed to General D.H. Hill. Federal officers quickly ascertained that the order was genuine, and took it to McClellan, who was receiving a deputation of Frederick citizens. McClellan turned aside to read it, became visibly elated, and shouted: "Now I know what to do!"

One of the citizens was a Confederate sympathizer who saw that McClellan had received important news relating to Rebel movements. He rode west, and found Stuart around South Mountain, to which his cavalry had been pressed on the 13th by two Union infantry brigades and Federal cavalry.

Stuart, recognizing the importance of the information, sent a courier to Lee at Hagerstown, and informed D.H. Hill at Boonsboro. Thus, on the night of the 13th, Lee and Hill knew that McClellan had positive information as to whereabouts of the army. As a precaution, Hill sent up Alfred H. Colquitt's Alabama-Georgia brigade to guard Turner's Gap on the evening of September 13.

No one knows how such an important order was dropped in the meadow at Frederick. "It was a shabby trick for fate to play us," Porter Alexander observed. D.H. Hill had his copy written by Stonewall Jackson and addressed to him, since Hill had been in his corps until this point. Lee's headquarters also sent Hill a copy, and always required a signed receipt for important orders. Thus, D.H. Hill was always suspected of receiving two copies, and somehow losing one.[10]

McClellan now had the most splendid opportunity of the war to destroy the Army of Northern Virginia. He had 65,000 men at Frederick, and could easily overwhelm the 30,000 men he thought Longstreet had west of South Mountain, only thirteen miles away. In fact, only D.H. Hill was there, with just 5,000 men. Likewise, Franklin's corps of 20,000 men was only twenty miles from Maryland Heights.

However, McClellan waited an astonishing eighteen hours before sending the first soldier to exploit his good fortune! This fateful hesitation saved the Army of Northern Virginia.

McClellan ordered the main army to march for Turner's Gap on Sunday, September 14, and Franklin to cross South Mountain six miles south at Crampton's Gap, then press southward to destroy McLaws's command and relieve the Ferry. Thus McClellan planned to spend the 14th getting over South Mountain, in preparation for a big fight beyond it on September 15.*

This gave Lee just enough time. He warned McLaws that Federals would be marching on his rear, notified Jackson to bring the siege of Harpers Ferry to a conclusion, told D.H. Hill to defend Turner's Gap, and instructed Longstreet to march at daybreak on the 14th to the aid of Hill. By the morning of September 14, the Confederates were fully alert, though by no means in position to stop a resolute Union attack: Longstreet's corps could not reach Hill before mid-afternoon.

McClellan detailed his army's right wing of about 30,000 men under Ambrose E. Burnside, in two corps (under Jesse L. Reno and Joseph Hooker), to seize Turner's Gap, and William B. Franklin's corps to capture Crampton's Gap. In the end there were two battles fought September 14 on South Mountain, one at Turner's Gap, the other at Crampton's Gap.

Franklin came up on Crampton's Gap about noon, and encountered Confederates behind a stone wall directly in front of the pass. It was a pitiful force: about 400 dismounted cavalry and infantry sent up by McLaws from Maryland Heights. Three small infantry brigades, about 1,600 men, were in reserve.

---

* The proper strategic move on the 14th would have been to send his entire army through Crampton's Gap (except a small decoy demonstrating at Turner's Gap). This would have given quick relief to the Ferry garrison, and eliminated any chance that McLaws could reunite with D.H. Hill and Longstreet. Then the remaining segments of the Army of Northern Virginia north of the Potomac could have been destroyed at leisure.

Franklin stopped before the tiny force, deploying a full division, and placing another in reserve. The Confederates opened fire, and for a while it looked like a stalemate, but some of Franklin's officers got exasperated with their commander's timidity, and ordered a charge. The thin Rebel line collapsed, and the men fled up the pass, scaring the reserves into flight as well. They fell back in confusion into narrow Pleasant Valley to the west, losing several hundred killed and wounded, plus 400 prisoners. But Franklin, deciding that getting through the pass was enough for one day, put his corps into bivouac.

During the night, McLaws moved up three additional brigades to strengthen the line across the valley. Meanwhile, Franklin's third division reached Crampton's Gap after the fighting ended. Thus, Franklin had 20,000 men against perhaps 5,000 Confederates.[*]

At Turner's Gap early on September 14, D.H. Hill was slow to respond to the danger, though he finally realized that the Federals could approach by three routes—up the main road, by way of Fox's Gap, a mile south, and by way of the Mount Tabor Church Road, coming in from the northeast through a deep gorge.

At first Hill had in place only Colquitt's brigade to defend the main road, and a thousand-man North Carolina brigade led by Samuel Garland. He had to commit Garland almost at once against Jacob D. Cox's Union division at Fox's Gap. Part of Cox's division reached an elevation behind the Tar Heels, sent down plunging fire, and killed Garland with the first volley. The brigade collapsed, retreated behind the mountain, giving up 200 prisoners, and was of no more use for the rest of the day.

Hill stopped Cox's soldiers from moving up the ridgeline and seizing Turner's Gap only by sending down several cannons and hastily forming a guard of staff officers, couriers, teamsters, and cooks behind the guns. George B. Anderson's North Carolina

---

[*] On the morning of September 15, General Franklin studied the thin line of Rebels stretched across Pleasant Valley and concluded it would be suicidal to attack. He estimated the Confederate force to be fully as large as his own corps!

brigade finally arrived and tried to regain Fox's Gap, but was pushed back. However, Cox didn't realize he had captured the gap, and he withdrew, waiting for the rest of Jesse Reno's corps to come up.

Hill originally had no one to defend the Mount Tabor Church Road, but he got a reprieve there, too. McClellan had assigned its capture to Hooker, and his corps didn't get into position until late in the afternoon. By that time, Hill had gotten the 1,200 men of Robert E. Rodes's Alabama brigade to the ridgelines on either side of the road, and held off Hooker's infantry with great determination for the remainder of the day.

Meanwhile Hill sent Roswell S. Ripley's Georgia–North Carolina brigade to reinforce George B. Anderson at Fox's Gap, but Ripley marched backward, to the rear of the mountain on the west side of Fox's Gap! Before he returned, the fighting was over.

About 3:30 P.M. the first of Longstreet's men arrived, George T. "Tige" Anderson's Georgia brigade and Thomas F. Drayton's Georgia–South Carolina brigade. Hill sent them down to assist Anderson. About 5 P.M., two of Reno's divisions, Cox's and Orlando B. Willcox's, struck Fox's Gap. Drayton was incompetent, and his brigade buckled after a short, sharp clash. The other two brigades didn't fare well, either, and the Rebels were soon in confusion.

At this juncture, John B. Hood's two-brigade division, just arrived, drove down from Turner's Gap, charged through Drayton's broken troops, and forced Reno's men to the crest of the mountain. Here the Federals held as fighting died out at nightfall, but not before General Reno fell, mortally wounded.

At Turner's Gap, reinforcements from Longstreet prevented Rodes from being entirely overwhelmed. But the Federals seized the commanding ridgeline to the north before nightfall. In that position Federal cannons could make the Confederate position at Turner's Gap untenable the next day.

McClellan knew he could force his way over South Mountain on the next day, especially since Sumner's five divisions had arrived that evening.

The Battle of South Mountain cost the Federals about 2,300 men, almost all killed and wounded. The Confederates probably lost about a thousand men killed and wounded, but McClellan claimed an additional 1,500 prisoners.

~~~ ~~~

Lee now faced some dismal choices. September 14 had been bad for his army; the 15th could be disastrous. Harpers Ferry was still holding out, blocking McLaws's retreat across the Potomac. McClellan's entire army could close up on McLaws's rear. It was evident that McLaws had to give up his position, and get back into Virginia before his force was destroyed. Meanwhile, the three divisions of Longstreet's command were hopelessly isolated north of the Potomac, and likewise must seek the south bank of the Potomac as soon as possible.

At 8 P.M. Lee sent a courier to McLaws informing him that "the day has gone against us," and that Longstreet and D.H. Hill were retreating to Sharpsburg, then crossing the Potomac at Shepherdstown, four miles south. He directed McLaws to find another crossing between the Ferry and Shepherdstown, and to get over as soon as he could.

Soon thereafter, a courier arrived with a message from Stonewall Jackson that changed everything. Jackson informed Lee that he looked "for complete success tomorrow. The advance has been directed to be resumed at dawn tomorrow." Jackson's message led Lee to believe that Harpers Ferry would surrender on the morning of September 15. [11]

The news rekindled Lee's audacity, and caused him to make one of the worst mistakes of his military career. He believed that if Jackson took Harpers Ferry, his force and Walker's division could reunite with Lee at Sharpsburg, only sixteen miles from the Ferry, while McLaws could cross the Potomac at the Ferry and likewise march to Sharpsburg.

Lee immediately canceled his previous orders and sent out instructions for the entire army to assemble at Sharpsburg. The campaign now depended on whether Stonewall Jackson could induce Colonel Miles to surrender in time for the Confederates investing the Ferry to get to Sharpsburg.

At dawn on September 15, Jackson ordered the attack to commence. Rebel artillery virtually surrounded the Union garrison, and began to exact terrifying damage. All parts of Bolivar Heights and the Ferry were covered by fire. The Federal cannon could not elevate enough to return fire on Walker's guns on Loudoun Heights. In an hour the Federal guns fell silent.

As Jackson's men began to move forward to storm the heights, the fire reopened. A. P. Hill at once moved two batteries to within 400 yards of the Federal defensive works and poured rapid enfilading fire into it. Union soldiers were slaughtered. Miles saw that further resistance would only produce useless killing. He ordered a horseman to carry a white flag across the lines to show that the garrison was surrendering.

It took a while to get stop-firing orders to the guns. Colonel Miles was mortally wounded. Jackson, eager to get away, gave generous conditions to General White. The officers went on parole with their side arms and private property. The soldiers kept everything they had, including blankets, except military equipment and weapons. Jackson left A. P. Hill's division to take the surrender, and ordered the rest of the force, including McLaws's and Walker's troops, to move at top speed for Sharpsburg. A. P. Hill paroled 11,500 men and captured 13,000 stand of arms, 73 pieces of artillery, and much military supplies. It was a brilliant success, skillfully handled.[*]

---

[*] Most of the cavalry, 1,300 men, under Colonel Benjamin F. "Grimes" Davis, an Alabamian who remained loyal to the Union, got out of Harpers Ferry on the night of September 14 by crossing the pontoon bridge over the Potomac and taking a road around the western base of Maryland Heights that McLaws had failed to block. Moving toward Hagerstown, the horsemen ambushed part of Longstreet's wagon train retreating toward Sharpsburg on the 15th, destroying about forty wagons. Colonel Miles could have evacuated a large portion of the Union infantry

Lawton's division got on the march at 3 P.M. and bivouacked that night four miles from Boteler's Ford at Shepherdstown. Jones's division was delayed due to the need to cook the next two days' rations. They started for Sharpsburg at 1 A.M. on the 16th. Even Jackson said the march that night was "severe." As the regiments reached Sharpsburg during the morning of September 16, each dropped down in exhaustion. Jackson, gray with dust, rode on to report to Lee. Lee was visibly relieved.

by the same unguarded road. McLaws's failure to post troops on this road exemplifies how the mistake of a subordinate can jeopardize even the best plans of an army commander. The error probably contributed to Lee's refusal afterward to give McLaws wider responsibilities.

★ 7 ★

ANTIETAM

Lee decided to fight along Antietam Creek on September 17, 1862, because he was confident his army could stop the Union attack, and he could then send Jackson around the enemy flank and defeat McClellan's army.

Lee convinced Jackson to accept this decision when he arrived at Sharpsburg on September 16. Lee, however, did not assess the terrain around Sharpsburg in advance to find out there was no space for a turning movement. The Potomac River swings in toward Sharpsburg northwest and southeast of the town, creating a narrow cul-de-sac with little maneuvering room on either side. Lee mistakenly thought the Potomac's course was westward from Sharpsburg, offering a wide avenue northwest for a swing around McClellan's army.*

Lee's erroneous assessment of the terrain explains the otherwise baffling conundrum of why Lee entered into battle, which brought disaster to the Confederate cause.

Lee and Jackson began planning on the afternoon of September 17 to send Jeb Stuart with all uncommitted forces around the Union right, or north. When Jackson found there was insufficient space

---

* As British general Sir Frederick Maurice wrote: "The ground he chose for battle, while admirably suited for defense, left him no opportunity for such a counterstroke as Longstreet had delivered at the second battle of Manassas. He could at best hope to beat off the Federals. But at the end of such a battle he would be no better off than he was on the morning of the 15th [of September]." See Maurice, 152.

between the Union batteries and the Potomac, he called off the movement. This clarifies a curious passage in G. F. R. Henderson's 1898 study of Stonewall Jackson. It relates that the Reverend Robert Lewis Dabney wrote in his first draft of an 1866 book on Jackson that Stonewall doubted the propriety of fighting the battle. Jackson's widow insisted that Dabney submit the draft to Lee. In a letter to Mrs. Jackson on January 25, 1866, Lee disputed Dabney's statement, saying that, when Jackson arrived at Sharpsburg from Harpers Ferry, "and learned my reasons for offering battle, he emphatically concurred with me."

Dabney eliminated whatever negative comments he attributed to Jackson, and in the finished book repeats Lee's language almost verbatim. Dabney was an aide to Jackson until after the Seven Days, and was generally accurate in reporting Jackson's thinking. However, he had little strategic sense, and may have confused what Jackson was saying. When Jackson found at Antietam that he didn't have sufficient space, his enthusiasm for the battle vanished. Perhaps this is what he conveyed to the Reverend Mr. Dabney, and Dabney misinterpreted it.[1]

If Lee had known the topographical constraints at Sharpsburg, he would have avoided the battle, as there were already other reasons why he should not have fought.

The British military analyst General J. F. C. Fuller, not knowing of Lee's misapprehension about the path of the Potomac, hunted for a reason why he fought such a "totally unnecessary battle," and attributed it to Lee's personal pride, which "could not stomach the idea that such an enemy [as McClellan] could drive him out of Maryland."[2]

Pride was not what motivated Lee, but an expectation of victory. But he failed to provide the one final element necessary for victory: space. There were three principal other reasons why Lee should have ordered a prompt retreat to Virginia on the morning of September 15.

One was that he could get only about 35,000 men in position at Antietam, whereas McClellan had more than 85,000. Moreover, all

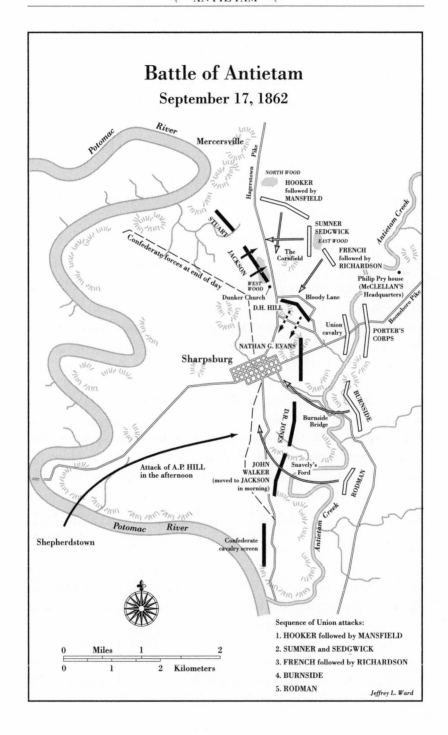

Battle of Antietam
September 17, 1862

Mercersville

NORTH WOOD

HOOKER
followed by
MANSFIELD

SUMNER
SEDGWICK

EAST WOOD

FRENCH
followed by
RICHARDSON

STUART

Confederate forces at end of day

JACKSON

The
Cornfield

WEST
WOOD

Dunker Church

Philip Pry house
(McCLELLAN'S
Headquarters)

Bloody Lane

D.H. HILL

Union
cavalry

PORTER'S
CORPS

NATHAN G. EVANS

Sharpsburg

BURNSIDE

D.R. JONES

Burnside
Bridge

Attack of A.P. HILL
in the afternoon

JOHN
WALKER
(moved to JACKSON
in morning)

Snavely's
Ford

RODMAN

Shepherdstown

Potomac River

Confederate
cavalry screen

0   Miles   1   2
0   1   2   Kilometers

Sequence of Union attacks:
1. HOOKER followed by MANSFIELD
2. SUMNER and SEDGWICK
3. FRENCH followed by RICHARDSON
4. BURNSIDE
5. RODMAN

Jeffrey L. Ward

of the men coming back from Harpers Ferry would be exhausted from hard marching.

The second reason was that the Confederate army was backed up against the Potomac River with a single ford over it. It had to stand or die.

Finally, even if he stopped McClellan, Lee would remain facing a much larger enemy who could receive huge reinforcements. Lee was backed into a corner, and would still have to retreat into Virginia to regain maneuverability.

McClellan squandered a golden chance to destroy Lee's small force of fewer than 15,000 men, after it retreated from South Mountain and halted behind Antietam Creek at Sharpsburg on September 15. But McClellan remained cautious and did not attack.

The next morning, September 16, Jackson's divisions reached Sharpsburg and dropped down, exhausted but in place. In the afternoon Walker's division arrived. McLaws's and Anderson's divisions were still south of the Potomac, but in position to come forward in the morning. A.P. Hill's division was finishing up paroling the Harpers Ferry garrison and sending off booty, but had orders to march to Sharpsburg at the earliest moment. The situation remained critical, but McClellan allowed this day of opportunity to pass as well with nothing more than a skirmish as he moved his troops into position for the battle on September 17, 1862.

Two major terrain features defined the battlefield. The first was Antietam Creek, about a mile east of Sharpsburg, a bold stream but fordable in places, which flowed south through a deep valley into the Potomac. The second was a broad, low ridgeline directly north of town, along which the Hagerstown Turnpike ran.

McClellan could have destroyed the Southern army in short order if he had taken advantage of his overwhelming numerical superiority. By attacking simultaneously down the Hagerstown Pike and along Antietam Creek directly east of Sharpsburg, he could have forced Lee to commit every one of his men. McClellan then could have sent two divisions across Snavely's Ford along the southern reaches of the creek, cut the highway to Shepherdstown, blocked the retreat of the Confederates to Boteler's Ford, just to the east, and crushed the Army of Northern Virginia front and rear.

This was the sort of battle Napoleon Bonaparte had fought numerous times, that military writers had described in detail, and that, copied by a reasonably competent general, was practically guaranteed of success.

But McClellan, the Young Napoleon, conducted a battle that was practically the opposite of the real Bonaparte's method.* His first, and most damning, mistake was to keep in reserve Porter's entire corps, plus all of his cavalry (totaling 4,200 horsemen), stacked up near the bridge over the Antietam just east of Sharpsburg on the Boonsboro Pike, with Franklin's corps coming up behind.

His second and almost as fatal error was to launch two attacks at separate parts of the line—but not at the same time. His first attack went in on the north on the Hagerstown Pike. After this attack had run its course, he assaulted across a stone bridge over the Antietam southeast of Sharpsburg. These uncoordinated actions permitted Lee to withdraw forces from the Boonsboro Pike and the south to contain the northward threat, and still get troops to deflect the later assault on the southern flank.

More than thirty years after the war, Porter Alexander was still astonished at McClellan's tactical blindness. The only thing that had saved the Southern army, he wrote, was "the Good Lord's putting it into McClellan's heart to keep Fitz John Porter's corps entirely out of the battle and Franklin's nearly out. . . . Common sense was shouting, 'Your adversary is backed against a river, with no bridge and only one ford, and that the worst one on the whole river. If you whip him now,

---

* Theodore Ayrault Dodge wrote in *Alexander* (New York: Houghton Mifflin, 1890, London: Greenhill, 1994), 657: "The maxims of war are but a meaningless page to him who cannot apply them."

you destroy him utterly, root and branch and bag and baggage. Not twice in a lifetime does such a chance come to any general.'"[3]

McClellan concentrated most of his army along the creek to the east, but sent Joe Hooker's and Joseph K. F. Mansfield's corps to the Hagerstown Pike, and ordered them to advance southward. Although McClellan conceived of this as a flanking attack, he broadcast his strategy by moving troops toward the pike on the 16th. This gave Jackson, in command on the north, time to turn the upper part of his north-south line to an east-west direction before the battle. This turn came at a point two-thirds of a mile northeast of the Dunker Church, a whitewashed brick building on the pike, about a mile north of town. Consequently, McClellan's attacks were all direct, frontal assaults.

A third McClellan mistake was to send in Hooker's corps alone, leaving Mansfield's corps idle a mile and a half to the rear. Jackson was then able to ignore Mansfield's two divisions and concentrate against Hooker.

Both sides' continued ambivalence toward having troops on the offensive dig defensive emplacements showed in the fact that nowhere on the battlefield did either side construct entrenchments or fortifications. Men did take advantage of depressions and out-crops of rock, or lined up behind existing walls. But commanders still held to the old tactical doctrine that troops should fight stand-ing up, in close line of battle, though these tactics had proved to be disastrous against the rifle. The seemingly logical step of throwing up breastworks to defend against an attack was a long time coming, and didn't attain doctrinal status until after the Battle of Fredericksburg in December 1862.

Antietam therefore was not an attack on a fortified position, but a pitched battle in an open field.

The battle opened at 6 A.M. on September 17. Hooker's 10,000 infantry in three divisions—under Abner Doubleday, George G. Meade, and James Ricketts[*]—struck down both sides of the

---

[*] Hooker commanded Irvin McDowell's old corps from Second Manassas, but only Ricketts remained in command of his division. Meade had replaced John F. Reynolds and Doubleday had taken over from John P. Hatch, wounded at Turner's Gap.

Hagerstown Pike and into a thirty-acre unharvested field of Indian corn just to the east.

They collided about three-quarters of a mile north of the Dunker Church with about 4,500 Confederates in two divisions, John R. Jones's west of the pike, and Alexander R. Lawton's in the Cornfield. Although Hooker committed all three divisions, the attacks still were uncoordinated, and each brigade assaulted singly. Even so the slaughter was unbelievable. The lines of battle sometimes stood within thirty or forty yards of each other and ex-

George G. Meade

(US Military History Institute)

changed volley after volley. In many places gunners brought cannons right up to the line and blew huge holes in the infantry with canister.

Within a few minutes thousands of men were dead or dying. In places long lines of men lay slain, still in the ranks in which they had stood alive only moments before.

Doubleday drove Jones's Rebels back a third of a mile. In the chaos, General Jones was stunned by an artillery air burst; though unwounded, he said he could not exercise command, and left the field. William E. Starke took over, but was hit three times and died within an hour. Colonel Andrew J. Grigsby assumed command, and led 1,100 men, all that was left of the division, in a desperate counterattack that regained the position they had held at the outset, and stopped Doubleday.

In the Cornfield—the stalks severed by bullets as if they had been reaped by a scythe—Lawton's division shattered each of Meade's brigades, but was decimated in the process. When Ricketts's division emerged from the East Wood into the southern part of the Cornfield, it suffered huge casualties from Marcellus

Douglass's small Georgia brigade, and the Georgians also lost nearly two-thirds of their number. To prevent a breakthrough, the Louisiana Tigers brigade under Henry Hays charged into the Federals, but also lost two-thirds of its strength in a few minutes.

General Lawton had seen that the Confederate line was in desperate danger from the opening blow, and almost immediately sent a courier to John Hood, asking for help.

Disregarding bursting shells and canister, and dead men lying in rows, Hood's two brigades pushed into the Cornfield, shot down gunners of a Federal battery, evicted the few Union infantry before them, and drove to a rail fence at the northern edge of the field. There they stopped, their ranks halved by bullets and artillery fire.

East of the Dunker Church, three brigades of D.H. Hill's 3,000-man division assisted Hood's assault, driving parts of Ricketts's division back into the East Wood, but were badly hurt in the process.

By 7:30 A.M. Jackson's and Hooker's commands had virtually destroyed each other. The survivors of Hooker's corps were scattered and incapable of further offensive action. The remnants of Jackson's two divisions were grimly hanging on; Hood's division was under heavy fire; and three of D.H. Hill's brigades were tottering.

McClellan had not left his headquarters at the Philip Pry house on a hill across the Antietam about two miles east of the Cornfield. Thus, he didn't know the conditions facing the men. But now, after Hooker had been defeated, he ordered forward Mansfield's corps, comprising two divisions with 8,000 men, formerly Nathaniel Banks's old corps. McClellan also directed Edwin V. Sumner's corps to come to Hooker's aid, but kept in reserve one of Sumner's three divisions, that of Israel B. Richardson.

Jackson didn't yet realize Mansfield was advancing, but he was worried about Hood, and sent a message to Lee that Hood must have help. Lee replied that he was already shifting a large part of the army to reinforce Jackson, stripping bare or almost bare other parts of the line. These were dire decisions, but calculated risks, since McClellan was not advancing along Antietam Creek.

Lee sent Tige Anderson's Georgia brigade from the Boonsboro Pike, John G. Walker's 3,200-man division from the lower reaches of Antietam Creek, and Lafayette McLaws's division, just coming up. He also was moving Richard Anderson's also-arriving division northward, to be used where necessary. Now only Shanks Evans's South Carolina brigade was directly blocking the Boonsboro Pike, and the tiny 2,400-man division of David R. Jones was guarding about a mile of the creek from the pike south. The lower Antietam Creek was virtually bare. Only just before it entered the Potomac was there a small cavalry flank guard, under T. T. Munford.

Mansfield had scarcely arrived at the northern edge of the Cornfield when a Confederate sharpshooter put a bullet into his chest. He died the next day, and General Alpheus Williams immediately took command.

Williams sent his own two-brigade division against Hood's men. And though one of the brigades suffered a thousand casualties and collapsed, the other, under George H. Gordon, mowed down most of Hood's division, and drove the few survivors west of the Dunker Church. A brother officer rode over to Hood and asked, "Where is your division?" Hood answered grimly: "Dead on the field."[4]

Meanwhile, two brigades of George Sears Greene's division attacked west toward the Dunker Church, half a mile away, and scattered D. H. Hill's three shaky brigades in this sector. They retreated in disorder, and took up a precarious position on the left flank of D. H. Hill's last two brigades—Robert E. Rodes's and George B. Anderson's—deployed in a zigzag, sunken farm lane running southeast about three-quarters of a mile southeast of the Dunker Church.

Greene lodged in the woods beyond the Dunker Church—a deep penetration into the center of the Confederate line. With a bit more push, the line could be broken, and the Army of Northern Virginia split in two. Greene sent back frantic pleas for help, but General Williams had committed his whole corps and could do little more.

It was now 9 A.M. In three hours of the most desperate fighting seen so far in the Civil War, 9,000 Confederates had fought twice their number to a bloody standstill. Jackson's wing of the army had been reduced to not much more than a thousand men in small groups, but most of two Union corps had disintegrated. In Hooker's corps General Ricketts could not assemble more than 300 men. Afterward, soldiers on both sides remembered this morning as the worst they experienced, before or after.

Nevertheless, disaster still stared the Confederate army in the face. For Sumner's two divisions were now coming forward. If he reinforced the spectacular gain made by Greene, the battle would be won.

McClellan decided it was safe to allow Burnside's four-division corps to attack the Confederate southern flank along the Antietam. But it took nearly an hour to deliver the order to Burnside and longer for him to go into action. He also ordered two divisions of Franklin's corps (William Farrar Smith's and Henry W. Slocum's) to bolster the northern flank. In sending these forces north, McClellan abandoned his plan to reinforce Porter with Franklin's corps in a culminating attack into Lee's center along the Boonsboro Road.

Sumner personally directed his lead division, under John Sedgwick. He didn't heed any advice about the situation, ignored Greene's strategic penetration, didn't wait for his second division, under William H. French, to come up, and launched Sedgwick in a bizarre and indecisive direction—due west from the East Wood, across the Hagerstown Pike, into the West Wood.

Furthermore, in this third piecemeal attack of the morning, he formed Sedgwick's three brigades in lines of battle one behind the other with only sixty yards' interval between each brigade, insufficient space to swing left or right to counter a strike on either flank.

Meanwhile, Jackson was trying to get his reinforcements in position. But as Sedgwick advanced across the now-bare Cornfield, the only forces on hand were Jubal Early's brigade, and the 200 or 300 men remaining in Jones's division, under Grigsby, a half-mile west of the Dunker Church.

Sedgwick's leading brigade stopped in the West Wood, leaving the division's left, or southern, flank entirely exposed. This was the point where Jackson aimed his counterstroke. He had sent a brigade of McLaws's division north, and, with the help of Grigsby's men, attacked Sedgwick's front. While the Federals were thus occupied, Early, McLaws, and Walker crashed into the southern flank of Sedgwick's line.

Sedgwick's brigades were too close together to turn to meet the Rebels, and the whole division collapsed south to north. The survivors rushed pell-mell northeastward to the shelter of thirty Union batteries which crowned high ground three-quarters of a mile north of the church. These guns checked the Confederates, who retired to the West Wood.

Greene's force, its northern flank exposed by Sedgwick's departure, had to withdraw.

Soon afterward, Jackson's medical officer, Hunter McGuire, found Jackson in the yard of the Dunker Church. The medical officer gave Jackson some peaches, his first food of the day, and reported the staggering preliminary casualty figures, expressing doubts that the survivors could withstand another assault. But Jackson shook his head, unconcerned, and pointed to the Federals huddled behind their guns a mile to the north, and said: "Dr. McGuire, they have done their worst."[5]

General French, not knowing where Sumner had gone, came out of the East Wood, formed his three brigades in order of battle, the brigade of Max Weber leading, and attacked southward.

Weber stopped below a low ridge in front of the crooked, sunken farm road where the Rodes's Alabama brigade and Anderson's North Carolina brigade, in all 1,200 men, were resting in comparative safety. Weber ordered his men to fix bayonets and charge.

The Confederate commanders decided not to give the order to fire until the Federals were so close that every bullet would take effect. John B. Gordon, commanding the 6th Alabama, ordered his men to lie down. "There was no artillery at this point upon either side, and not a rifle was discharged," Gordon wrote. "The stillness was literally oppressive, as in close order, with the commander still

John B. Gordon

riding in front, this column of Union infantry moved majestically in the charge." As the Federal brigade came within easy range, some of Gordon's men asked impatiently for permission to fire. Not yet, Gordon answered. "Soon they were so close that we might have seen the eagles on their buttons, but my brave and eager boys still waited for the order," Gordon continued. "Now the front rank was within a few rods of where I stood. It would not do to wait another second, and with all my lung power I shouted 'Fire!'"

The effect was appalling. The entire Union front line went down. The Union commander's horse fell dead in a heap, although the officer was unhurt.[6]

Colonel F.M. Parker of the waiting 30th North Carolina had warned his men he would give the order to fire only when the Federals crossed the ridge and the men could see the enemy's belts. Aim at these, he told them. When Parker yelled "Fire!" 150 men of the 4th New York fell at almost the same moment. In five minutes the brigade suffered 450 killed and wounded. Many of the survivors ran away, but some dropped behind the crest, lay down, and returned fire.

French's second brigade, under Dwight Morris, advanced through the chaos. The men had been in service barely a month. Some fired into the backs of the Union soldiers lying in front of them; others broke and ran; still others joined Weber's men on the ground under the brow of the ridge.

French's last brigade, under Nathan Kimball, approached at the double-quick, bayonets fixed, and likewise met a hail of

Confederate bullets. Rebels in the rear passed up loaded rifles to the men in the front. Federal dead and wounded covered the crest. Within minutes, 1,750 men of French's division had been killed or wounded, and thousands of survivors streamed panic-stricken to the rear. The position they had failed to seize gained the name it would bear forever thereafter: the Bloody Lane.

D.H. Hill's men were exhilarated, but exhausted, and suffered heavy losses themselves, from rifle fire and artillery shells coming in from east of the creek.

While this intense contest raged, Richard Anderson's division came up to reinforce D.H. Hill, while McClellan at last released Israel B. Richardson's division. It moved into the East Wood. A Federal shell wounded Confederate general Anderson severely. Command fell to Roger A. Pryor, a former member of the U.S. Congress, who was incapable of deploying the division. Only a few members took up positions in the Bloody Lane; the remainder stayed in the rear.

Richardson, seeing that Kimball's force was being shattered, hastened both Thomas F. Meagher's Irish brigade and John C. Caldwell's New York–Pennsylvania brigade to its support. Both were torn to pieces in minutes, but survivors clung to the ridgetop, and the 29th Massachusetts of Meagher's brigade made a surprise attack against Rodes's brigade. Though quickly halted, the assault unnerved the defending Rebels.

Lieutenant Colonel J.N. Lightfoot, commanding the 6th Alabama after Colonel Gordon was wounded, asked Rodes's permission to withdraw from a salient where the men were being subjected to enfilade fire. Rodes agreed, but Lightfoot misunderstood the order, and told his neighboring commanders that the whole brigade was to withdraw. Within seconds Rodes's entire brigade evacuated the Bloody Lane, permitting the Federals to pour devastating enfilade fire into the North Carolinians still holding the rest of the lane, killing many and forcing the others to flee.

Soon afterward Charles Carleton Coffin, a Northern journalist, inspected the Bloody Lane. "The Confederates had gone down as the grass falls before the scythe," he wrote. "Resolution and energy still lingered in the pallid cheeks, in the set teeth, in the gripping hand. I recall a soldier with the cartridge between his thumb and finger, the end of the cartridge bitten off, and the paper between his teeth when the bullet had pierced his heart. . . . A young lieutenant had fallen while trying to rally his men; his hand was still firmly grasping his sword, and determination was visible in every line of his face. I counted fourteen bodies lying together, literally in a heap, amid the corn rows on the hillside. The broad, green leaves were sprinkled and stained with blood."[7]

Richardson's men occupied the Bloody Lane and moved into the gaping void in the Rebel line. Confederate cannons on the hill to the south stopped the first rush, while Rodes and D. H. Hill pulled together a few men to create a semblance of a line.

One more thrust would divide the Army of Northern Virginia with no hope of reunion. But the Federals had been so badly hurt that they did not advance far. And McClellan, though he could see from the Pry house the Rebel collapse in the Bloody Lane, sent no forces to exploit the breakthrough.

Part of the reason was that General Longstreet had drawn together a small diversionary force around the Dunker Church under Colonel John R. Cooke, a Harvard-educated engineer, who had his own 27th North Carolina and the 3d Arkansas of Walker's division, plus 250 Georgians and North Carolinians from McLaws's division under Lieutenant Colonel William MacRae.

While the Bloody Lane battle was still storming, Longstreet had ordered Cooke to attack. The assault crossed the plateau east of the Dunker Church, and drove deep into the rear of Richardson's position. A rabble of Federals that had taken shelter behind some haystacks surrendered as the assault swept through them. Rebel officers told them to stay where they were until they could be moved to less-exposed ground.

Federal officers saw the attack coming and met it with Richardson's third brigade, under John R. Brooke. Cooke, seeing that his tiny force had no hope of carrying the enemy position, ordered a withdrawal. The prisoners who had been left among the haystacks shot down many Confederates as they retreated. Cooke brought back only half of the 675 men he commanded and only 50 of the 250 men of McLaws's division.

Nevertheless, the boldness of the strike frightened Sumner and McClellan into believing that Lee was planning a major attack on the northern flank. McClellan still believed that Lee possessed enormous strength. Thus, Smith's and Slocum's divisions of Franklin's corps formed up to deter a Rebel assault, not to renew the Federal attack. Despite the defensive posture, Smith launched three regiments in William H. Irwin's brigade in an unsupported advance toward the Dunker Church. Cooke's and MacRae's survivors shot this attack to pieces in minutes, killing or wounding 224 Federal soldiers.

With this gratuitous bloodbath, the action on the northern flank ended. By 1 P.M. the survivors on both sides lay stunned and exhausted. But the Confederate line had held.

Richardson ordered his men behind the ridgeline just north of the Bloody Lane. Shortly thereafter a shell wounded him severely (he died six weeks later). McClellan replaced him with Winfield Scott Hancock, and told him to hold his ground.

Lee and Jackson were actually trying to attack around the northern flank of the Union army, and Jackson went up to investigate early in the afternoon. He alerted troops for a possible movement, and began calling up whatever artillery was in the vicinity, mostly Stuart's guns. He told General Walker he wanted 4,000 to 5,000 men to attack. "We'll drive McClellan into the Potomac," Jackson said.[8]

⁓⁓

Two reasons have been noted for the extremely poor performance of General Burnside along the southern reaches of Antietam Creek. One is that he was angry because McClellan had detached Hooker's corps from his wing. The other is that Burnside was incompetent.

Burnside had overwhelming superiority, 12,500 infantry in four divisions against not more than 2,000 Confederates remaining after Lee's withdrawals. If Alfred Pleasonton's cavalry had been out scouting, Burnside would have known that A. P. Hill's division was marching hard from Harpers Ferry, but could not arrive before mid-afternoon, and at most would have 2,000 exhausted men to send into battle.

Burnside had plenty of time to get across the lower Antietam, close off Lee's retreat, and destroy his army. Instead, Burnside concentrated most of his effort at the most difficult crossing point on the stream, the 125-foot stone Rohrbach Bridge—to be forever remembered as the Burnside Bridge—less than a mile southeast of Sharpsburg. Placed on the heights opposite the bridge, and shielded by a stone wall and a rock quarry, were 400 Georgians under Colonel Robert L. Benning, a former member of the Georgia Supreme Court.

But south of Benning were only a few skirmishers, a couple cannons, and Munford's small cavalry force near the Potomac. Yet in this sector was Snavely's Ford, where passage was easy. If Burnside had masked one or two divisions behind Snavely's Ford while feigning an attack against the Burnside Bridge, he could have marched across the ford onto the rear of the Confederate army almost without opposition.

McClellan's battle plan actually called for this very tactic: a demonstration to pin down the Rebels at the bridge, and a reinforced division under Isaac P. Rodman to force passage downstream.

But human error or perhaps Burnside's petulance caused the plan to go awry. McClellan's engineers selected Rodman's crossing point at a ford two-thirds of a mile below the Burnside Bridge (following the course of the creek). Neither Burnside, his tactical commander Jacob D. Cox, nor Rodman investigated the ford in advance, and when Rodman marched down to it on the 17th, he discovered it was impassable because a high bank rose from the water's edge. Rodman commenced a search for Snavely's Ford (half a mile away!), which took him until around 1 P.M. to find and then cross, against virtually no opposition.

Meanwhile, Burnside and Cox devoted their attention to the Burnside Bridge. The Antietam Valley is narrow here, and the road on the east, or Union, side ran close to the creek for 250 yards before turning sharply to cross the bridge. The Georgians on the opposite hill could fire into the flank of any Federal force for nearly the entire distance it was in sight.

After one brigade of Cox's Kanawha Division failed to rush the bridge, emerging at the creek about 350 yards north of it, Burnside and Cox ordered Jacob Duryea's 300-man 2d Maryland to approach along the road and storm the bridge. As soon as the Marylanders came along the road in a column of fours, the Georgians struck with a hail of bullets, while Confederate batteries on the Boonsboro Pike rained down shells. Within moments the regiment lost 44 percent of its men, and the remainder ran for cover.

Edward Ferrero's brigade received the order to assault next. Ferrero chose his two toughest regiments, the 51st New York and the 51st Pennsylvania, totaling only 670 men. He realized another attack along the road would bring disaster, and ordered the men instead to charge straight down the grassy hill just above the bridge. Georgian bullets pounded the Federals before they were halfway down. The officers, seeing that their men could never rush the bridge in a single sprint, swung the regiments left and right under cover just shy of the bridge.

By now Benning's men were almost out of ammunition, and one in four were dead or wounded. A light Union howitzer had been able to get down the hill to an area where it could fire point-blank at the far end of the bridge. As the cannon spouted double-shotted canister, and Union riflemen on the hilltop poured terrific fire on the opposite hill, the Georgians began running away. Colonel Robert B. Potter of the 51st New York saw his chance and led his men onto the bridge, followed quickly by the Pennsylvanians. In moments they were across and up the slopes.

It was 1 P.M. The bridge was in Union hands. The cost had been 500 men killed or wounded; the Rebels had lost 120.

Lee had anxiously monitored Burnside's attack. He knew Jones's division had no possibility of stopping Burnside's corps. But he made no transfers from the north, knowing A. P. Hill was on the way. Hill arrived around 2:30 P.M., wearing his red battle shirt, and reported that his first three brigades would be up soon. Later, veterans of that march reported that Hill urged laggards forward with the point of his sword. Hill's division was coming up almost literally at the last minute.

About this time, a shattered wreck of a battery appeared in the streets of Sharpsburg. A few dirty, staggering gunners followed the exhausted horses. The battery had fought valiantly all day, and had suffered severe losses. The battery commander, Captain William T. Poague, came up to Lee for orders. Among the begrimed private soldiers was Lee's youngest son, Rob, nineteen years old. Lee told Poague to return to the front.

"Are you going to send us in again?" Rob asked his father. "Yes, my son," Lee answered, "you all must do what you can to help drive these people back." The battery turned and headed back into battle.[9]

Shortly after 3 P.M. Cox ordered the 5,500 men he had lined up just above the creek to advance, Rodman's division on the left, Orlando B. Willcox's on the right, while 3,000 men backing them in the Kanawha Division came behind, with Samuel D. Sturgis's division across the Antietam in reserve. Lee had about 2,000 men in place. A.P. Hill's brigades were not yet on the field.

Burnside's aim was to advance on Sharpsburg and the plateau immediately south of it. This would crack the Confederate right flank, and get astride the road to Shepherdstown and Boteler's Ford. He had plenty of time; he had at least four hours to darkness.

Directly east of Sharpsburg, General Jones had posted Richard B. Garnett's Virginia brigade and Joseph Walker's South Carolina brigade. To the south in mostly open fields a few skirmishers were scattered, and south of them were three small brigades: Thomas F. Drayton's Georgia–South Carolina, James L. Kemper's Virginia, and Robert Toombs's Georgia.

Willcox advanced northwestward up the road to Sharpsburg. Rebel skirmishers hiding in farmsteads and along fences delivered deadly rifle fire, but had too little strength to stop the advance. Twenty-eight Confederate cannons on high ground east and south of town shelled the advancing Federals, but many of the Rebel guns were knocked out by heavy counterbattery fire from long-range Federal rifled artillery east of the creek.

Willcox's men reached the high ground just east of Sharpsburg, and forced Confederate artillery to withdraw. Walker gathered the remaining Rebels behind a stone fence for a last-ditch defense. Willcox's infantry evicted them in a fierce and bloody fight, and drove the survivors back into Sharpsburg.* It was 4 P.M., and nothing was left to keep the Federals from pressing into the town and cutting Lee's army in half. However, Willcox's men were exhausted and nearly out of ammunition. He stopped to rest them and to locate more cartridges.

Meanwhile, matters were taking a serious turn for the Federals on their left. Rodman's two brigades advanced toward the ridge south of Sharpsburg, charging into fire from a dozen Confederate cannons and valiant, but greatly outnumbered, Rebel infantry. Kemper's Virginians and Drayton's South Carolinians and Georgians—590 men—drew up at a stone wall and rail fence on the ridge crest.

Colonel Harrison S. Fairchild's New York brigade lay down in a shallow depression, trying to escape the Rebel fire. David Thompson of the 9th New York saw a rolled overcoat bound into the air and fall into the furrows of the field. "One of the enemy's grape-shot had plowed a groove in the skull of a young fellow and had cut his overcoat from his shoulders," Thompson wrote. "He never stirred from his position, but lay there face downward—a dreadful spectacle. A moment after, I heard a man cursing a comrade for lying on him heavily. He was cursing a dying man."

Soon thereafter, Fairchild ordered the brigade to stand up and attack. "In a second," Thompson remembered, "the air was full of the hiss of bullets and the hurtle of grape-shot. The mental strain was so great that I saw at that moment the singular effect mentioned, I think, in the life of Goethe on a similar occasion—the whole landscape for an instant turned slightly red."[10]

---

* The position the Federals occupied is where the National Cemetery is now located.

Fairchild's brigade climbed over a sharp hill and encountered the Confederate line fifty yards away. Both lines stood their ground briefly, swapping terrible volleys, the bullets knocking down whole ranks on both sides. Then the New Yorkers charged, collided in a fierce but short hand-to-hand fight, and drove the Rebel survivors back in confusion, some running into Sharpsburg. At the cost of half his brigade, more than 450 men, Fairchild was on the verge of breaking the entire Confederate right flank.

Meanwhile Colonel Edward Harland's Connecticut–Rhode Island brigade advanced on Rodman's left flank, unaware that the first elements of A. P. Hill's division had crossed the Potomac and were moving on it through the tall Indian corn that covered the fields. Hill's division had left Harpers Ferry that morning with 3,300 men. But the pace was killing and Hill had no more than 2,000 exhausted but determined men in his three leading brigades—under James J. Archer, Maxcy Gregg, and Lawrence O'B. Branch—when they reached the battlefield around 3:30 P.M.

As Harland moved forward, someone spotted Rebel troops off to the south, and Rodman sent an aide to warn Harland, whose men were just entering a large cornfield. As Rodman spurred forward to warn Fairchild, a sharpshooter's bullet struck him with a mortal wound in the chest.

Meantime, Harland's advance regiment, the 8th Connecticut, captured one of Hill's batteries on the ridgeline, but ran into crossfire from North Carolinians of Hill's division, lost half its number, and fell back in disorder.

Because Burnside and Cox had deployed only half of their available infantry, the left flank of the Union line had now diminished to just two regiments with a total of 1,000 men: the experienced 4th Rhode Island and the new 16th Connecticut.

Maxcy Gregg's South Carolina brigade, only 750 men still in the ranks, had emplaced behind a stone wall on the western edge of the cornfield. The two Union regiments had advanced to a point only a hundred feet away when Gregg's officers ordered the men to level their rifles, and, in one voice, yelled "Fire!" The effect was fright-

ful. Federals went down in bunches. The experienced Rhode
Islanders replied in desperate volleys, but the green Connecticut
men milled around in confusion, as the South Carolinians poured
volley after volley into them. Within moments they fled in panic to
the rear, drawing the 4th Rhode Island with them.

General Cox saw the soldiers streaming out of the cornfield,
realized his entire line was in danger, and at once ordered Willcox's
men to withdraw from the edge of town. A brigade of the Kanawha
Division moved forward, but A. P. Hill now had Gregg's, Archer's,
and Branch's brigades in order of battle, and they outflanked the
brigade, which quickly withdrew toward the Antietam. General
Branch, riding near the front, dropped dead with a bullet through the
head. This raised the number of dead and wounded generals to nine
Confederate and nine Union.

Cox feverishly built a new line covering the Burnside Bridge
and the heights west of the creek, bringing over Sturgis's division for
the job. The Federal assault on the Confederate right, or south, had
collapsed, a victim of Burnside's delays, the commitment of too few
troops to the final push, and the flank blows of A. P. Hill's tired but
triumphant soldiers.

While Burnside's divisions were rushing to the rear, Jackson at
last attempted the flanking movement on the north that he and Lee
had planned. But dominating the narrow space between the Potomac
and four Union brigades on the enemy line were thirty-four heavy
enemy guns. Jackson could muster only twenty-one mostly smaller
pieces, and they fell silent in a quarter of an hour under Federal
counterbattery fire. With no space beyond the range of the guns to
move his men, Jackson concluded it would be impossible to turn
Meade's northern flank. He stood down his 5,000 infantry, and sent
his artillery back to their starting places.[11]

Night fell at last. The Army of Northern Virginia had fought the
Union Army of the Potomac to a standstill. The Federal army had
suffered about 2,150 killed, 9,500 wounded, and 760 missing—a
total of 12,410, one-fourth of the men who had gone into action. The
Confederate army had lost 1,500 dead, 7,800 wounded, and 1,000

missing (mostly dead)—a total of 10,300, or 31 percent of those on the firing lines.

McClellan had committed only 50,000 of his men, and these in disconnected assaults at various places and times, allowing Lee sufficient time to get enough men to each danger point to stop the assaults. More than a third of McClellan's army did not fire a shot. Even so, the men who did get orders to fight came close to breaking the Confederate line and bringing the army to disaster.

The Army of Northern Virginia now entered a changed, much more bitter era. The aura of inevitable victory which had surrounded it had vanished. It had fought McClellan to a draw in one of the most tenacious defensive battles in the history of warfare. Robert E. Lee had maximized the effect of his slender forces by seeing points about to be threatened, and masterfully transferring men to them before disaster struck. He had revealed his genius for defensive warfare. He was prouder of Antietam than any other battle he directed, because he believed his men there faced the greatest odds they ever encountered. But Lee and Jackson had been unable to turn this stalemate into victory because they couldn't swing around McClellan's army and dislocate it.

Soon the Confederate army would have to retreat. To the world, this would spell defeat. Abraham Lincoln was waiting for the slightest Union success to proclaim emancipation of the slaves and the transformation of the war into a crusade. This would guarantee the persistence of the Northern people in the war and keep Britain and France from recognizing the Confederacy.

It was the bloodiest day in American history, and the day the war began to turn against the South.

⁕ 8 ⁕

FREDERICKSBURG

On the morning of September 18, 1862, Lee and Jackson tried once more to strike around McClellan's northern flank. Despite their losses, they still hoped to deal McClellan a decisive blow. Jackson rode out to inspect the sector again, but confirmed what he had seen the day before: the Potomac's course left no space for a movement not swept by Federal artillery. The two officers reluctantly gave up the idea of an offensive.[1]

The only course now was to retreat across the Potomac. McClellan did not contest the withdrawal, on September 19, but Jackson threw back a small Union force that ventured across the river on September 20.

Lee entertained ideas of swinging westward, crossing the Potomac, and challenging McClellan once more. But, realizing his army was too weak and wounded, he pulled it back into camps north of Winchester, and gave his men a much-needed rest. The Confederate government delivered food, clothing, blankets, and some shoes, though not enough to resupply all the men, while a chronic shortage of horses and mules continued.*

---

* In the Confederate army, homespun was replacing factory-made clothing. With gray dye imports mostly cut off by the blockade, women at home and army commissary agents had turned to walnut hulls and copperas (ferrous sulfate), which produced a dye of a peculiar brown tint, dubbed butternut, now being seen as the "real" Confederate color. Brogans had taken the place of boots; overcoats had vanished; and soft, shade-giving slouch hats (which also made "capital pillows") had replaced the kepi. Shoulder-hung haversacks were universal. Tents were found mostly at headquarters, the men sleeping in pairs, in blankets and rubber sheets,

Confederate officers combed the countryside for stragglers; convalescents returned; and a new conscription law provided a steady, if small, stream of recruits. By December Lee's total force reached 78,000 men and 255 guns. Lee also reorganized the army formally into corps, one led by Jackson, the other by Longstreet, and both these officers were promoted to lieutenant general.

Antietam was not the indisputable Northern victory Abraham Lincoln had hoped for.* But it was significant enough to give him the opening to issue his Emancipation Proclamation on September 22, 1862, to be effective on January 1, 1863, but only in the Confederacy, not in the four Union slave states. He also suspended the writ of habeas corpus, a protection in the Constitution designed to prevent illegal detention by government authorities. Lincoln denied habeas corpus to anyone giving "aid and comfort to Rebels."

---

which, on the march, they carried rolled over their shoulders. The men cooked with frying pans or skillets. One Rebel wrote: "Reduced to the minimum, the private soldier consisted of one man, one hat, one jacket, one shirt, one pair of pants, one pair of drawers, one pair of shoes, and one pair of socks. His baggage was one blanket, one rubber blanket, and one haversack." By comparison, Union soldiers were provided for generously. Under the quartermaster general, Montgomery C. Meigs, the army consumed one-half of the total output of Northern industry. Meigs exploited a new process of machine-sewing of shoes, and introduced a standardized shelter half. Any soldier could match his half with that of any other soldier and create a two-man "pup tent," virtually eliminating large tents and the wagons necessary to carry them. And though Meigs introduced French-style field food-preparation equipment, Union soldiers, like Confederates, preferred to cook over an open fire using pots and pans. See Wiley, *Johnny Reb*, 112, 116, 307; Henderson, vol. 1, 221–22; Hattaway and Jones, 139–40.

* Antietam was not so clear-cut a result as the Federal success in Kentucky at about the same time. It was this campaign, not the equivocal attainment at Antietam, that bolstered Lincoln and his government. Confederate general Braxton Bragg had invaded Kentucky in August 1862 and had gotten between the Union army and its principal supply base, Louisville, Kentucky. Instead of seizing the city, Bragg turned east to Bardstown, allowing the Federal commander, Don Carlos Buell, to rush to Louisville, refit a superior army there, and move against Bragg. Bragg got only 16,000 of his 53,000 men on the field of Perryville on October 8, 1862, but the Rebels nevertheless outdid 55,000 Union troops. Even so, Bragg retreated into southern Tennessee, the campaign a fiasco, due, not to the failure of Confederate arms, but the failure of Bragg's will.

The Emancipation Proclamation opened up recruitment of former slaves as soldiers in the Union army. The first regiment of free blacks went into service in New Orleans on September 27, 1862. Before the war was over, 179,000 enlisted free black men served in the Union army.

⁓ ⁓

Lincoln gave McClellan one more chance to redeem himself, ordering him on October 6 to "cross the Potomac and give battle to the enemy." But McClellan stalled until October 26, and then marched in a leisurely fashion to Warrenton by November 6. Lee kept Jackson in the valley, and dispatched Longstreet to Culpeper to shield the Virginia Central Railroad and Gordonsville.

Warrenton was as far as McClellan got. Lincoln, exasperated with McClellan's "slows," replaced him with Ambrose E. Burnside on November 5, the day after the congressional elections, in which the Republicans suffered losses but retained control of Congress.

Burnside honestly protested that he was not qualified. But Lincoln was more interested in Burnside's lack of political ambitions, knowing that even with a Federal victory, he would pose no threat to Lincoln in the 1864 presidential election.[*]

Burnside knew he had to produce quick action, and proposed that the army move to Fredericksburg, where it could be supplied through Aquia Creek on the Potomac twelve miles away. From Fredericksburg, he planned to push directly toward Richmond, protecting Washington as he advanced. The plan was astonishing in its lack of imagination. It required the North to exert direct force all the

---

[*] Burnside (1824–81) had graduated from West Point in 1847. He had commanded a brigade at First Manassas and had captured Roanoke Island and New Bern in North Carolina early in 1862, but had shown little enterprise at Antietam. Lincoln also relieved Fitz John Porter, a crony of McClellan, and placed Joseph Hooker, returned to duty after being wounded at Antietam, in command of Porter's old corps.

way to Richmond, beating the Confederate army at every point it chose to stand.

A far better objective would have been to turn on one of the wings of Lee's army, and destroy it. Burnside by happenstance had landed his 119,000 men and 374 guns between Jackson in the lower valley and Longstreet at Culpeper. Burnside could have marched on either wing before the other could move to its assistance. But Burnside didn't see his opportunity.

Halleck and Lincoln agreed to the Fredericksburg plan provided Burnside moved fast, crossed the Rappahannock River upstream, marched down the south bank, and captured from the flank and rear the heights a mile south of Fredericksburg and parallel to the river. These heights were the key to the town, and enveloping them was greatly preferred to assaulting them from the front. However, Burnside, despite warnings, approached Fredericksburg from directly across the river.

Lee figured out Burnside's plans quickly, but was unable to get more than a token force to Fredericksburg before Edwin V. Sumner's advance elements arrived at Falmouth, opposite Fredericksburg, on November 17. Sumner wanted to ford the river and seize the town at once, but Burnside told him to wait for pontoon bridges, which didn't arrive until November 25.

Lee sent Longstreet's corps to Fredericksburg on November 19, where it occupied the heights south of town. Burnside thus missed his opportunity to drive the Confederates out of position and open a road to Richmond. Only then did he awaken to the difficulty of assaulting the heights. But, to get around them, he searched in the wrong direction for a crossing, looking below the town, where the river was tidal, broad, and thoroughly unsuitable—at Skinker's Neck, twelve miles below the town, and Port Royal, eighteen miles downstream, where the river was a thousand feet wide. Yet to the west, the country was hilly and wooded, and the river narrow with several good fords. A crossing in this sector was feasible.

Lee at first had not planned to stand at Fredericksburg, intending to retreat to the North Anna River, about twenty-five miles south.

There Lee believed the nature of the ground would make a counter-stroke possible. But because Burnside was so slow, Lee decided to defend Fredericksburg. Jackson opposed the decision, and urged Lee to follow his original plan.

By standing at Fredericksburg, Jackson told D. H. Hill, "we will whip the enemy but gain no fruits of victory."[2]

Jackson saw that Fredericksburg was unsuitable for a decisive triumph. The heights south of Fredericksburg were excellent as a defensive bastion, but the position offered no depth, and the Union supply line was short. The Confederates could stop a Union assault, but would have no space to swing around the defeated army and break it apart. The key was Stafford Heights, directly across the river from the town. From this elevation, the Federals—with more artillery than Lee and a much higher proportion of long-range rifled guns—could dominate every inch of the battlefield and destroy any move against the Union flank.

Jackson knew that the Confederates could not achieve a victory by merely stopping the Federal army. Even forcing it to sustain high casualties would not be enough. Antietam had proved that. At least one Federal army had to be destroyed to ruin Northern morale, open an uncontested route to the North, and bring Southern independence.

Jackson's method to achieve this was to withdraw to the North Anna River, where there was room for maneuver and a chance, after Burnside had attacked and failed, to swing around him, cut off his supplies and line of retreat, and destroy his army.

Jackson had proposed this strategy three times already. Against John Pope on the Rapidan Lee had delayed until Pope got wind of an envelopment, and ran back to the Rappahannock. At Second Manassas, Jackson had enticed Pope into attacking Groveton Heights, giving Longstreet a bare flank to go around Pope's army, and block it from crossing Bull Run. Lee had waited until too late on the second day, and Pope escaped with most of his army. In Maryland, Jackson wanted to confront the Union army east of South Mountain, forcing it to attack and lose or forfeit Philadelphia and possibly Baltimore. Instead, Lee withdrew westward into the

Cumberland Valley, where nothing decisive could be attained, and had to stand on the defensive after McClellan got a copy of the orders dispersing his army.

Now Jackson proposed the strategy for the fourth time. Again Lee rejected it.

Why did Lee not see see the advantage of backing up to the North Anna? There he could follow the pattern he had planned at Antietam: a successful defense, followed by a flank attack. Why did he opt for a solely defensive posture at Fredericksburg that had no possibility of a decisive outcome?

The only answer Lee gave was to preserve the supplies existing in that portion of Virginia between the Rappahannock and the North Anna. But these supplies were modest at best. The conclusion must be that Lee did not accept Jackson's theory of battle. Lee chose to deal with the enemy before his eyes. He could not destroy the Union army at Fredericksburg, but he could stop it. That, to Lee's mind, was enough. In his campaigns, Lee had sought to defeat the enemy in his front. He never had aimed either at attacking the will of the enemy people to pursue the war or at wholly destroying the enemy army.

Jackson protested Lee's decision, but Lee was adamant, and Jackson obediently moved his corps to Fredericksburg.

Burnside organized his army into three "grand divisions" consisting of two corps each under Sumner, Joseph Hooker, and William B. Franklin.[*]

---

[*] Sumner commanded the 2d and 9th Corps, containing 31,000 men; Hooker, with the 3d and 5th Corps, had 36,000; and Franklin, with the 1st and 6th Corps, commanded 42,500. Burnside's cavalry amounted to 3,500 men. Thus Burnside's force totaled 113,000 men. About 30,000 additional troops were unused, the 12th Corps guarding the Potomac, and the 11th Corps holding Manassas, while a small force remained at Skinker's Neck. See Allan, *Army of Northern Virginia*, 469; *Official Records*, vol. 21, 90.

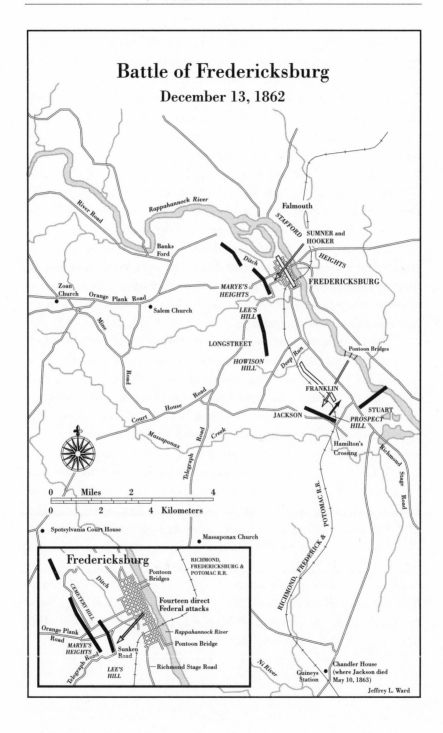

Battle of Fredericksburg
December 13, 1862

River Road

Rappahannock River

Falmouth

STAFFORD

SUMNER and HOOKER

Banks Ford

Ditch

HEIGHTS

FREDERICKSBURG

Zoan Church

Orange Plank Road

Salem Church

MARYE'S HEIGHTS

LEE'S HILL

Mine

Road

LONGSTREET

HOWISON HILL

Deep Run

Pontoon Bridges

House Road

FRANKLIN

Court

STUART

Massaponax

Creek

JACKSON

PROSPECT HILL

Telegraph Road

Hamilton's Crossing

Richmond Stage Road

0   Miles   2   4

0   2   4   Kilometers

Spotsylvania Court House

Massaponax Church

Fredericksburg

CEMETERY HILL

Ditch

Pontoon Bridges

RICHMOND, FREDERICKSBURG & POTOMAC R.R.

Orange Plank Road

MARYE'S HEIGHTS

Telegraph Road

Sunken Road

LEE'S HILL

Fourteen direct Federal attacks

Rappahannock River

Pontoon Bridge

Richmond Stage Road

RICHMOND, FREDERICKSBURG & POTOMAC R.R.

Ni River

Guineys Station

Chandler House (where Jackson died May 10, 1863)

Jeffrey L. Ward

Sumner threatened to bombard Fredericksburg if it didn't surrender. Longstreet replied through the mayor that the Confederates would not occupy the town, but would deny it to the Federals. Sumner didn't carry out his threat, but Lee advised the town's 5,000 people to evacuate while they had a chance. The weather had turned unseasonably cold and snowy, but nearly all the population abandoned their homes and sought shelter in farmhouses, churches, barns, or woods to the south.

When Jackson's men arrived at Fredericksburg around December 1, Lee sent them to block Burnside from crossing below the city. Jubal Early's division went to Skinker's Neck, and D.H. Hill's division to Port Royal. Rebuffed, Burnside thought up a new strategy: if he crossed the river below Fredericksburg, he might drive around Longstreet's right and seize Hamilton's Crossing, five miles southeast of the town. This would interpose the Union army between Longstreet and Jackson.

The plan might have worked, but Burnside did not move fast enough, giving Jackson the chance to respond.

As the situation changed before his eyes, Burnside forgot that the power of his battle plan had been to avoid the enemy's strength, dislodge him from his strong position, and destroy him indirectly. Instead, he abandoned the guile that had set him on his course in the first place, and sought to destroy the enemy by brute force.

A far better course of action would have been to cross at Fredericksburg with one grand division to occupy the attention of Longstreet's corps on the hills south of town, then to use another grand division, with the third in reserve, to pass over the river east of town, and to press for Hamilton's Crossing before Jackson could react. Only A.P. Hill's division, a mile and a half southwest of the crossing, was close enough to get into blocking position quickly, and it might have been overwhelmed. Such a move would have prevented Jackson's occupation of the highly defensible Prospect Hill, directly west of the crossing, and forced Longstreet to move off the heights farther west to confront the Union army.

The center of Longstreet's position was Marye's Heights, 130 feet high, facing across largely open fields to the built-up portion of the town clustered along the river 600 to 700 yards away. To the southeast was another hill, 210 feet high, where General Lee and Longstreet had their observation post, and which was thereafter known as Lee's Hill. To the east, separated by the depression of Deep Run, was Prospect Hill, lower and more approachable than Lee's Hill and about four miles from Marye's Heights. In front of Lee's and Prospect Hills were largely open fields running to the river, a mile to a mile and a half away.

Telegraph Road ran through a sunken course for about 500 yards directly at the foot of Marye's Heights, the road's northern edge bordered with a four-foot-high stone wall. Just east of Marye's Heights, Telegraph Road (now U.S. Route 1 Business) turned south toward Richmond through the gorge of Hazel Run.

Lafayette McLaws, in command at Marye's Heights, saw that the sunken road and stone wall offered a splendid defensive position. He ordered a ditch to be dug along the wall, deep enough for men to stand in and fire while remaining sheltered, and for the dirt to be banked against the wall on the north to give additional protection. Defending the stone wall were 2,000 men from Thomas R.R. Cobb's Georgia brigade of McLaws's division, and the 24th North Carolina of Robert Ransom's division. On Marye's Heights behind were the rest of McLaws's and Ransom's divisions, about 4,000 men.

Longstreet placed the balance of his corps on other hills east and west of Marye's Heights.

Since Stonewall Jackson was charged with defending Skinker's Neck and Port Royal, he did not occupy Prospect Hill.

Although the sunken road had taken on the trappings of a defensive emplacement, and although the artillery batteries had dug pits for their guns at various points on the hills, Lee had deliberately avoided building many fortifications and earthworks for the infantry, in order to deceive Burnside. Lee felt that the natural position on the heights was so strong that fortifications might convince Burnside it was impregnable. By feigning weakness Lee hoped to entice Burnside into attacking.

Burnside finally was ready to strike in the early hours of December 11, 1862. He ordered two pontoon bridges to be thrown across the river, 400 to 440 feet wide, at the upper or western end of town, a third at the lower end, and another two (later three) a little more than a mile farther downstream, near where Deep Run empties into the Rappahannock.

Burnside directed that the bridges were to be built in two or three hours. Thereafter Sumner's grand division of 31,000 men was to cross on the upper pontoon bridges, while Franklin's grand division of 42,500 men was to move over the lower bridges. Hooker's grand division of 36,000 men was to remain on the north side of the river, ready to support either Sumner or Franklin as needed.

A small group of Mississippi and Florida riflemen under William Barksdale, in pits and basements along the river, stopped construction of the upper pontoon bridges for much of the day. Though Union soldiers quickly drove Rebel defenders from the lower sites, allowing engineers to build the pontoon bridges, Burnside refused to allow anyone to cross until all the bridges had been built.

At last, around 4:30 P.M., volunteers filled ten pontoon boats at the upper site, paddled across, drove the Rebel riflemen away, and permitted the engineers to throw the bridges across. But Barksdale's men had gained practically a whole day, and robbed Burnside of the only essential element in his plan: speed.

Burnside now forgot his original purpose. Instead of striking for Hamilton's Crossing before Stonewall Jackson could react, Burnside devoted the whole of December 12 to moving most of Sumner's and Franklin's grand divisions across the river, Sumner's men occupying the town and spending the day plundering homes and businesses, while Franklin's forces formed up facing Prospect Hill.

This showed that Burnside was going to strike at Marye's Heights and Prospect Hill. Longstreet was already in place in the former location, but Jackson had to concentrate on the latter. By noon he had hidden the divisions of A. P. Hill and William B.

Taliaferro in the woods on the hill, while ordering up D.H. Hill's division from Port Royal, and Jubal Early's from Skinker's Neck. They arrived shortly after dawn on December 13, forming a reserve behind A.P. Hill and Taliaferro, thus uniting the entire Confederate army of 78,000 men on the heights.

When Burnside appeared on the eastern flank around 5 P.M. on December 12, General Franklin, along with his corps commanders, John F. Reynolds and William Farrar Smith, urged him, despite the loss of surprise, to strike with at least 30,000 men toward Hamilton's Crossing the next morning, and turn Lee's flank at any cost. That was the only reasonable course still open. Although it was no longer possible to split Jackson's corps, only Stuart's cavalry was guarding the open region east of Prospect Hill. If Franklin attacked there, Jackson would have to come off his formidable defensive position on Prospect Hill to meet him.

Burnside seemed to agree with the plan. But no orders reached Franklin until 7:30 A.M. on Saturday, December 13, and they were confusing and contradictory. While telling Franklin to keep his "whole command" ready for movement around Jackson's flank, Burnside told him to send "a division, at least," to seize Prospect Hill by direct assault, with the aim of rolling up the Confederate flank from east to west.

Franklin, Reynolds, and Smith concluded that the commanding general wanted them to capture Prospect Hill by direct assault. Only then might Burnside order a descent on Hamilton's Crossing.

Burnside adopted identical tactics against Longstreet's corps behind Fredericksburg. He ordered Sumner to direct "a division or more" up the Orange Plank Road (now Virginia Route 3) and along Telegraph Road "with the view to seizing the heights to the rear of the town." The Plank Road met Telegraph Road near the foot of Marye's Heights where the stone wall commenced, then continued over the heights.

Confronted with the rapid response of Jackson on the eastern flank, Burnside had given up his original plan, and forfeited the battle before it began. He ordered separate isolated direct attacks directly into massed Confederate forces on Marye's Heights and on Prospect Hill, four miles apart, so that neither could be decisive or could support the other. More, he set out to assault the two points best prepared to receive him.

Jackson had emplaced fourteen cannons on the extreme right of Prospect Hill, just above Hamilton's Crossing, and twelve guns north of the Richmond, Fredericksburg, and Potomac Railroad tracks, which ran along the base of the ridgeline. He mounted twenty-one more cannons about 200 yards behind the tracks.

Because Prospect Hill extended for only a mile and a half, only one division could be placed in battle positions on it. Jackson had selected A. P. Hill's division for this task, and Hill had deployed three of his six brigades on the front line, his other three into a second line behind. Hill made one major error: between two brigades he left a gap of about 600 yards where marshy woodland, overgrown with underbrush, extended north beyond the railroad tracks. This unguarded section offered a covered route by which the Federals might approach the ridgeline.

A. P. Hill did not inform Jackson about the gap. Otherwise, Jackson would have sealed it. On the morning of December 13, Jackson rode the line and stopped to study the boggy wood that projected toward the Union forces. "The enemy will attack here," he said grimly. But with battle imminent, it was too late to make major tactical realignments.[3]

In heavy fog and in the open fields between Jackson's position and the river, Franklin lined up George G. Meade's Pennsylvania division of Reynolds's corps on the left, with John Gibbon's division on the rear right flank, and Abner Doubleday's division on the left, or east, to defend against Stuart's cavalry. Franklin put Smith's entire corps of three divisions to the west, where they were left alone the entire day.

About 8:30 A.M., just as Meade's three brigades started forward, Major John Pelham, Stuart's brilliant artillery chief, advanced two cannons—an English-made Blakely rifle and a twelve-pound Napoleon smoothbore—on Meade's flank and opened fire. A dozen

Federal guns responded to "the gallant Pelham," as Lee described him in his official report, and disabled the Blakely. But the twenty-four-year-old officer moved his remaining cannon frequently, making it difficult for Federal gunners to counter him, and multiplying the effectiveness of the weapon. Pelham's action so distracted Franklin that he kept Abner Doubleday's entire division guarding the left flank all day. At last Stuart, afraid Pelham and his crew would be destroyed by the frantic Union fire, ordered him to withdraw.

After Pelham pulled back, the Federal guns commenced a furious cannonade on Jackson's line, hoping to taunt the Rebel guns into replying and thereby give away their positions. However, Jackson ordered his cannons to remain silent until Meade's infantry attack came into range. He also sent eight guns from the army artillery reserve to join Pelham on the flank, and told them, likewise, to wait. Around 10 A.M. the fog lifted.

At about 11:30 A.M. Franklin, hoping the shellfire had disabled the Confederate guns, ordered Meade's brigades forward. The broad lines of blue advanced in excellent order and silence. Not a gun fired on them. But the Rebel gunners were waiting, ranges set, their hands on the lanyards. When the Federal lines reached within 800 yards of the Confederate positions, the gun commanders got the order to fire, and flames and smoke erupted from every Rebel cannon. Shells tore great gaps in Meade's lines. The guns on Pelham's flank poured in deadly enfilade fire. The bluecoats wavered, halted, and recoiled beyond range. The attack failed, but the Federal gunners had located most of the Confederate cannons, and for the next hour they inflicted great damage in counterbattery fire.

Meanwhile, Gibbon went to the assistance of Meade, forming a column of brigades on Meade's right, or west, facing W. Dorsey Pender's North Carolina brigade, while Meade deployed two of his brigades on his front, with the third behind in close support. About 1 P.M. both divisions advanced. Confederate cannons were fewer now, but those still operating responded bravely. The twelve Rebel guns north of the RF&P tracks fired until Gibbon advanced on them, then pulled back.

But as the men of both divisions came within range, they were staggered by a hail of bullets from rifles on the hill. Gibbon's men got no farther than the railroad tracks, losing 1,200 men in a few minutes. Meade's soldiers to the east discovered the wooded marsh in front of them to be free of Confederate missiles and, moreover, to be hidden from view of the Rebels on the hilltop. Meade's soldiers squeezed into this undefended sector and advanced toward the hill. The Federals drove right into the center of A. P. Hill's position, captured about 300 Rebels, routed two regiments, and forced James Henry Lane's North Carolina brigade back into the woods.

On Lane's rear, Edward L. Thomas's Georgia brigade came forward and halted Meade's westernmost brigade, while James J. Archer's Alabama-Georgia-Tennessee brigade held Meade's easternmost brigade in a hot fight. But Meade's center brigade, meeting no resistance, advanced onto Prospect Hill, and bore down on Maxcy Gregg's unsuspecting South Carolina brigade in reserve. When Gregg's men saw the enemy approaching, they grabbed their arms and began firing. But Gregg thought the force was Confederate, and rushed forward to stop the firing. Almost at once he was killed. One of Gregg's regiments collapsed, but the rest held firm.

Meade's division had marched into a quagmire. One brigade had penetrated into the center of the Confederate line, and the other two were battling on the flanks. But all were without support. Jackson wasted no time, ordering Early and Taliaferro to rush men forward to restore the line. E. N. Atkinson's Georgia brigade and Robert F. Hoke's Alabama–Georgia–North Carolina brigade crashed into the Federals, sending the entire division fleeing down the slope in panic and disorder.

The Rebels rushed forward, shouting what a Union chaplain described an "unearthly, fiendish yell," driving the bluecoats before them, pressing across the railroad line, and out into the plain. Gibbon's division likewise fell back in the chaos of the charge. General Lee, watching the counterstroke from Lee's Hill, turned to Longstreet and said emphatically: "It is well that war is so terrible— we should grow too fond of it!"[4]

The Confederates were excited, but not organized. Men from Birney's division rushed forward and, aided by Federal artillery fire, stopped them. It was now about 2:30 P.M. Franklin decided to make no other effort, though only two divisions and a portion of a third had been seriously engaged. Burnside expected Franklin to renew the attack. Franklin's failure to do so led to his subsequent removal from the war. But another attack, if undertaken, doubtless would have failed.

While Franklin was still fending off Pelham's single gun on the eastern flank, Burnside ordered Sumner to attack Marye's Heights just behind Fredericksburg. William H. French's division of Darius N. Couch's corps was waiting in the shelter of Fredericksburg's buildings. Formed as the second line was Winfield S. Hancock's division.

Between the edge of the town and Marye's Heights about 600 yards of a largely open gentle slope intervened, although a few isolated houses and gardens were scattered about. A couple hundred yards beyond the town was a deep drainage ditch or canal, twenty feet wide and four feet deep, passable only at the bridges on the roads crossing it. Just beyond the canal, the land rose, giving the Federals good cover to deploy. Once they rose above the slope, they were exposed as long as they stood upright for the 400 yards to the Confederate cannons on the hills and the rifles behind the stone wall. About halfway, however, was a slight, terrace-like rise or bank, which could shield men lying down.[*]

---

[*] Johnson and Buel, vol. 3, 118, reproduces a picture from a contemporary photograph which shows clearly Marye's Heights, as seen by the advancing Union soldiers, the location of the stone wall, the ditch or canal, and the ghastly field the Federal soldiers were obliged to traverse. Ibid., 89, reflects a wartime photograph taken from the elevation (Willis's Hill) just to the right, or east, of Marye's Heights, where the National Cemetery is now located. It shows in sharp detail the scene from the opposite, or Confederate, viewpoint, including the sunken road, the stone wall, and the open terrain between it and the town.

Nathan Kimball's Indiana–New Jersey–Ohio–West Virginia brigade crossed the ditch first and formed up on the other side, followed 200 yards behind by the Delaware–New York–Pennsylvania brigade of John W. Andrews, then the same distance back the Connecticut–New York–Pennsylvania brigade of Oliver H. Palmer.

Confederate artillery commanded the whole sector. The nine guns of the Washington Artillery of New Orleans were mounted on Marye's Heights, and other cannons were emplaced on Lee's Hill. Porter Alexander had his large battalion of twenty-six guns just west of the heights, but had not emplaced all the pieces, so as to be able to move fast to any danger spot. Before the battle, Longstreet, noticing one of Alexander's idle cannons, suggested he add it to those guarding the plain in front of Marye's Heights.

"General," Alexander answered, "we cover that ground so well that we will comb it as with a fine-tooth comb. A chicken could not live on that field when we open on it."[5]

As Kimball's brigade started toward Marye's Heights, preceded by a cloud of skirmishers, a Federal battery advanced to the edge of town and opened fire, while cannons on Stafford Heights issued a tremendous barrage, trying to silence the Confederate artillery. But the Rebel gunners, protected by small earthworks, ignored the counterbattery fire, and poured murderous fire on the advancing Union infantry.

The Union skirmishers, in the lead, endured such galling fire that, when they reached the slight bank or terrace, they lay down behind it, still a hundred or so yards from the stone wall. Behind came Kimball's brigade, marching upright in close formation.

Lieutenant William Morris Owen, adjutant of the Washington Artillery, wrote: "We could see our shells bursting in their ranks, making great gaps; but on they came, as though they would go straight through and over us. Now we gave them canister, and that staggered them. A few more paces onward and the Georgians [and North Carolinians] in the road below us rose up, and, glancing an instant along their rifle barrels, let loose a storm of lead into the faces of the advance brigade. This was too much; the column hesitated, and then, turning, took refuge behind the bank."[6]

Kimball's brigade lost 520 men in twenty minutes and disinte-grated. Coming immediately behind, Andrews's brigade suffered the same deadly fire, but it broke sooner and lost 342 men. Palmer's brigade, coming next, lost 291 men before withdrawing.

Eleven more almost identical charges followed at about fifteen-minute intervals, the last charges coming after night had fallen. Each brigade lost on average about half of its total numbers, and a few were virtually obliterated. The survivors either sought what lit-tle cover there was on the ground, hid behind the few houses and outbuildings on the plain, or fled back into Fredericksburg.

Burnside never crossed the river, but continued to insist on the charges continuing, though it became apparent after French's divi-sion disintegrated in the first attacks that any further charges were madness. Only Joe Hooker—of all the Union generals—tried to talk Burnside into calling off the hopeless attacks, and Burnside turned a deaf ear to him.

Horrible barricades of dead, dying, and wounded covered the ground from a hundred yards back from the sunken road all the way to the elevation at the canal.

In at least one case, the Federal soldiers stretched out on the ground were so incensed by new brigades attacking through them that they fired into their backs, killing and wounding their own men.

As the day went on, the fire from the sunken road grew. General Cobb was killed by a sharpshooter; Joseph B. Kershaw took com-mand, and brought down into the road his South Carolina brigade. General Ransom sent in additional North Carolina regiments from his division. Four ranks of infantrymen were in the road. As one rank fired, it moved back to the rear to reload, while the other ranks fired in turn. The procedure kept up almost continuous volleys. Any Union soldier who lifted his head was likely to be hit.

The horrible day ended at last. Burnside had attacked at only two points. He had ignored great sections of the line, and left idle large portions of his army. The assaults against the sunken road were simply massacres. They only emphasized what already had been proved long before: attacks against riflemen standing in bulletproof entrenchments were almost bound to fail.

The battle finally convinced Lee and all the other doubting officers in both armies that field fortifications were mandatory in defensive positions. At the end of the battle, Lee ordered his army to raise the entrenchments already in place. "My army is as much stronger for these new entrenchments as if I had received reinforcements of 20,000 men," he said.[7] But no general found an alternative to the line of battle, and frontal attacks against entrenched positions continued to the end of the war, with the attendant casualties.

Burnside intended to attack again the next day, proposing that the three-division 9th Corps under Orlando B. Willcox, with Burnside personally leading, would repeat the movement against Marye's Heights that had failed so miserably on the 13th. Sumner, Hooker, and Franklin talked him out of it.

On December 14 Burnside allowed his wounded to lie unattended in the no-man's-land between the two armies. The men writhed in misery or dragged themselves inch by inch toward the rear. Everywhere they were calling, "Water, water." It was too much for Confederate sergeant Richard Kirkland to stand. Nineteen years old, Kirkland assembled canteens of water and walked onto the battlefield opposite the sunken road, knelt before the nearest wounded Union soldier, and gave him water. For an hour and a half in the afternoon, Kirkland continued his mission of mercy, carrying water back and forth from the Confederate lines to the Federal soldiers. Throughout the whole period, not a Federal rifle was raised against him.[8]

On December 15, Burnside sent a flag of truce for burial of the dead and to retrieve those wounded who had lain on the ground for forty-eight hours yet managed to survive. Lee readily consented, and soon Union surgeons, ambulances, and burial details mingled with the Confederates in the field.*

---

* Johnson and Buel, vol. 3, 100; *Southern Historical Society Papers*, vol. 10, 460; Freeman, *R. E. Lee*, vol. 2, 470–71. On December 14, the 2d Wisconsin of Abner Doubleday's division went on picket duty and made a bargain with the Rebels opposite to stop firing, allowing men on both sides to move about without cover.

The cost of the battle was startling. The Federals lost 12,600 men, most of them killed or wounded. The Confederates suffered 5,300 casualties, most of them when Meade's division exploited the gap A.P. Hill had allowed on Prospect Hill. The major losses at Marye's Heights occurred on the hill, where the men were more exposed, not in the sunken road, where the stone wall protected them. Of the 1,400 Confederate casualties at Marye's Heights, fewer than 300 came in the sunken road. The casualty figures gave graphic proof of the value of field fortifications.[9]

On the night of December 15 Burnside withdrew his army to the north side of the river. Jackson had been correct. The Confederates had achieved a spectacular victory, but gained no strategic fruits. The Federals had not been thrown into disorder, and had not been forced into retreat. They could easily replace their losses, and still retained the initiative. Once more Lee had fought a bitter battle, but had not achieved a decisive victory.

When the 24th Michigan relieved the Wisconsin outfit on the morning of December 15, however, it at once fired on the exposed Confederates, causing a number of casualties. Angry Rebels opened intense fire that continued until 4 P.M., when a Confederate soldier challenged a 6th Wisconsin man to a fistfight in the middle of the road to Richmond. Soldiers on both sides gathered to watch the fight, which, by consensus of the onlookers, ended in a draw. Thereafter, the two sides put down their arms and entered into a brisk trade—especially Northern coffee for Southern tobacco. See Johnson and Buel, vol. 3, 142. Here was conclusive evidence that the issues dividing North and South were political, and that the people on both sides were compatible. Mortal enemies do not challenge one another to fistfights.

CHANCELLORSVILLE

As the year 1863 began, the outward condition of the Confederacy appeared formidable. But ominous cracks had appeared. Though Lee's Virginia army had stepped back only fifty miles from the Potomac in the East, the Federals had evicted the Confederates from Kentucky and seized most of Tennessee, much of Louisiana, part of Arkansas, and all but a short stretch of the Mississippi River.

On January 1, Abraham Lincoln issued his formal Emancipation Proclamation, giving freedom to slaves living in states in rebellion. This had little immediate effect, except to seal off any hope of intervention by Britain and France.

More dangerous to the cause was the declining strength of the Confederacy's principal force, the Army of Northern Virginia. At first glance, General Lee's record had been spectacular since taking command of the army only seven months previously. Lee had sustained 48,000 casualties, while inflicting 71,000.[1] Yet these figures disguised a shattering reality: during the period the Confederate army had given up 4,000 prisoners, while it had captured 29,000 Union soldiers. Since prisoners could be exchanged, the actual Confederate losses, killed and wounded, amounted to 44,000, while the actual Federal losses were 42,000. Lee had suffered *more* real losses than the Federals. With less than a third the white population of the North, the South could not long endure Lee's system of waging war.

On January 19, 1863, Union general Burnside at last made a move. Knowing he could not repeat a frontal attack at Fredericksburg, he tried to cross the Rappahannock over the narrow fords to the west. But Burnside's generals had lost confidence in him, and the weather contributed to their objections. Violent rain fell on January 20, and continued for days. The Federal advance stalled in deep mud.

After the "mud march," Burnside returned to camp at Falmouth blaming his generals for the failure, especially Joseph Hooker, whom he ordered dismissed from the service for "unjust and unnecessary criticisms of the actions of his superior officers and of the authorities." He relieved Generals William B. Franklin and William Farrar Smith, plus six division or brigade commanders. Burnside told Lincoln he could not continue in his job unless the president approved. Faced with this ultimatum, Lincoln quashed Burnside's order and removed him from command.

Many Union officers wanted McClellan reinstated. But Lincoln knew this would be tantamount to a military dictatorship, and refused. Lincoln dismissed Franklin for his lack of effort after two of his divisions had been repulsed by Jackson at Fredericksburg. Edwin V. Sumner was growing old and feeble, and was considered to be a McClellan partisan. "Fighting Joe" Hooker was popular, but he had brazenly told a newspaper reporter that President Lincoln should be replaced by a dictator.

The choice came down to Hooker and division-commander George G. Meade. The odds-on favorite was Meade, but Lincoln selected Hooker because he had no political ambitions, and would not be a rival in the 1864 presidential election. Lincoln named Hooker on January 26, 1863, and wrote him: "I have heard . . . of your recently saying that both the army and the government needed a dictator. Of course it was not for this, but in spite of it, that I have given you the command. Only those generals who gain successes can set up dictators. What I now ask of you is military success, and I will risk the dictatorship."[2]

President Lincoln turned to crises at home. His transformation of the war into a crusade to free the slaves virtually stopped volunteering for the army. Lincoln responded by pushing through Congress a conscription act, which he signed into law on March 3.

The administration applied the law to suppress dissent as well. Wherever army provost marshals encountered opposition, they jailed the disaffected and denied them trial. This caused immense opposition, and chilled Democrats who had previously supported Lincoln's war effort. Leadership of the Democratic Party fell into the hands of those strongly opposed to Lincoln, namely "Peace Democrats" like Fernando Wood, a former mayor of New York City, and "Copperheads," especially in the Midwest, who were weary of the bloodshed and ready to end the war through compromise.

Hooker abandoned Burnside's cumbersome grand divisions, forming seven corps directly under himself, but could do little more until the cold weather passed. Both armies moved into winter quarters and waited.

The Army of Northern Virginia suffered severely from want of supplies, primarily caused by the incompetence of the commissary-general, Colonel Lucius B. Northrop. This officer refused to improve his system, but remained in office because he was supported by President Davis. Only the efforts of families of the soldiers, who sent food from home, prevented severe repercussions.

Lee began to lose men shortly after the start of the year. The Federal garrison commander at New Bern, North Carolina, had raided westward in December, temporarily breaking the Weldon and Wilmington Railroad at Goldsboro, and arousing fears that the Federals were contemplating a permanent closing of this vital Confederate supply line. On January 3, Lee sent down Robert Ransom's small division to block further attacks, and on January 14 detailed North Carolinian D.H. Hill to direct military operations there.

In February, the Federal 9th Corps, under William Farrar Smith, moved by sea to Fort Monroe. This raised alarm that the Federals were planning to march up the James River Valley toward the capital, or were thinking of advances in the Carolinas.

Lee sent south George Pickett's division and soon after John Bell Hood's division, both of Longstreet's 1st Corps, and on February 17 sent Longstreet himself. This left Lee with about 60,000 men and 170 guns to meet Hooker's 138,000 men and 428 guns.

Although the 9th Corps soon departed to the west, General Longstreet became excited about the suggestion of Secretary of War James A. Seddon to attack Suffolk, a few miles west of Norfolk. The Federals were garrisoning Suffolk with 20,000 troops. Though they interfered somewhat with the efforts of Confederate commissary agents to requisition hams and bacon from the rich hog-growing region west of Suffolk, the force presented no strategic danger.

The principal Federal objective was the Army of Northern Virginia. Even if Longstreet succeeded in seizing Suffolk, it would have no effect on Hooker. Lee wrote Gustavus W. Smith, commanding the Richmond defenses: "Partial encroachments of the enemy we must expect, but they can always be recovered, and any defeat of their large army will reinstate everything."[3]

But President Davis, seconded by Seddon and Longstreet, ignored Lee's pleas, and Lee did not pursue the matter. Longstreet failed to capture Suffolk, yet held more than 20,000 troops out of the colossal confrontation about to take place between Lee and Hooker. This quarter of the army might have made a profound difference. Suffolk also demonstrated why Lee usually remained with Longstreet instead of Jackson during active operations. When alone, Longstreet appeared incapable of independent action and had little initiative.

Longstreet revealed his willingness to sacrifice strategic needs to further his own ambition. But Lee exhibited weakness by not demanding concentration upon the main danger to the Confederacy: Hooker's army. Lee always bowed to the civilian leadership, despite its frequent wrongheadedness.

One reason for Lee's lack of resistance was a serious illness that struck him in late March 1863. He called it a severe cold, but the symptoms included an elevated pulse rate and pain in his chest, back, and arms. After two weeks in bed, Lee still felt weak and unsteady, and never completely recovered. His ailment may have been angina pectoris, caused by atherosclerosis, or gradual constriction of the blood flow in his arteries. The attack was the signal for the onset of cardiovascular problems that resulted in his death from a stroke in 1870.

Lee was planning another invasion of the North to take place around May 1. We know that he had discussed such a campaign with Stonewall Jackson, for Jackson set his chief engineer, Jedediah Hotchkiss, to work in January 1863 to produce a detailed map running from Winchester to Harrisburg, Pennsylvania.[4] Although Lee, in a letter to Davis in mid-April, only listed a desire to sweep the Shenandoah Valley and throw Hooker's army "into the Potomac," Jackson's remarkable map shows that the two generals were contemplating something far more ambitious.

Unfortunately for the Confederacy, Hooker struck first. The opening act of the 1863 campaign was a cavalry clash on March 17 at Kelly's Ford, twenty-three air miles upstream from Fredericksburg. The Federal cavalry, now much improved and amounting to 11,500 troopers, came off well against Jeb Stuart's horsemen, now totaling only 4,400, primarily because of a shortage of horses. At Kelly's Ford, the Union cavalry pushed back the Rebels, who lost John Pelham, killed from a shell burst. Despite their success, the Federals pulled back. The only result was to show Lee that Hooker was looking westward, at least in part, to make his advance.

Lee was sure a turning movement would hinge on United States Ford, nine miles northwest of Fredericksburg as the crow flies. Lee picked this ford because it gave access to Chancellorsville, three miles south, an intersection where four roads came together, including the Orange Plank Road and Orange Turnpike. If Hooker could get on the Plank Road and turnpike (present-day Virginia Route 3), he might drive against Lee's left flank and squeeze him out of Fredericksburg.*

Lee was right, which demonstrated how well he could divine the enemy commander's strategic moves. However, Hooker originally hoped to fake a major operation at or near United States Ford, and to send the bulk of his army over the Rappahannock east of Fredericksburg, then swing southwest and cut the RF&P Railroad. His aim was to block Lee's major supply line and prevent him from attacking the main Federal supply base at Aquia Creek. Hooker had been motivated by counterespionage, which spread the false word that Lee had a large pontoon bridge, and was going to cross the river and strike for Aquia Creek.

Hooker also planned to send most of his cavalry to seize Gordonsville and other points on the Virginia Central Railroad, then turn east, cut the RF&P near Ashland, just north of Richmond, and block the retreat of the Rebel army. Since Northrop's supply system had difficulty keeping more than a few days' rations with the army, Hooker figured any cutting of the rail line would force Lee to fall back on his depots.

Hooker's master plan called for the infantry to dislodge Lee from Fredericksburg, while Union cavalry blocked his movement southward. Yet a cavalry strike was strategically senseless. The war

---

* The Orange Plank Road and the Orange Turnpike ran together out of Fredericksburg for about five miles to a point just east of Zoan Church, about four and a half miles east of Chancellorsville. There the Plank Road arched southward but at Chancellorsville rejoined the older, straighter, but ravine-broken turnpike. The two roads ran together for about two miles west to Dowdall's Tavern and Wilderness Church, where the Plank Road again diverged south and pursued a more southerly course to Orange Court House. The turnpike continued westward three miles to Wilderness Tavern and Wilderness Run, where it split in two directions, one road leading to Orange, the other to Culpeper. Present-day Virginia Route 3 pursues the course of the old turnpike from Fredericksburg west, while Virginia Route 610 traces the easterly arc of the Plank Road from Zoan Church to Chancellorsville, and Virginia Route 621 that part diverging at Dowdall's.

had shown that horsemen could only hold a blocking position when dismounted, thereby sacrificing their mobility. The Confederates could reopen the railroads by sending infantry to oust any cavalry raiding force.* Besides, Lee had no history of retreating, and empty stomachs were nothing new to the Confederates. If the Rebel army did not run, a cavalry strike would be a blow in the air. Worse still, much of the Federal cavalry strength would be unavailable to serve as Hooker's eyes and ears.

Hooker had planned for his cavalry to move two weeks before his infantry advanced, but rains set in on April 15, making the Rappahannock unfordable. In response Hooker came up with a new plan. According to Porter Alexander, it was "decidedly the best strategy conceived in any of the campaigns set on foot against us."[5] It took full advantage of the fact that the Union army outnumbered the Confederate more than two to one.

Hooker directed that two Union corps (the 1st and 6th) under Major General John Sedgwick were to cross the river at Fredericksburg near where Franklin's grand division had crossed on December 11 and 12, and hold the main Confederate army on the heights south of town.

Meanwhile three additional corps (the 5th, 11th, and 12th), composed of 42,000 men under Major General Henry W. Slocum, were to march upstream and cross—not at the obvious United States Ford, where Rebel outposts were on guard—but all the way up the river at Kelly's Ford. From there the Union force would turn back down the right bank, and seize from the south both U.S. Ford and Banks Ford, five miles west of Fredericksburg. Capturing these two

---

* Federal cavalry were largely armed with the Sharps single-shot breech-loading carbine. It gave a rate of fire higher than the infantry rifle musket, but its bullet had an effective range of only about 175 yards, and followed an extreme parabolic trajectory that made it difficult to control. Since the infantry rifle had an effective range of 400 yards, cavalry at best could deflect an infantry attack temporarily, not hold a position. Also, since the cavalry strike was to be in the enemy rear, the horsemen would soon run out of supplies, especially ammunition. Their presence in the rear could only be sustained provided the main Federal army moved quickly to their support.

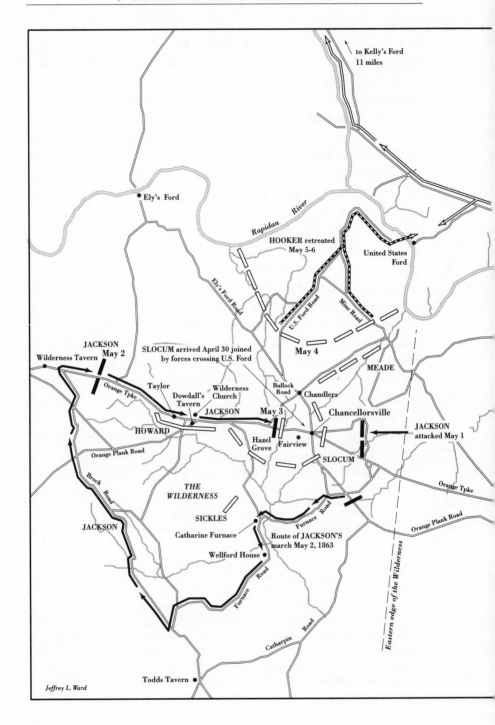

to Kelly's Ford
11 miles

Ely's Ford

Rapidan River

HOOKER retreated
May 5-6

United States
Ford

Ely's Ford Road

U.S. Ford Road

Mine Road

JACKSON
May 2

Wilderness Tavern

SLOCUM arrived April 30 joined
by forces crossing U.S. Ford

May 4

MEADE

Orange Tpke

Taylor

Wilderness
Church

Bullock
Road

Chandlers

Dowdall's
Tavern

JACKSON

May 3

Chancellorsville

HOWARD

Hazel
Grove

Fairview

JACKSON
attacked May 1

Orange Plank Road

SLOCUM

Brock Road

Orange Tpke

*THE
WILDERNESS*

SICKLES

Catharine Furnace

Route of JACKSON'S
march May 2, 1863

Orange Plank Road

JACKSON

Wellford House

Furnace Road

Furnace Road

Catharpin Road

Eastern edge of the Wilderness

Jeffrey L. Ward

Todds Tavern

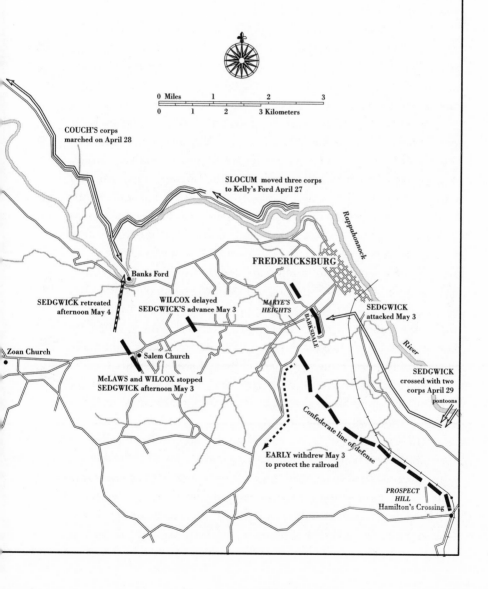

The Chancellorsville Campaign
April 27–May 6, 1863

0 Miles 1 2 3
0 1 2 3 Kilometers

COUCH'S corps
marched on April 28

SLOCUM moved three corps
to Kelly's Ford April 27

Rappahannock

FREDERICKSBURG

Banks Ford

SEDGWICK retreated
afternoon May 4

WILCOX delayed
SEDGWICK'S advance May 3

*MARYE'S
HEIGHTS*

BARKSDALE

SEDGWICK
attacked May 3

SEDGWICK
crossed with two
corps April 29

pontoons

Zoan Church

Salem Church

McLAWS and WILCOX stopped
SEDGWICK afternoon May 3

River

Confederate line of defense

EARLY withdrew May 3
to protect the railroad

*PROSPECT
HILL*
Hamilton's Crossing

fords would put the Union army's wings back into contact, while unhinging the Rebel line at Fredericksburg.

In the broad, rolling fields opposite Banks Ford, Hooker intended to confront Lee. The Federal army could be fully deployed in this wide, open countryside, where its vastly superior numbers and guns would be unbeatable. Lee would have to fight under impossible conditions, or retreat.

Kelly's Ford was twelve miles above the junction of the Rappahannock and the Rapidan Rivers. Lee would not expect a movement that far upstream: to turn back east would require fording the Rapidan. Hooker calculated that he could get on Lee's flank almost without opposition.

On April 27, the three corps under Slocum marched in great secrecy toward Kelly's Ford. The next day Major General Darius N. Couch's 17,000-man 2d Corps (except John Gibbon's division, which remained in camp at Falmouth to deceive the Confederates) marched to the north sides of U.S. and Banks Fords. Couch's job was to convince the Confederates that he was preparing to force crossings at these points. All twelve batteries of the Union army's reserve artillery moved up opposite Banks Ford, intending to cross as soon as Slocum's men secured the south bank and threw over the pontoons.

Early on April 29, Sedgwick with 40,000 men constituting the 1st and 6th Corps, crossed the Rappahannock, shielded by fog, at two points about three miles below Fredericksburg opposite Stonewall Jackson's corps. They dug in at the riverbank, and made no attempt to storm either Prospect Hill or Marye's Heights.

Hooker's last corps, the 18,700-man 3d Corps under Major General Daniel E. Sickles, remained on Stafford Heights, ready to reinforce either wing as required.

Outposts reported the movement on the western flank to Lee on April 28, but he believed the force was moving on the Shenandoah Valley. By the morning of April 29, all three Union corps were across Kelly's Ford and moving back east without Confederate detection.

Hooker designated only 1,300 Union horsemen, under Alfred Pleasonton, to scout ahead of Slocum's infantry, sending all the rest south under General George Stoneman to strike at Confederate communications. Confederate cavalry commander Jeb Stuart at first could not figure out Union intentions, guessed Slocum's force at a third its actual strength, and thought it was heading toward Gordonsville.

The Federals waded two fords on the Rapidan, Germanna (on present-day Virginia Route 3), seven miles south of Kelly's Ford, and Ely's (on present-day Virginia Route 610), nine and a half miles southeast of Kelly's.

On the afternoon of April 29 couriers informed Lee of the passage of the fords. He now realized that Stuart was wrong, and the Federals were descending on his left flank. He at once dispatched Richard H. Anderson's division to the Chancellorsville crossroads.

Stuart, also realizing that he was out of place, moved with Fitzhugh Lee's brigade, 3,300 men, eastward to assist Lee, leaving only W. H. F. "Rooney" Lee's brigade of 1,000 troopers to deal with

(NATIONAL ARCHIVES)

Wilderness, near Chancellorsville

the 10,000 Union cavalry in the Confederate rear. Stuart concentrated his now-superior cavalry where it was most needed—at the front of both armies. This gave Lee quick information about all Federal movements, and denied information to the Federals, since Pleasonton could not penetrate Stuart's cavalry shield. Lee ignored Union cavalry breaks of the railway lines, and General Stoneman's move degenerated into a giant, but useless, raid.

By the morning of April 30, Stuart had captured prisoners from the three Union corps, and Lee first learned the magnitude of the force opposing him on the west: two-thirds the size of his whole army. Since Anderson could not stand alone, Lee ordered Anderson to select a strong position and dig in. Anderson moved back four and a half miles east of Chancellorsville to Zoan Church and began to construct defensive entrenchments.

Soon afterward, Slocum's advance forces arrived at Chancellorsville. The location consisted solely of a large two-story brick house with pillars in front, and a large clearing around it. Meanwhile Couch's soldiers occupied U.S. Ford, and threw over pontoon bridges. Slocum's instructions had been to continue on to seize Banks Ford, about six miles northeast of Chancellorsville. But during the morning of April 30 Hooker ordered the entire right wing to halt and await an enemy attack. This was Hooker's first fatal error.*

During the day the remainder of the three Union corps closed up on the Chancellorsville crossroads. They had marched forty-six miles and had achieved a stunning surprise. Hooker had maneuvered the Confederate army out of position without a battle. Heavy reinforcements were coming up by way of U.S. Ford, two divisions of Couch's 2d Corps and all of Sickles's 3d Corps, which arrived on the morning of Friday, May 1, giving Hooker 70,000 men and 208 guns on Lee's flank.

But success was incomplete until the Federals secured Banks Ford, which would serve both to reconnect the two wings of the

---

* It is unknown why Hooker believed the right wing might be attacked, since only Anderson's division was in place and clearly it was no match for three corps.

Union army, and get the Union wing out of a wild and dangerous region known as the Wilderness.

The eastern edge of the Wilderness lay a couple miles east of Chancellorsville. The original forest stretched fourteen miles along the Rappahannock and eight to ten miles to the south. It had been cleared over the previous half century to supply charcoal for iron furnaces in the area. A dense second growth of briars, underbrush, pine, cedar, and low-branched hardwood trees had created a place where visibility extended only a few feet and walking was difficult. Only the roads and a few isolated places had been kept clear. In such an area, Hooker's greatest strength, his artillery, was useless.

If Hooker was going to deploy his army effectively, he had to get out of the Wilderness.

April 30 was a difficult day for Lee. He had assumed that 40,000 or so Union soldiers had arrived on his left flank, about the same force as Sedgwick was entrenching in front of Jackson east of Fredericksburg. Yet neither commander was advancing.

But Lee decided that Hooker's major effort was coming on the west. It was clearly the most dangerous, because, if Slocum advanced much farther, he would possess Banks Ford, be free of the Wilderness, and be directly on the Confederate left flank.

Hooker's second fatal error was to allow Sedgwick to decide whether or not to attack. Sedgwick saw that Prospect Hill was occupied by the Rebels, and he elected to remain still. The principal purpose of Hooker's move against Lee's flank was to strike at a weakly held point. It was now obvious that the only way to guarantee that the flank remained weak was to send in a powerful frontal attack against the main line of Confederate resistance—along Marye's Heights and Prospect Hill. This would hold Lee's army in place. But Sedgwick did not recognize the opportunity. By failing to insist on such an attack, Hooker permitted Lee to transfer the bulk of his army to the endangered western flank.

Seeing that Sedgwick remained idle, Lee ordered Lafayette McLaws's division to march at once to aid Anderson at Zoan Church, leaving only William Barksdale's Mississippi brigade to defend Marye's Heights. He also ordered Jackson to march three divisions of his corps at daylight the next day, May 1, to Zoan Church, take charge of the western flank, and "repulse the enemy." Jackson left his fourth division, under Jubal Early, along with William N. Pendleton's reserve artillery, to watch Sedgwick.

By nightfall of April 30, Lee had turned his back on Sedgwick and commenced concentrating 47,000 men and 144 guns on the west to confront Hooker. He left only about 10,000 men on the Fredericksburg heights under Early.

Hooker had entirely miscalculated Lee's response. His order of the day on April 30 read: "Our enemy must either ingloriously fly or come out from behind his defenses and give us battle on our own ground, where certain destruction awaits him."[6] Despite the reference to battle, Hooker was certain that Lee would "ingloriously fly." His whole strategy had been predicated on this expectation. But in the unlikely event that Lee did not retreat, and turned on Hooker, the Union commander did not plan to attack. Rather, he intended to stand on the defensive, and receive Lee's attack.

The previous defeat at Fredericksburg had seared itself into Hooker's consciousness. He had learned the lesson of the Minié-ball rifle: that attacks usually failed. But Hooker made the wrong decision, to take a passive role, leaving the possibility for action in Lee's hands. It was Hooker's third fatal mistake.

Hooker had planned only a modest advance on May 1—to get out of the Wilderness and to seize Banks Ford. Hooker started his move at 11 A.M., sending separate columns eastward on the Orange Plank Road to the south, the turnpike in the center, and the River Road to Banks Ford to the north.

Meanwhile, Stonewall Jackson got his corps to Zoan Church at 8 A.M. May 1, and took command. Jackson was well aware of the nature of the Wilderness. He also knew that the Confederates would be unable to counter the Federal artillery if it deployed in the open spaces to the east. Jackson immediately made one of the most masterful decisions of his military career: he ordered the Rebel troops to abandon the defensive emplacements they were building, and to advance directly against the Federal army.

If he could push Hooker back into the Wilderness, Jackson knew that the Federal artillery would be badly crippled. He recognized that the woods could provide excellent defensive positions, and the unlimited logs and brush would make attacks difficult. But bottling up the Union guns would even the odds. And, by pressing the Federals back into the Wilderness, he would block Hooker from reaching open country, where his army would be invincible. In a single stroke, Jackson turned a desperate situation that threatened destruction of the Army of Northern Virginia into an opportunity for a spectacular victory.

Jackson's advance stunned Hooker. Instead of using his immensely superior power to drive Jackson back, Hooker withdrew to Chancellorsville, forming defensive lines behind an arc of crude but strong earthworks just east and south of the crossroads.

It was an astonishing, unbelievable response, which angered Hooker's generals immensely. When General Couch reported to Hooker on the night of May 1, Hooker said: "I have got Lee just where I want him. He must fight me on my own ground." Couch later wrote: "To hear from his own lips that the advantages gained by the successful marches of his lieutenants were to culminate in fighting a defensive battle in that nest of thickets was too much, and I retired from his presence with the belief that my commanding general was a whipped man."[*]

General Lee arrived in the afternoon of May 1, and he rode out to study Hooker's left, or north, to determine whether there was any chance to turn the Federal line there and cut the Union army off from

---

[*] Johnson and Buel, vol. 3, 161; Bigelow, 259. Porter Alexander remarked on "the perfect collapse of the moral courage of Hooker, as commander in chief, as soon as he found himself in the actual presence of Lee and Jackson." See *Fighting for the Confederacy*, 216.

U.S. Ford. But Lee found too many Federal troops and too little space to swing around the northern flank.

Around 7:30 P.M. Lee met with Jackson. It was obvious that the Army of Northern Virginia had two options: to attack Chancellorsville frontally, or to move by the flank to the south. Both generals believed Hooker's front was too powerful, but sent two engineers to make sure. The officers reported back that a direct attack would be unconscionable.

This left only a flanking movement. But what could be the objective? As Lee and Jackson discussed the matter, Jeb Stuart rode up and announced Fitzhugh Lee had discovered that the Federal right was stretched out facing south along the Plank Road west of Chancellorsville. Moreover, this line was "floating in the air": it rested on no secure defensive position, and the Federal corps commander there, Oliver O. Howard, had established no defensive line facing west. Thus, the Federal position could be turned by moving south and west of Chancellorsville, and coming up on the Plank Road or turnpike beyond Hooker's westernmost elements. The Confederates then could strike straight east along the Plank Road directly onto the flank of the Union army!

As heady as this prospect was, it presented great danger as well. A march around the southern flank would divide the Rebel army, leaving either segment too small to fight a pitched battle if Hooker struck one or the other.

Nevertheless, both generals recognized that a flanking movement presented the only means to drive Hooker back across the Rappahannock. Lee approved the movement, and appointed Jackson to carry it out, with Stuart to shield the march with his cavalry. Jackson rose, smiling, touched his cap, and said: "My troops will move at 4 o'clock."[7]

Neither the route of the march, the exact objective, nor the number of troops to be used had been decided on. Lee's original idea was for a simple flanking movement to dislodge Hooker and force him to retreat. But the dangerous situation in which Hooker had placed his army opened for Jackson the possibility of destroying his entire force.

Early on the morning of Saturday, May 2, 1863, Jackson awoke from a short sleep and interrogated his chaplain, Tucker Lacy, whose family owned land in the region, about a route to follow. Lacy remembered that Charles C. Wellford, owner of Catharine Furnace, lived a couple of miles southwest. Jackson at once called his mapmaker, Jedediah Hotchkiss, to seek out Wellford. Hotchkiss and Lacy woke Wellford, who pointed out a covered route, and appointed his young son, Charles, as guide.

By the time Hotchkiss returned, Jackson was conferring again with Lee. Hotchkiss traced the route recommended by Wellford. There was a moment of silence. Lee then said: "General Jackson, what do you propose to do?" Jackson replied: "Go around here," pointing to the line Hotchkiss had shown. Lee: "What do you propose to make this movement with?" Jackson, without hesitation: "With my whole corps." Lee replied: "What will you leave me?" Jackson: "The divisions of Anderson and McLaws."

This was the moment of truth. Lee had rejected Jackson's earlier proposals for a massive strike on the enemy flank. But here was an opportunity that might never come again. Hooker had placed himself in a perilous position, with only one river crossing. If Jackson got on his rear, he might force the Federals away from the ford. Hooker then would have nowhere to turn and might be annihilated.

Lee was astonished by Jackson's boldness, but recognizing that Jackson had seen a chance to transform the situation, he answered calmly: "Well, go on."[8]

Jackson's corps began to move forward about 7 A.M. As the head of the column marched southwest toward Catharine Furnace, Stonewall Jackson rode a short distance behind with his staff. Lee stood by the road to say good-bye. Jackson drew rein, and they talked briefly. Jackson pointed ahead; Lee nodded; Jackson rode on.

One of the most brilliant and successful flank marches in the history of warfare had begun.

The Confederate men were in high spirits, expectant, knowing Jackson was embarked on another of his mysterious marches, and that they were a part of history. But the actual journey was largely uneventful, a long, hard hike of about twelve miles, along narrow dirt roads cut through the forest. There was little dust because of recent rains, and Stuart's horsemen protected the men from any disturbances by Federal patrols to the north. All day long, Rebel cavalry kept pushing through the woods just far enough to receive fire from the Federals, then withdrawing.

After Jackson set off, Lee ordered the two remaining divisions to convince the Federals they were preparing to attack.

Despite the effort to deceive, Union observers discovered Jackson's march soon after it got under way. David B. Birney, commanding a division in Daniel Sickles's corps, had moved some of his men to a cleared elevation, Hazel Grove, a little more than a mile southwest of Chancellorsville. About 8 A.M. some of his scouts reported that a long column was moving southwest on the Furnace Road, running south of Hazel Grove.

Birney reported the sighting, but Hooker jumped to the conclusion that the Confederates were retreating to Gordonsville. Hooker warned Henry W. Slocum, commanding the 12th Corps facing Lee, and Howard, commanding the 13,000-man 11th Corps on the west, about a possible attack on their flanks. But he didn't regard the threat as great, and neither Slocum nor Howard gave it much credence, although Howard received—and ignored—a number of reports of Rebel movements to his south throughout the day.

Around noon Hooker authorized Sickles to advance on Catharine Furnace and attack Lee's "trains." Birney's division moved forward, followed by Amiel W. Whipple's. But Anderson's division, just east of the furnace, and the 23d Georgia, detached from Jackson's column to guard the furnace, opposed the advance vigorously. During this firefight, Jackson's men and wagons passed beyond reach of the Union probes.

Jackson's corps marched to the end of the Furnace Road, three and a half miles southwest of the Orange Plank Road, then turned back northwest on a lesser-traveled woods road (now Virginia Route 613) coming onto the Brock Road (also now Route 613) about a mile south of its junction with the Plank Road (now Virginia Route 621).

About 1 P.M. some 2d Virginia Cavalry horsemen turned east up the Plank Road and saw the right of the 11th Corps's line. Jackson and Fitz Lee rode up the Plank Road to an elevated point a mile southwest of Dowdall's Tavern, near the junction with the turnpike. Jackson saw that the Union entrenchments lay a few hundred yards away, facing south.

Jackson had planned to turn up the Plank Road to attack, believing that the end of Howard's positions was farther east. Now he continued north on the Brock Road for another mile and a half to the turnpike (now Virginia Route 3), then turned east, certain he then would be beyond the farthest western Federal element.

As Jackson's corps was completing its march around Hooker, General Sickles decided he could break the Confederate column he and Hooker believed was retreating toward Gordonsville. He surrounded the 23d Georgia at Catharine Furnace, capturing most of the members, but called for reinforcements, since he believed Confederate rear guards would be alert and dangerous. Accordingly, Hooker told Howard to send Francis C. Barlow's 1,500-man brigade of Adolph von Steinwehr's division. This force marched to the furnace.

Howard's corps, now numbering 11,500 men, about half of them immigrants from Germany, was spread out for nearly two miles along the Orange Turnpike or Plank Road. Most emplacements faced south, not west, though the most westerly portion was facing west: two regiments of Leopold von Gilsa's brigade of Charles Devens's division, behind a weak abatis of felled small trees and bushes. It was just north of the turnpike and a little more than a mile west of Dowdall's Tavern. With the regiments were two cannons posted to enfilade the road, not the forest stretching out to the west. Another regiment, the 75th Ohio, was a considerable distance east of von Gilsa, in reserve. The remainder of Devens's division was on either side of Talley's house and farm, half a mile east of von Gilsa's position. Devens's men faced south along the pike, the division's four guns trained on the road, not the woods.

About a quarter of a mile east and north of Talley on high cleared ground around the Hawkins farm was Carl Schurz's two-brigade division.* Most of Schurz's division also faced south, but two regiments of Alexander Schimmelfennig's brigade faced west. It, like von Gilsa's force, was shielded by a light abatis.

The final brigade, commanded by Adolphus Buschbeck, of von Steinwehr's division was facing south at Dowdall's Tavern, where a considerable area was clear of trees. There was a shallow shelter trench or ditch, several hundred yards long, facing west just north of the road, with several cannons behind it. The trench, however, was unoccupied.

Between Howard's 11th Corps and Slocum's 12th Corps around Chancellorsville was a mile of unoccupied ground, previously held by Barlow's brigade, now marching to assist Sickles.

Below Catharine Furnace were two divisions of Sickles's corps, with Barlow's brigade, and one regiment of Pleasonton's cavalry, perhaps 16,000 men, believing they were pursuing Lee's fleeing army. Pleasonton, realizing his cavalry was of little use chasing Rebels in the thickets, had kept his other two regiments at Hazel Grove.

In summary, two weak lines of Howard's corps faced west, but most of his men and guns were facing south. Sickles's corps was so far south as to be beyond possibility of taking part in the fight, and could be cut off if Jackson could push far enough east. The remainder of Hooker's army faced largely east or south, defending against Lee's two divisions, and was in no position to block Chancellorsville from the rear. Only one division, Hiram G. Berry's of Sickles's corps, was in the vicinity of Chancellorsville, and might be called on in an emergency.

---

* This position, less than half a mile west of the point where the Orange Plank Road branched off to the southwest, was also known as the Taylor house, located north of the road, whereas the Talley house and fields were south. Just north of the junction of the turnpike and the Plank Road was the Wilderness Church, and a quarter of a mile to the east of the road junction was Dowdall's Tavern, also carried in some reports as Melzi Chancellor's house.

Jackson was well aware that the key to destruction of Hooker's army was U.S. Ford. He intended from the outset to get his corps between Chancellorsville and the ford. However, he couldn't move directly to the ford, because he didn't know what Union forces might be there, and such a move would sever all connection with Lee. Therefore, Jackson's only feasible line of attack was eastward along the turnpike and Plank Road.* This would roll up the 11th Corps and drive Jackson into the rear of the corps of Couch, Sickles, and Slocum. Once there, Jackson hoped to turn onto Bullock Road, about a mile west of Chancellorsville, and seize Chandler's cross-roads (or White House), a spot three-fourths of a mile northwest of Chancellorsville. This point controlled both roads to U.S. Ford, and would cut off Hooker's retreat, sever Hooker's connection with any Union forces around the ford (1st Corps arrived there during the afternoon), and place Hooker between Jackson and Lee.

Thus, Jackson's advance was on Hooker's right flank, not on his rear athwart his line of retreat.

Jackson deployed his men, making as little noise as possible. In the first line went Robert E. Rodes's division. In the second line two hundred yards back was Raleigh E. Colston's division. Behind, partly in column, came A. P. Hill's division.

Since Howard's corps was on the turnpike and the Plank Road, the main thrust was going to be made by three brigades of Rodes's division near it—George Doles's Georgia brigade, lined up just south of the road; Edward A. O'Neal's Alabama brigade, just north; and Alfred Iverson's North Carolina brigade, to O'Neal's left.

On the far right or south, in the first line, was Alfred H. Colquitt's Georgia brigade. Directly behind was S. Dodson Ramseur's North Carolina brigade. A short distance to the south was E. P. Paxton's Stonewall Brigade of Colston's division, positioned to march straight up the Plank Road to Dowdall's Tavern as

---

* The Plank Road and the turnpike ran together for a little more than two miles from Chancellorsville to Dowdall's Tavern, where the Plank Road turned off southwest and the turnpike continued on west. The part running together was generally known as the Plank Road, and is so carried here.

the assault lines moved out. Paxton's job was to clear out any Union detachments that might be south of the main line along the turnpike.

Neither Colquitt's, Ramseur's, nor Paxton's brigades were likely to face significant Federal forces. Their advance was imperative, however, since their path would lead them over both Hazel Grove and Fairview, an elevated, open area about two-thirds of a mile southwest of Chancellorsville. These two heights were the only places where many guns could be emplaced, and their capture would imperil Hooker's entire position. Also, seizure of Hazel Grove would separate Sickles's large force from Hooker's main body, and probably lead to its surrender.

Jackson did not realize the significance of Hazel Grove and Fairview at that moment, but he ordered all of his troops to push resolutely ahead, allowing nothing to stop them. Jackson's orders were explicit: if any part of the first line needed help, the commander could demand aid from the second line without further instructions. Under no circumstances was there to be a pause.

At about 5:15 P.M. all was ready, and Stonewall Jackson released his eager, excited, and enthusiastic soldiers. They descended upon a Union army still unaware of their presence. The Federals first received an intimation of trouble when deer and rabbits, stirred up by the Confederate lines, rushed in fright through their positions.

The turnpike turned slightly southward along the route Doles's brigade advanced. The Georgians were just north of the road when, about a mile ahead, they encountered von Gilsa's soldiers preparing their evening meal. The Federals hastily formed a line of battle. Doles smashed straight into von Gilsa's position. The Federals stood through three volleys, but fell apart, the men rushing backward in total disorder. The two Federal cannons fired a few rounds, but the Georgians shot down the horses, and the gunners fled. Von Gilsa's regiments facing south, hit by volleys from front, flank, and rear, disintegrated without firing a shot. A few Union soldiers rallied around the 75th Ohio, but it, too, turned and fled.

The great bulk of the men of Devens's division facing south abandoned their positions and ran headlong toward Chancellorsville. General Howard, watching the disaster unfold from the elevation about Dowdall's Tavern, noted that "more quickly than it could be told, with all the fury of the wildest hailstorm, everything, every sort of organization that lay in the path of the mad current of panic-stricken men had to give way and be broken into fragments." Howard's aide was struck dead by a shot, and Howard's horse sprang on his hind legs and fell over, throwing the general to the ground.[9]

A few Union soldiers rallied around Schurz's divison at the Hawkins farm, but the stand was brief. The attacking Rebels emerged from the woods, the men in front halting and firing. As they reloaded, another set of Confederates ran before them, halted and fired, in no regular line, but with lethal swiftness. Rebel brigades enveloped Schurz's position, and sent the entire division fleeing eastward.

As Rodes's three brigades on or near the turnpike pressed loudly and eagerly toward Dowdall's Tavern, Colquitt on the south advanced only a few hundred yards, then halted, in direct disobedience of orders. He had gotten a report that Federals were on his southern flank. Paxton's brigade was positioned to deal with any stray Union soldiers in the area, but Colquitt's halting forced Ramseur's and Paxton's brigades to stop as well. Ramseur, in exasperation, assured Colquitt that he would take care of any Federals that appeared. At last Colquitt moved. But three brigades, 5,000 men, were now so far behind Jackson's advance that they couldn't catch up. Colquitt's disobedience prevented seizure of Hazel Grove and Fairview and the severing of Sickles's large force from the main army.

Terror was now sweeping Howard's corps. The Rebels in Colston's second line were so eager that they were pushing through Rodes's lead brigades.

Buschbeck's men at Dowdall's Tavern had moved into the shallow trench and were facing westward. They were the last organized Federal line in front of Jackson, but were nervous and tentative as the Rebels advanced inexorably on them. Jackson, knowing that once this force was scattered nothing was left, assailed Buschbeck's line along his whole front, while rolling troops around both flanks. A sheet of fire struck some Federals in the trench. As they went down, men on either side vacated the trench and ran away, many throwing away their arms, and joining the stream of soldiers, horses, cannons, and wagons rushing for the rear. Thousands of soldiers did not stop until they reached and crossed U.S. Ford.

Rodes's and Colston's lines were getting intertwined, but the Rebels still advanced steadily. Jackson rode into the mixed ranks and ordered them to press on, irrespective of the confusion. But Rodes was an orderly man, and not gifted with the vision of his commander. About 7:15 P.M., fearing confusion, Rodes called a halt about a mile and a half west of Chancellorsville, notifying Jackson to send forward A. P. Hill's division to take up the assault while he moved his and Colston's divisions back to Dowdall's Tavern to re-form.

This unnecessary stop gave the Federals an opportunity to take a breath and organize a defense. Darkness was falling. Rodes's halt ended any chance of resuming the advance while daylight remained.

Hooker, at the Chancellor house, did not get news until 6:30 P.M., when Captain Harry Russell, one of his aides, heard violent noise and, turning his glass westward, yelled, "My God, here they come!" Russell believed the fleeing Federals were part of Sickles's corps. It was only when Hooker and his aides rushed into the mass that they discovered the truth.

Hooker nearly panicked, sending word to Sickles to save his men if he could. If Colquitt had not stopped, Sickles could have been cut off from the main army.

Because Rodes had halted, Hooker had an hour to repair the rout of his army. Hiram Berry's division was near, and Hooker ordered it to move west along the Plank Road and challenge Jackson. This was one of the bravest acts in the history of the Army of the Potomac: the men advanced resolutely toward the enemy, even as thousands of other Union soldiers rushed around them and fled to the rear.

Captain T. W. Osborn, chief of Berry's artillery, later wrote: "As we passed General Hooker's headquarters, a scene burst upon us which God grant may never again be seen in the Federal army of the United States. The 11th Corps had been routed and were fleeing to the river like scared sheep. The men and artillery filled the road, its sides and the skirts of the field. . . . Aghast and terror-stricken, heads bare and panting for breath, they pleaded like infants at the mother's breast that we should let them pass to the rear unhindered."[10]

Around 8 P.M. Berry's men started entrenching in the valley of a small stream about half a mile west of Chancellorsville and just north of Fairview. At Fairview twenty Federal artillery pieces, several of them 11th Corps guns stopped by Hooker's staff, were being unlimbered and pointed westward. Soon after, Alpheus Williams's division of the 12th Corps also arrived, and extended Berry's line southward to cover Fairview and the guns.

Meanwhile, Sickles's men rushed northward, while Pleasonton at Hazel Grove organized a defense around some artillery there. These guns held off a few Confederates from A. P. Hill's division who reached Hazel Grove in the darkness. In this fashion, Sickles's corps reconnected itself to Hooker's main force.

A. P. Hill found only James Lane's North Carolina brigade available to deploy immediately. It was 8:45 P.M. before the brigade was lined up on either side of the Plank Road a mile west of Chancellorsville.

General Jackson arrived at the front, planning to send parts of Hill's division northeast to seize Chandler's crossroads by way of Bullock Road, running directly to it from the advanced Confederate positions. There were no significant Union forces to stop such a movement.

Jackson could still cut off the Union army from the Rappahannock. The night was clear and a full moon rose, giving sufficient light for troops to move. Moreover, the Union soldiers were thoroughly demoralized, and could have offered little resistance.

Jackson had not yet established connection with Lee, which he meant to do by pushing Lane's brigade straight forward to and through Chancellorsville. When Lane asked for orders around 9 P.M., Jackson raised his arm in the direction of the enemy, and exclaimed: "Push right ahead, Lane, right ahead."

Soon thereafter A. P. Hill arrived, and Jackson gave him his orders: "Press them," Jackson emphasized. "Cut them off from the United States Ford, Hill; press them."[11] Hill announced he was unfamiliar with the country leading to the ford, and Jackson ordered Captain J. Keith Boswell, well acquainted with the roads and paths of the Wilderness, to guide him.

Jackson accompanied Hill and his staff in advance of Lane's line to get further knowledge of the terrain in the direction of U.S. Ford. They heard Federal voices and axes cutting trees for abatis. Firing erupted in front of them. Jackson and his party hurriedly moved off the Plank Road and turned into the little-used Mountain Road a few yards north.

Only a few minutes before, Union general Pleasonton, fearing Confederates were about to overrun Hazel Grove, ordered the 8th Pennsylvania Cavalry to stem the enemy advance. The lead squadron collided with the front ranks of the Confederates on the Plank Road. Numerous Union horsemen went down from Rebel volleys. The charge disintegrated, and the survivors fled, but riderless horses and horseless riders rushed about in the dark woods for some time, creating chaos.

Lane's soldiers were still alert from the cavalry charge, and as Jackson's party rode along the Mountain Road, the 18th North Carolina mistook the sounds for Federal cavalry. The order was given to fire, with Jackson's party not more than twenty paces away. Captain Boswell and an orderly fell dead. Three bullets struck Jackson. One penetrated his right palm; another went into the wrist of his left hand; and a third splintered the bone of his left arm between the shoulder and elbow, severing an artery. Jackson's horse bolted for the Federal lines, but Jackson turned it back.

Jackson weakened quickly from loss of blood, though Hill and his aides stopped some of the bleeding with a knotted handkerchief. After getting Jackson back to the compound, Jackson's medical officer, Hunter McGuire, and other doctors amputated his left arm just below the shoulder.

Shortly after Jackson was hit, Union artillery fire wounded General Hill in the legs. He relinquished command to Rodes, and then to Jeb Stuart, now the only unwounded major general on the western flank. Stuart did not take over command until after midnight, however, because he was at Ely's Ford.

This transfer of command was fatal to Jackson's plan to swing most of his corps north to block U.S. Ford. Stuart was aware of the confusion caused by the loss of Jackson and Hill, and suspended operations until daylight.

The failure to complete Jackson's movement presented Hooker with an opportunity. He had Meade's 5th Corps already in place to the north of Chancellorsville, and John F. Reynolds's 1st Corps came up during the night. The two Union corps had 30,000 men, more than Stuart's entire force. Hooker could have ordered the 25,000 men he had gotten lined up just west of Chancellorsville to demonstrate and hold Jackson's corps in place. Then the 1st and 5th Corps could have swung around Jackson's left, or northern, flank.

However, Hooker had not thought of turning the tables on the Confederates. He ordered 1st and 5th Corps to construct a defensive line to protect U.S. Ford.

This line was incomplete by morning, and a narrow opportunity presented itself to Stuart. If he had assaulted northward at daylight on May 3, he still might have split Hooker from the river, though it would have been much more difficult than in the chaos of the night before.

But Lee was not interested in trusting such a movement to Stuart. He surely had agreed to Jackson's plan to separate Hooker from U.S. Ford. But he must have realized that the time for such a blow had passed by the morning of May 3. With only a cavalry major general and infantry brigadiers in command of Jackson's troops, the sooner he could reunite both wings of the army the better. When Lee got word of Jackson's wounding early on May 3, he directed Stuart to press eastward "in order that we can unite both wings of the army."[12]

To get the two wings together, Stuart resolved to strike the Union forces directly. He directed Porter Alexander, the senior artillery commander, to locate suitable gun positions. Alexander found few in the heavily wooded Wilderness, but he recognized the importance of Hazel Grove, isolated from the main Union line, and vulnerable to a Confederate strike. If he could get guns on this elevation, he could not only hit Union infantry lined up against Jackson's corps, but enfilade the Union guns at Fairview, three-fourths of a mile to the northeast. If the Federals could be evicted from Fairview, Hooker's entire position would become untenable.

Consequently, seizure of Hazel Grove was the crucial tactical move of the day. Hooker made it easy by missing its importance, ordering evacuation early on May 3. The Rebels occupied the point before 7 A.M. "There has rarely been a more gratuitous gift of a battlefield," Alexander later remarked.[13]

Soon thereafter, Alexander covered the height with forty cannons. These, plus twenty more that he and other artillery officers emplaced on the Plank Road, fired on Union infantry facing west, but concentrated on the forty Federal guns atop Fairview. Although most of the Union pieces were entrenched, the Rebel guns beat them down, a process speeded because the Federal guns soon ran out of ammunition, and Hooker did not see to their being resupplied.

Because of the fortuitous concentration of Rebel cannons at Hazel Grove, Stuart's proper tactical move was not to fling his infantry headlong against the Federal positions, but to select a point on the Union line where Alexander could focus his fire, and to batter that point until it was weakened. Then he should have launched an infantry strike at the point, to penetrate the enemy rear. Elsewhere he should have made only feint attacks to hold the enemy in place. Once a Confederate infantry force broke through the weakened part of the Union line it could have evicted the enemy cannons on Fairview. This would have forced Hooker to withdraw.

Instead, Stuart ordered direct infantry assaults against the entire Federal line. During the night, the Union infantry had worked diligently to build breastworks, some shallow, but all protected by abatis of felled trees and heavy brush.

Stuart's attacks were some of the bloodiest and most violently contested in the war. The Federal defenses slowed the Confederate assaults and contributed to the enormous casualties, though Rebel determination was so great that the Union forces suffered as well. Even so, most Rebel assaults failed. However, the Union soldiers began to run out of ammunition, and Hooker made no efforts to replenish it. This caused them to fall back as the Rebels continued their advance.

Stuart lost 30 percent of the men he had engaged. Confederate casualties, which had been few until these assaults, reached a higher proportion of the men involved (21 percent) than Federal losses (15 percent). The struggle was so terrible that several Confederate veteran outfits refused to advance into the hail of Union shells and bullets. And a number of Federal commanders marched their men off the battlefield without orders. There were so many instances of this that President Lincoln decided not to punish the officers responsible.

Lee's attacks from the southeast were pressed less hard, and the losses were accordingly lighter.

About 9 A.M. on May 3 the Union guns at Fairview withdrew, and an hour later Confederate infantry seized the height. This broke Hooker's position, not Stuart's sanguinary attacks. Hooker now ordered the withdrawal of his entire force northward. The Confederates were exhausted and made no attempt to pursue.

Hooker kept about 35,000 of his soldiers—far more than Stuart's whole force—entirely out of the fight, and he neither resupplied his infantry facing Stuart or his guns on Fairview with ammunition, nor protected the guns adequately with infantry. Hooker was painfully injured around 9 A.M. when a Rebel solid shot shattered a pillar on the porch of the Chancellor house and flung part of it against Hooker's head and body. The blow apparently affected Hooker's judgment, and this may account in part for his poor decisions.

Hooker's withdrawal allowed the two wings of Lee's army to reunite. But before Lee could launch an assault against Hooker's positions guarding U.S. Ford, he had to respond to the threat on his rear by General Sedgwick, who finally moved from Fredericksburg on the morning of May 3.

Sedgwick had 24,000 men facing Early with only 3,500 men on Prospect Hill southeast of Fredericksburg. Sedgwick could easily have driven through Hamilton's Crossing, turning the entire Confederate position, and struck straight at Lee's rear. Instead Sedgwick marched up the plain in front of the Confederate positions on the hills below Fredericksburg, and attacked frontally the same sunken road below Marye's Heights that had ruined Ambrose Burnside's offensive in December 1862.

As John Bigelow Jr., historian of the Chancellorsville campaign writes, "The result was the singular spectacle of a body of troops practically on the enemy's flank moving to the enemy's front in order to attack him."[14]

At Fredericksburg, John Gibbon's division, which until then had remained on Stafford Heights, joined Sedgwick, raising his total force by 6,000 men.

Though Sedgwick could have marched around Marye's Heights, he commenced the same insane assault against the heights as Burnside had done. This time, however, only a single Confederate brigade was in place, William Barksdale's Mississippians. The first Union assaults failed, the Federals suffering nearly a thousand casualties in less than five minutes. But Thomas M. Griffin, commanding the 18th Mississippi in the sunken road, foolishly accepted a Federal request for a cease-fire to remove wounded. This permitted Union officers to observe how few Rebels were holding the road. The Federals then attacked in heavy force, and captured and destroyed nearly the whole Mississippi regiment.

Early withdrew down the Telegraph Road toward Richmond to protect the RF&P Railroad. Only Cadmus M. Wilcox's Alabama brigade of Anderson's division, which had been guarding Banks Ford, was in position to delay Sedgwick's advance directly on Lee's rear. Sedgwick took a long time organizing a strike west on the Plank Road, giving Wilcox time to build two strong blocking positions, which delayed Sedgwick long enough for Lee to get Lafayette McLaws's division to Salem Church, six miles east of Chancellorsville, and build a strong defensive line. Here McLaws and Wilcox stopped Sedgwick in a sharp engagement, despite Sedgwick's two-to-one superiority.

Sedgwick remained immobile all the next day (May 4), giving Lee the opportunity to organize a converging assault that finally drove Sedgwick across Banks Ford, now occupied by the Federals, in the early evening.

Neither Sedgwick nor Hooker, with an army still twice the size of Lee's, did anything to counter the Confederate attack. Hooker had been overmastered by Lee, and could think of nothing to do but run.

Lee intended to attack Hooker, but on the night of May 5–6 Hooker took advantage of a huge storm to pull his entire force north of the Rappahannock, abandoning his entrenchments. Hooker marched his beaten army back to Falmouth, and Lee returned to the heights behind Fredericksburg.[15]

The South had lost its opportunity to destroy the Army of the Potomac. Now Jackson was dying. He had been moved back to Guineys Station (now Guinea) on the RF&P to recuperate, but had contracted pneumonia. Jackson lingered until Sunday, May 10, 1863. In his last hours his mind wandered back to battle, and he called out: "Order A. P. Hill to prepare for action! Pass the infantry to the front! Tell Major Hawks—" He became silent for a while, then said quietly and clearly: "Let us cross over the river and rest under the shade of the trees." Stonewall Jackson was dead.[16]

The South had achieved its most spectacular victory in the war. Hooker's army reeled in defeat and frustration back across the Rappahannock. Lincoln and the Northern people wondered whether it was even possible to defeat the Army of Northern Virginia.

Yet the South paid too high a price for Chancellorsville, for it lost Stonewall Jackson. The 11th Corps commander, Oliver O. Howard, the man who—next to Joe Hooker—suffered most in prestige and recrimination at Jackson's hands, described the South's loss best: "Providentially for us, it was the last battle that he waged against the American Union. For, in bold planning, in energy of execution, . . . in indefatigable activity and moral ascendency, Jackson stood head and shoulders above his confrères, and after his death General Lee could not replace him."[17]

Shortly after Jackson's wounding, Lee had lamented that Jackson had lost his left arm, while he had lost his right. Yet the loss was far greater than that. Lee also lost the one officer of the Confederacy who possessed the drive and the vision to win the war.

Jackson had finally succeeded in convincing Lee to make a decisive blow on the enemy's flank and rear. Jackson was struck down literally at the moment he was ordering conversion of this maneuver into a total victory by placing his corps between Hooker and U.S. Ford.

Jackson, alone of all commanders on either side, had found a tactical solution to the power the Minié ball had brought to the defense: to sustain whatever direct attacks the enemy might make, knowing they would fail, or, in the absence of attacks, to demonstrate on his front, and then to swing a powerful force on the enemy's flank to dislodge him, and create chaos and disruption in his rear.[*]

Military geniuses are rarely characterized by a capacity for deep, original thought. Few have invented new weapons, or new methods of military organization. What has marked brilliant commanders over the centuries is something far more simple—and far

---

[*] William Tecumseh Sherman also learned this lesson, but his epiphany came later, leading to his 1864 victory in the Atlanta campaign.

more subtle. They have recognized the one fundamental principle of successful warfare: that victory depends upon avoiding the enemy's strength and upon striking where the enemy is not. Because certain generals practiced this principle when opposing generals did not, they won great victories, and created or destroyed vast empires.

Jackson was a military genius. He had found a way to avoid making frontal attacks against the massed power of the Union army. This was the essence of his intellectual breakthrough. But Lee had not absorbed the lesson. And this sealed the fate of the Confederacy.

(LIBRARY OF CONGRESS)

Wounded Federal troops at Fredericksburg.

✴ 10 ✴

THE MARCH INTO
PENNSYLVANIA

With Hooker cowering at Falmouth, Lee was eager to sweep around his western flank and drive once more into the North. To wait at Fredericksburg would invite another Union turning movement, possibly another indecisive battle, and, in time, defeat.

Lee soon realized that Jefferson Davis thought otherwise, but wouldn't admit it to Lee. Since the start of the war, the president's strategy had been to stand on the defensive, believing the South could outlast the North. Offensive maneuvers were not necessary.

Now Ulysses S. Grant was threatening Vicksburg, the Confederacy's last strongpoint on the Mississippi and its only rail connection with the trans-Mississippi states. Days after Lee and Jackson had won at Chancellorsville, Grant had evicted a Confederate garrison at Grand Gulf on the Mississippi, and started marching toward Vicksburg, twenty-five miles to the north.

The move set off a huge alarm in Richmond, with Secretary of War Seddon diverting troops to reinforce John Clifford Pemberton, the Confederate commander at Vicksburg, and ordering the nominal commander in the west, Joseph E. Johnston, to take charge personally.

The threat to Vicksburg aroused fright among Southern civilians, but practically none among Confederate generals. Lee saw the city only as a means to interdict Federal traffic on the river. Longstreet felt the South would be little worse off if Vicksburg were lost, and Johnston regarded middle Tennessee as much more important.

However, Confederate politicians bemoaned the possibility that the trans-Mississippi states might be "cut off" from the rest of the South, though goods coming from the region were so few that their loss would not cripple the Confederate war effort.

Davis asked Lee whether he could send some of his troops to defend Vicksburg. Lee reacted sharply, saying his army should be reinforced, not weakened. He asked that Confederate forces standing idle along the southern coasts be brought north and added to the Army of Northern Virginia. He got few results, though he did secure the return of George Pickett's and John Bell Hood's divisions, detached during the previous winter.[*]

Meanwhile, Grant moved to Jackson, Mississippi, forty-five miles to the east of Vicksburg, and quickly drove out a small Rebel force under Joe Johnston, cut the railroad to Vicksburg, and isolated the city. General Pemberton, instead of breaking out to join Johnston, challenged Grant on May 16, but, losing, fell back into Vicksburg's defenses. This made it easy for Grant to surround the city and commence a siege, whose only outcome could be the surrender of the garrison.

On the same day, Lee met with Davis and his cabinet to discuss an offensive into Maryland and Pennsylvania. Lee explained that the reason for the invasion was to tap the abundant food supplies of the North. He was unwilling to admit aloud that he was seeking a decision in the war. The cabinet agreed that Lee could cross the Potomac and "threaten Washington, Baltimore, and Philadelphia."[†]

---

[*] But two of Pickett's brigades were left to defend Richmond, reducing the division from 8,000 men to about 5,000.

[†] Woodworth, 228–32; Freeman, *R.E. Lee*, vol. 3, 19. General Longstreet proposed a different strategy: to transfer a portion of Lee's army to Braxton Bragg, crush the Union army of William S. Rosecrans in Tennessee, and march against Cincinnati, thus relieving pressure on Pemberton at Vicksburg. Porter Alexander endorsed the idea. See Johnson and Buel, vol. 3, 245–46; Porter Alexander, *Military Memoirs*, 363–66; *Fighting for the Confederacy*, 219–20; Freeman, *Lee's Lieutenants*, vol. 3, 42–45; Longstreet, 327–28. Longstreet and Alexander were correct that the South could transfer troops quicker than the North could move an equivalent force to meet them. But the argument fails for two reasons: (1) it would not be decisive, and

Lee set about reorganizing his army. He couldn't replace Jackson, and didn't try to. Instead, he added a third corps, taking one division from Longstreet's corps, another from Jackson's, and forming a third from two brigades on detached duty, and two brigades from A. P. Hill's six-brigade division. Longstreet had returned to resume command of the 1st Corps. Lee promoted Richard S. Ewell to lead Jackson's 2d Corps. Ewell had lost his left leg at the Battle of Groveton, but now could walk on his wooden leg and could mount and ride a horse. Lee named A. P. Hill as commander of the 3d Corps. Ewell and Hill were promoted to lieutenant general. Neither Ewell nor Hill was accustomed to Lee's style of command. Usually, Lee consulted and discussed tactics with his officers then often seemed to "suggest" a course of action. Many times, it was hard to determine if in fact Lee had given an order at all. Ewell and Hill were used to Stonewall Jackson, who ordered directly and precisely what he expected to be done.[*]

(2) the South did not have the military leadership in the West to carry it out. Even if Rosecrans could have been defeated, Grant induced to call off his siege of Vicksburg, the Rebel army freed to march to the Ohio River, and Hooker deceived enough to remain immobile at Fredericksburg (a great many ifs), the effect on the North's willingness to wage the war would not have been decisive. In 1863, the vast bulk of Northern industry was concentrated from Baltimore to New Hampshire along the eastern seaboard. Capture of Cincinnati would have damaged Northern war production little. More important, the focal point of the North was the East Coast, where most of the people lived, and specifically Washington, where the government resided. If an invasion was to occur, this was where it should strike. "What benefit could the North gain from Grant's siege of Vicksburg or Rosecrans's capture of Chattanooga if Lee could deliver a crushing defeat to the Army of the Potomac in Pennsylvania?" Glenn Tucker wrote (Tucker, 19). Regarding leadership, Bragg had marched into Kentucky with a superb army in 1862, but had turned away from Louisville when he could have seized it, and had retreated after he had won victories at Perryville and Murfreesboro, Tennessee. Likewise, the supreme commander in the West, Joseph E. Johnston, had nowhere near the drive, imagination, or capability of Lee.

[*] The reorganization of the army's artillery was completed about this time. Each corps had five battalions, averaging sixteen guns each. One battalion was assigned to each division and two battalions to the artillery reserve, but all could be assembled for cannonades. General William N. Pendleton remained the chief of the army artillery, but his general artillery reserve was broken up and never reestablished.

To command Hill's division, Lee elevated Dorsey Pender of North Carolina. To command the new division in Hill's corps, he promoted Henry Heth, a Virginian and West Pointer (1847) who had joined the Army of Northern Virginia only in February but had proved both reliable and steady leading a brigade in A. P. Hill's division. Meanwhile Edward Johnson took over Raleigh Colston's division, as Lee decided that Colston was unsuited for command.*

The new organization was more flexible. It consisted of about 70,000 men: Lee had been unable to get substantially more reinforcements. Aside from Hood's and Pickett's divisions, only two brigades were added (J. Johnston Pettigrew's North Carolinians and Joseph R. Davis's Mississippians and North Carolinians). The ghastly losses in the past year had gravely reduced the Southern leadership pool. Two of his corps commanders were untried; three of his nine divisions were under new leaders. There were seven new brigadier generals, and six infantry brigades were led by senior colonels.

Moreover, James Longstreet was no longer the faithful subordinate he had been before tasting independent command earlier in the year. As Douglas Freeman wrote, "Longstreet had returned to the army, secretly swollen with the idea that he was the man to redeem the falling fortunes of the Confederacy."[1]

Now that Jackson was dead, Longstreet expected to have more say in military decisions. Though he had shown little initiative in the campaign against Suffolk, Longstreet had learned the lesson Jackson had been preaching: the tactical defense was the only way to win a battle. That is, the Confederates should not initiate an

---

This structure subsequently was adopted by Prussia, Austria, France, and Britain, and was the genesis of the division and corps artillery organization that became standard in the U.S. Army. See Porter Alexander, *Military Memoirs*, 367, 370.

* On the morning of May 3, 1863, Stuart ordered Colston to move his division toward U.S. Ford. Colston replied that the position was too strong to be seized. Stuart was disgusted that a general should say he could not take a position without trying. Stuart placed Colston's division under General Rodes. Lee apparently judged Colston's failure to be hopeless, and relieved him on May 20. See Freeman, *Lee's Lieutenants*, vol. 3, 661.

attack, but take up good positions and await a Federal assault. He believed he had extracted a promise from Lee to maintain the tactical defensive in Pennsylvania. Lee denied he made such a promise, but did intend to induce the Union army to attack him. As events were to show, however, he reverted to his old offensive habit the moment he faced a challenge.

One of Lee's principal aims was to convince the increasing number of people in the North seeking peace to press for an end of the war. He urged Davis to spread the idea that the South would return to the Union if acceptable conditions were met. "When peace is proposed to us," Lee wrote Davis, "it will be time enough to discuss its terms."[2] Such a plan might gain support in the North, but it depended—as was the case in the invasion in 1862—on the Confederacy's being able to win a victory on Northern soil. If the South lost and had to retreat, the peace initiative would collapse.

On June 3, 1863, Longstreet's 1st Corps began moving to Culpeper, northwest of Chancellorsville, and, the next day, Ewell's 2d Corps followed. Hooker, informed by spies, sent his cavalry to find out whether Lee was concentrating at Culpeper.

Jeb Stuart, always ready for a pageant, talked Lee into authorizing a grand cavalry review on June 8 in a huge field just east of Culpeper. From Stuart's point of view, the day-long affair was wonderful, but he was surprised the next morning when Union cavalry streamed across the Rappahannock heading for Culpeper. Lee saw at once that the Federals were trying to scout out the presence of Confederate infantry, and ordered Stuart to intercept them.

Stuart moved to Brandy Station, on the Orange and Alexandria Railroad, about six miles northeast of Culpeper, and there collided with the Union horsemen under Alfred Pleasonton. For hours, both sides contested Fleetwood Hill, a long ridge just north of the station, each side charging back and forth. It was the greatest and grandest

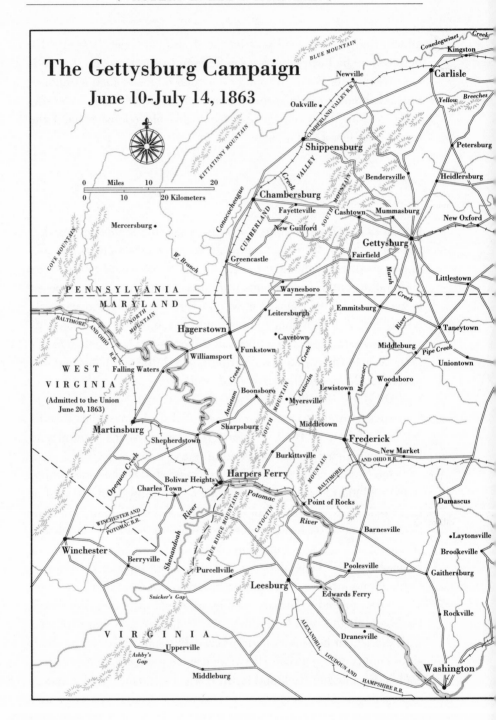

The Gettysburg Campaign
June 10-July 14, 1863

BLUE MOUNTAIN

Conedoguinet Creek
Kingston
Carlisle
Newville
Oakville
Yellow Breeches
Petersburg
Shippensburg
Bendersville
Heidlersburg
Chambersburg
Fayetteville Cashtown Mummasburg
New Oxford
New Guilford
Mercersburg
Gettysburg
Fairfield
Greencastle
Littlestown
Waynesboro
Emmitsburg
PENNSYLVANIA
MARYLAND
Leitersburgh
Taneytown
BALTIMORE AND OHIO R.R.
NORTH MOUNTAIN
Hagerstown
Cavetown
Middleburg Pipe Creek
Uniontown
Williamsport
Funkstown
WEST Falling Waters
Lewistown Woodsboro
VIRGINIA
Boonsboro
(Admitted to the Union
June 20, 1863)
Myersville
Middletown
Martinsburg
Sharpsburg
Shepherdstown
Frederick
Burkittsville
New Market
AND OHIO R.R.
Bolivar Heights
Harpers Ferry
Charles Town
Point of Rocks
Damascus
WINCHESTER AND
POTOMAC R.R.
Potomac
Barnesville
Laytonsville
Winchester
Berryville
Brookeville
Purcellville
Poolesville
Gaithersburg
River
Leesburg
Edwards Ferry
Snicker's Gap
Rockville
VIRGINIA
Dranesville
Upperville
Ashby's
Gap
Washington
Middleburg

KITTATINNY MOUNTAIN
CUMBERLAND VALLEY R.R.
VALLEY
Conococheague Creek
SOUTH MOUNTAIN
CUMBERLAND
W. Branch
COVE MOUNTAIN
Marsh Creek
River
Antietam Creek
Catoctin Creek
SOUTH MOUNTAIN
Monocacy
CATOCTIN MOUNTAIN
BLUE RIDGE MOUNTAINS
Shenandoah River
Opequon Creek
ALEXANDRIA, LOUDOUN AND HAMPSHIRE R.R.
BALTIMORE

0 Miles 10 20
0 10 20 Kilometers

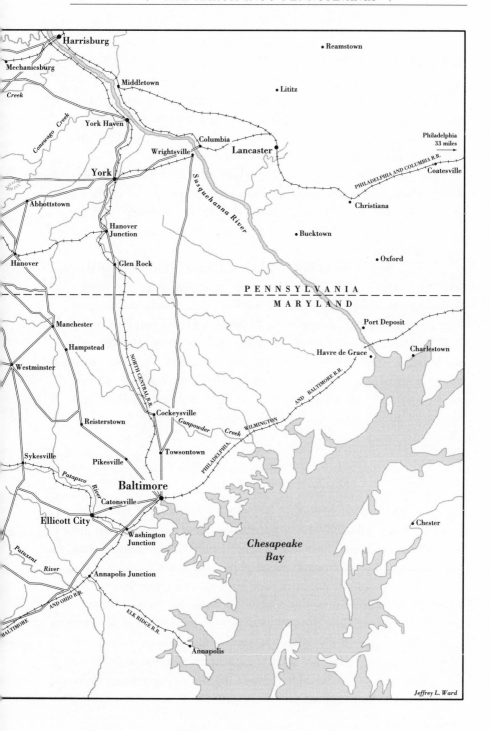

Jeffrey L. Ward

cavalry action of the war, but accomplished nothing. Union general Abner Doubleday later explained why: "Every cavalry charge, unless supported by artillery or infantry, is necessarily repulsed by a countercharge; for when the force of the attack is spent, the men who make it are always more or less scattered, and therefore unable to contend against the impetus of a fresh line of troops, who come against them at full speed and strike in mass."[3]

Late in the afternoon, the Federals drew off, without reconnoitering, though Stuart's response proved the presence of Lee's infantry at Culpeper. The losses were 930 for the Federals, 485 for the Rebels, including Lee's son, Rooney, who suffered a severe, but not fatal, leg wound.

Seeing that Hill was still at Fredericksburg, Hooker wanted to send the bulk of his army across the Rappahannock, overwhelm Hill, then turn back northward behind Lee's main body at Culpeper, intercepting communications with Richmond. Lincoln and Secretary of War Stanton did not dare to have Lee between Hooker and Washington, and ordered Hooker to abandon the idea. Within a week, Hooker proposed that, if Lee invaded the North, he should march south and attack Richmond. Again Lincoln refused, "Lee's army, and not Richmond, is your sure objective point."[4]

On June 10, Lee set in motion his second invasion of the North. Ewell's corps crossed the Blue Ridge, and marched toward Winchester, Virginia, near the northern end of the Shenandoah Valley. Longstreet's corps advanced along the eastern flanks of the Blue Ridge, to shield A. P. Hill, now bluffing at Fredericksburg but who was to march into the valley as soon as Hooker moved. Longstreet was to follow. Stuart's cavalry were to hold the gaps of the Blue Ridge until Lee's advance across the Potomac drew the Federals after him. Lee told Stuart his primary job was to keep the Federals as far east as possible, protect the lines of communication, and scout out enemy movements.

Responding to Lee, Hooker turned his army away from Fredericksburg on June 13 and started to Washington. Shortly after the last Federals departed, Hill broke camp and marched northwest.

On June 13 and 14, Ewell surrounded Union general Robert H. Milroy's Union garrison at Winchester. Milroy tried to slip away in the early hours of June 15, but only a small part of his command got through. The remainder, about 4,000 men, surrendered. An uncontested route was now open to the North.

John D. Imboden's 2,100-man and Albert G. Jenkins's 1,600-man cavalry brigades went with Ewell. Jenkins was to stay in front of the army, Imboden to guard the left. While Imboden's cavalry broke up parts of the Baltimore and Ohio Railroad, Jenkins, moving well ahead of Ewell's infantry, arrived in Chambersburg, Pennsylvania, twenty-five miles north of the Potomac, on June 15, and exacted heavy contributions of horses, cattle, grain, and other goods, paying in Confederate money. If locals refused Southern currency, officers issued receipts setting forth the name of the owner, and the fair market value of the products taken. While there, locals stole some of Jenkins's horses, and he sternly demanded compensation from the Chambersburg city fathers. They paid, in Confederate money. Jenkins took the bills with a smile, appreciating the joke.*

Union general Darius N. Couch had been detailed to Harrisburg, Pennsylvania, to organize a defense of the Susquehanna River, but before he could reach Carlisle, eighteen miles west, Jenkins was already there. Terrified farmers fled across the Susquehanna, driving horses and cattle before them.

Meantime, Ewell's infantry arrived at Williamsport on the Potomac on June 15, and began to cross into Maryland, while A. P. Hill

---

* Doubleday, 96. Lee's General Orders No. 73 stated: "It must be remembered that we make war only upon armed men, and that we cannot take vengeance for the wrongs our people have suffered without lowering ourselves in the eyes of all whose abhorrence has been excited by the atrocities of our enemies. . . . The commanding general therefore earnestly exhorts the troops to abstain . . . from unnecessary or wanton injury to private property." Although there were some violations of the order, no charges of rape and few of plundering were leveled. See Freeman, *R. E. Lee*, vol. 3, 56–57; Douglas, 245.

was still located near Fredericksburg, ninety-five air miles away. Lincoln recognized the vulnerability. "The animal must be pretty slim somewhere in the middle," he wrote Hooker.[5] However, Lee had judged his opponent accurately. A bold and resourceful enemy commander could have cut the Army of Northern Virginia in half, but Hooker was neither.

Panic was sweeping the North. Governors and civilian leaders demanded immediate action. In a gesture of despair, Lincoln called on nearby states to raise 120,000 men for temporary service. Few came forward; even if they had, there was no time to prepare them for war, and there were few additional arms. Meanwhile, Union forces moved from Fort Monroe to White House on the Pamunkey River east of Richmond, and made gestures to attack the Confederate capital, now virtually bereft of troops. But President Davis called out militia, and the Federal diversionary raid fizzled.

Edward Johnson's and Robert Rodes's divisions of Ewell's corps reached Chambersburg on June 23. Ewell's other division, under Jubal Early, took the road eastward and halted on June 23 at Waynesboro, fifteen air miles south of Chambersburg, and twenty miles west of Gettysburg. Confederate foraging parties spread out far and wide from the advancing columns.

Hooker closed in on the defense of Washington, making no effort to pursue Lee. By June 15 most of his army was milling around Centreville, Manassas, and Fairfax Court House. The same day Longstreet moved from Culpeper north to Ashby's and Snicker's Gaps in the Blue Ridge.* Lee hoped to tempt Hooker into marching against the gaps, giving the Confederates a chance to crush the Army of the Potomac in open country, or get between it and Washington, forcing Hooker to attack.

But Hooker would not respond, despite the success of Pleasonton's cavalry in pushing Stuart's horsemen back to the gaps in a series of running fights around Middleburg, Upperville, Aldie,

---

* Today U.S. Routes 17 and 50 go through Ashby's Gap, and Virginia Route 7 passes through Snicker's Gap.

and Philomont. Hooker had orders from Lincoln and Stanton to keep his army between Lee and the capital.

Unable to taunt Hooker into action, Lee ordered Hill's corps to follow Ewell, and pulled Longstreet's corps into the valley to guard the Confederate rear. Hooker moved infantry toward Ashby's and Snicker's Gaps, but two Rebel cavalry brigades under Beverly H. Robertson continued to hold them. Meanwhile, the 10,000-man Federal garrison at Harpers Ferry abandoned the indefensible town and occupied Maryland Heights just north of the river.

On June 23, Lee proposed to Davis that General Pierre Beauregard transfer some of the troops under his command to Culpeper. From there he could threaten Washington. This would force Hooker to detach part of his army, giving Lee superior forces in Pennsylvania. Lee had delayed proposing this strategy until his army was already embarked on an invasion aimed at a decision in the war. Lee feared that Davis would forbid a full commitment if he knew Lee's intentions in advance. But Davis refused to call up Beauregard.

Lee now worked out his strategy. The army, Ewell in the lead, was to advance northward from Chambersburg to Harrisburg and the Susquehanna and destroy rail communications with the west. Hill was to stay east of South Mountain, the extension into Maryland and Pennsylvania of the Blue Ridge, to keep the enemy at a distance.

Stuart had been stung by newspaper criticisms of his action at Brandy Station, and sought some grandiose act to restore his reputation. He proposed leaving Imboden's and Jenkins's cavalry brigades to cover Ewell's advance into the North, while the two brigades under Robertson were to guard the passes over the Blue Ridge, then close up on the rear of the army. Stuart wanted to move the remainder of his cavalry, 6,000 men, on Hooker's rear, and return to the army if he passed into Maryland. Lee assented, but with the caveat that Stuart must rejoin the army at once if Hooker actually crossed, and take his place on the army's right flank as it moved north.

Stuart started out on another of his "rides." But this one earned him infamy and recrimination. Lee's intention was that Stuart disrupt Hooker's rear until he could capture Harrisburg, then for Stuart to hurry back to the main army. Stuart, on the other hand, intended to achieve another spectacular feat, riding entirely around Hooker's army and rejoining Lee somewhere around York, Pennsylvania.

Early on June 25 Stuart advanced to Haymarket, just east of Thoroughfare Gap in the Bull Run Mountains, where he came upon Winfield S. Hancock's corps. It was evident that the Union army was moving for the Potomac on all roads. Stuart should have returned at once to shield the army and report on Federal movements. Instead, he went on, placing Hooker between himself and Lee, and eliminating any chance of scouting for the army.

Hooker had finally decided to follow Lee. Now feeling Washington was safe, Hooker selected a path on the east side of South Mountain, but parallel to Lee's movements. If Lee turned toward Baltimore or Washington, he believed he could occupy gaps in the range and stop him.

The Union army began to cross the Potomac at Edwards Ferry, six miles east of Leesburg, on June 25, and marched toward Frederick, Maryland. But Hooker also sent Henry W. Slocum's 12th Corps toward Harpers Ferry to act against Lee's line of communications. Lee, realizing he could not maintain a supply line back into Virginia, severed all ties. The Army of Northern Virginia must live off the country.*

Longstreet forded the Potomac at Williamsport on June 24, while Hill crossed at Shepherdstown, passed over the battlefield of Antietam the year before, and united with Longstreet at Hagerstown the next day. Two days later, they arrived at Chambersburg and Fayetteville, eight miles east.

---

* Lee's letter of June 25, 1863, to President Davis said: "I have not sufficient troops to maintain my communications, and, therefore, have to abandon them." See *Official Records*, vol. 27, pt. 3, 931; Freeman, *R.E. Lee*, vol. 3, 51; *Southern Historical Society Papers*, vol. 4, 99. The Confederates had carried only enough artillery ammunition to fight one heavy battle. This was enough, since a victory would transform the military situation, and Lee believed he could bring up more ammunition with a cavalry escort if need be.

Now supported, Ewell sent Johnson and Rodes to Carlisle, which they occupied on June 27, while Jenkins's cavalry struck farther east, reaching Kingston, thirteen miles from Harrisburg, and skirmishing only four miles from the city.* Panic gripped the civilian population, many fleeing Harrisburg, while business stopped in Philadelphia.

Meanwhile on June 26, Early marched eastward through Gettysburg, a town of about 3,000 people, passing word back to Hill's corps that a desperately needed source of shoes was there. Early pressed on to York, then to Wrightsville, twenty miles southeast of Harrisburg, seeking to secure the bridge over the Susquehanna there so as to operate against Harrisburg from the rear. But Early found the bridge ablaze, set by militia from Columbia across the river. The flames fired lumberyards on the river's bank and threatened to engulf the town. The Confederates joined in to help the citizens save Wrightsville from burning.

Hooker, deciding it was useless to keep a large force at Harpers Ferry, asked General Halleck to add the Ferry garrison to Slocum's corps and employ the combined force to follow on Lee's rear. But Lincoln expected Lee to repeat the pattern of the 1862 invasion and send back forces to capture the Ferry garrison. He said the troops had to stay. Hooker, believing his army should be concentrated, offered his resignation, assuming it would be rejected on the eve of battle.

But Lincoln had been waiting for a chance to fire Hooker ever since Chancellorsville. He had only refrained because Salmon P. Chase, secretary of the treasury, was a sponsor of Hooker and politically powerful. Now Lincoln, on June 28, accepted Hooker's resignation and replaced him with George Gordon Meade, then

---

* At Carlisle, a committee of citizens asked Ewell whether he had any objection to the people praying for the president of the United States. "Certainly not," Old Dick replied. "Pray for him. I'm sure he needs it." See Douglas, 246. Around Carlisle, General Edward Johnson lined up captured Pennsylvania militiamen—whom he was about to send home—and ordered them to take off their regulation U.S. Army shoes and socks. His own barefoot soldiers, Johnson remarked, had work to do, while the crestfallen militia could find other shoes when they got home. See Freeman, *Lee's Lieutenants*, vol. 3, 36.

commanding 5th Corps. Meade (West Point, class of 1835) was an intelligent officer with much experience, but had attained no great successes in the war.

As Meade took command and moved north, Jeb Stuart, now isolated in Virginia, had to make a wide detour. He was two days behind the Federal army, crossing the Potomac near Dranesville, only fifteen miles upstream from Washington. Once over, he seized a large wagon train, burned a Baltimore and Ohio Railroad bridge, and chased some Union cavalry from Westminster, but always remained behind the Union army. His troops served no function as Lee's eyes and ears.

On June 28, Lee, at Chambersburg, having not heard from Stuart or from Robertson's cavalry left to guard the passes of the Blue Ridge, took no news as good news, and ordered Ewell to march on Harrisburg from Carlisle, with Longstreet and Hill to follow, probably the next day.

That evening, however, Lee received word that one of Longstreet's spies had found three Union corps in Frederick, and two more near South Mountain, a few miles west, and that Meade was now commanding the army.

Lee reacted in a strange and destructive way. He immediately ordered Ewell to abandon his march on Harrisburg, deciding that the whole army must be concentrated and moved east of South Mountain to keep the Federals on the same side. His aim was to block a Union move into Cumberland Valley onto his rear, and thereby prevent cutting his supply line. Yet Lee had already abandoned this supply line, and had no rear to protect!*

As one courier galloped off to Ewell, another rushed back to order Robertson—still idly guarding the unthreatened passes of the Blue Ridge—to bring forward his cavalry. On the morning of June

---

* It is all the more astonishing that Lee thought Meade might move into the Cumberland Valley because he knew Lincoln and Halleck would require Meade to keep the Union army between him and Washington, and a march into the valley would unmask the capital. In fact, Meade had no intention of moving onto Lee's rear. Thus, Lee did not need to concentrate east of South Mountain.

29 Lee directed Ewell to march directly from Carlisle toward Cashtown or Gettysburg. Hill was to move eastward to these towns, to be followed by Longstreet, who was to guard the rear until the arrival of Imboden's cavalry, two days' journey to the west. Meantime, Lee still had not heard from Stuart.*

Lee's decision to concentrate in the vicinity of Cashtown or Gettysburg was senseless strategically. It meant the abandonment of the superb position he had gained by his march into Pennsylvania. The Army of Northern Virginia was well north of the Federal army, thus demonstrating that Stuart's absence had not inhibited Lee's movements or caused him to place the army in a dangerous position.

Long before Meade could have reacted, Lee could have crossed the Susquehanna, seized Harrisburg, broken the bridges, turned the river into a moat, and had a long head start down the undefended road to Philadelphia, the Union's second city, with 600,000 inhabitants, much industry, and location astride the main north-south railroad arteries of the North.

The Union army would have been powerless to stop such a movement, but would have been bound to try—compelled to chase after the Rebel army in an exhausting, debilitating footrace. Anywhere along the way, either before or after capturing Philadelphia, at any superior defensive position with open flanks, Lee's army could have halted, rested, built formidable entrenchments, reconnoitered effective turning routes, and waited.

The Federal army would have been compelled to attack on a field selected by the Confederates and favorable to their arms. The

---

* Many writers have criticized Stuart, with much justification, for his failure to get to the Confederate army in time to provide information on the whereabouts of the Federal army. But Lee was equally at fault. He had Imboden's force of 2,100 cavalry that could have been ordered from the left to the right flank the instant the Confederate army crossed the Potomac. This force could have provided accurate information on the Union army until Stuart or Robertson came up. Instead, Lee allowed Imboden to operate far to the west, where there were no Federal forces. Likewise, he allowed Robertson to remain four days in the passes of the Blue Ridge after his army had crossed the Potomac.

Union army almost certainly would have been defeated, and the Rebels could have swept around its flanks and possibly destroyed the entire force.

Why did Lee not see this? Why did he react in such an automatic but aggressive manner the moment he got unexpected news? Furthermore, after he ordered his army to concentrate, why did he not stand and wait for the Federals? Why did he advance blindly without reconnoitering the way ahead? As Porter Alexander remarked, "When all our corps were together, what could successfully attack us?"*

There are two answers to these questions. First, Lee was a bellicose man, easily aroused to the passion of battle, and always had abandoned his larger strategic aims and turned to challenge his enemy directly and aggressively whenever he was confronted with a surprise or when he thought, rightly or wrongly, that his plans had miscarried. He had done it at Beaver Dam Creek, Frayser's Farm, and Malvern Hill in the Seven Days. He had done it at Antietam. Now he was doing it again.

The second reason for Lee's action was that he no longer had Stonewall Jackson to advise him. Jackson would have recognized the strategic opportunities the Southern army possessed, spread out as it was in an arc from Chambersburg to Carlisle, York, and Wrightsville. He would have urged caution. Even if he could not have induced Lee to strike for Philadelphia, he surely would have argued convincingly to concentrate the Confederate army somewhere near Carlisle.

---

* Porter Alexander, *Fighting for the Confederacy*, 230. A broader unanswered question is, Why was Lee surprised at the appearance of Meade in the first place? He knew the Federals would be compelled to come after him. After all, Rebel cavalry had been roaming about Pennsylvania, extracting food and horses from farmers, for two weeks! And his infantry were almost at the gates of the state capital, Harrisburg. The fact that Lee had heard nothing from Stuart should not have led him to believe the Federal army was still in Virginia.

There Lee would have had ample time to scout out and occupy a formidable defensive position, while the Union army would have been forced to come forward and fight on ground of Lee's choosing. Instead, the Confederates rushed pell-mell east, south, and southwest to concentrate, in hard and exhausting marches, Longstreet and Hill fifteen miles, Ewell twenty, Early forty! They had no chance to reconnoiter a suitable battlefield in advance, or even to know what lay in front of them.

Richard Anderson

On June 29, Harry Heth's division of A. P. Hill's 3d Corps marched to Cashtown and Mummasburg, east of South Mountain, followed by Dorsey Pender's division, with two divisions of Longstreet's corps coming behind on the 30th. Richard Anderson's division of Hill's corps waited at Fayetteville with orders to move on July 1. Longstreet's third division, under George Pickett, remained to protect the rear until Imboden's arrival. Lee himself rode with Longstreet's troops.

Meantime, Early at York recalled a brigade waiting at Wrightsville, and started for Gettysburg on the morning of June 30. At the same time, Rodes's division marched from Carlisle to Gettysburg by the direct route, Ewell going along, while Johnson's division moved on the westerly route to convoy trains of requisitioned food. By nightfall, Rodes and Early arrived at Heidlersburg, ten miles north of Gettysburg, and Johnson reached Greenwood, ten miles east of Chambersburg on the Cashtown road.

With no cavalry to inform him, Lee didn't know that Federal horsemen under General Pleasonton were fanning out northward, aware of the Confederate threat to Harrisburg, and trying to shield a possible movement of the Union army in that direction. On June 29, John Buford's cavalry division of 3,000 men passed near Fairfield, six miles south of Cashtown, and saw the bivouac fires of a small Rebel detachment that Johnston Pettigrew, leading Heth's advance brigade, had set out as a flank guard. Withdrawing to Emmitsburg, Buford told Pleasonton that the Rebels were advancing from Fairfield. Pleasonton informed General John F. Reynolds, commanding the left wing of the army (1st, 3d, and 11th Corps).* Reynolds told Meade. Pleasonton, wanting to find out precisely what the Rebels were up to, ordered Buford to take his division into Gettysburg the next day, June 30, and hold it until the Federal infantry arrived.

On June 30 Harry Heth at Cashtown sent Pettigrew's brigade on eight miles to Gettysburg, hoping to find the shoes that Early had reported there. Atop a ridge a mile west of town, Pettigrew saw through his field glasses the long dark column of Buford's cavalry approaching on the road from Emmitsburg. Obeying orders not to get into a fight alone, Pettigrew withdrew about four miles, rode back to Cashtown, and reported on the encounter to Heth and Hill.

Hill concluded that the Federal cavalry were only an observation detachment. Seeing an opportunity, Heth interjected: "If there is no objection, General, I will take my division tomorrow and go to Gettysburg and get those shoes."

"None in the world," Hill replied.[6]

General Buford rode to the crest of the hill from where Pettigrew had spied his advance, and watched the Confederate infantry retire. He informed Reynolds and Meade that large bodies of Confederates were coming out of the South Mountain pass down the Cashtown road, confirming other reports that the Rebels had

---

* Meade placed the right wing, the 2d, 5th, 6th, and 12th Corps, under Henry W. Slocum of 12th Corps.

abandoned the threat against Harrisburg and Philadelphia, and were concentrating toward Baltimore and Washington.

Buford was sure Reynolds would move infantry up to block the Confederates the next day, and determined to hold his ground on the mostly cleared western elevation—known as McPherson Ridge—until Union infantry could arrive.

On the evening of June 30, the Federal army was spread out along the Maryland-Pennsylvania border. Closest was 1st Corps, under Abner Doubleday, on Meade's extreme left, six miles southwest of Gettysburg at Marsh Creek, and the 11th Corps, under Oliver O. Howard, a couple miles south of Emmitsburg. Meade's other five corps were scattered south and southeast for twenty miles. The Army of the Potomac counted about 80,000 men in its seven corps, plus 13,000 cavalry. The Army of Northern Virginia had about 60,000 men in its three corps, and 10,000 cavalry, though Stuart was off with most of the horsemen.

The news of Rebel infantry at Fairfield and reports of them streaming down from Cashtown caused Meade to conclude that Lee was coming after him. Any idea of a bold advance vanished. On June 30, Meade ordered the entire Union army back to Pipe Creek, eighteen to twenty miles southeast of Gettysburg, to take up a defensive position twenty miles long from Middleburg on the west to Manchester on the east. Along Pipe Creek, Meade could shield both Washington and Baltimore, but not Harrisburg or Philadelphia, and could not interfere with Lee if he decided to continue advancing north or east.

Reynolds probably never received the Pipe Creek order, and followed Meade's original orders to advance to Gettysburg.

On the night of June 30, Hill informed Lee of Pettigrew's encounter with Federal cavalry, and sent a courier to Ewell advising that he was going to advance on Gettysburg the next morning. At 5 A.M. on Wednesday, July 1, Heth's division marched out, followed by Dorsey Pender's division. Though Lee had cautioned both Ewell and Hill not to bring on a general engagement until the rest of the infantry came up, Hill, without any positive information about what lay ahead, and with no other purpose than to supply his men with shoes, set in motion the greatest battle ever to be fought on the American continent.*

Lee did not stop him. If he had exhibited even the most elementary caution, he would have held Hill in place until the Confederate army could ascertain what it was facing at Gettysburg. Though Stuart's cavalry were still missing, Jenkins's cavalry were scouting ahead of Ewell's corps, and could have reconnoitered to determine if Buford was alone or if Union infantry were coming forward.

One thing should have been clear: the Federals would think long and hard before crashing into the Rebel army, and Lee had plenty of time to decide whether and where to fight a battle.

---

* *Official Records*, vol. 27, pt. 2, 317, 444. Porter Alexander remarked (*Military Memoirs*, 381): "Hill's movement to Gettysburg was made of his own motion, and with knowledge that he would find the enemy's cavalry in possession. Ewell was informed of it. Lee's orders were to avoid bringing on an action. Like Stuart's raid, Hill's venture is another illustration of an important event allowed to happen without supervision. Lee's first intimation of danger of collision was his hearing Hill's guns at Gettysburg."

☀ 11 ☀

GETTYSBURG

The Confederates stumbled into the Battle of Gettysburg primarily because of the impulsiveness of A. P. Hill and the lack of control of Robert E. Lee. Once in, Lee did not want out.

When Heth's division approached Gettysburg on the Cashtown road, otherwise known then as Chambersburg pike, his infantry pushed Buford's vedettes across Willoughby Run, a mile west of town and at the foot of McPherson Ridge. Buford sent word of the advance to General Reynolds with 1st Corps at Marsh Creek, six miles southwest, at about 6 A.M.

Reynolds ordered both 1st Corps and 11th Corps, just south of Emmitsburg, to march at once for Gettysburg. Reynolds went himself with the 1st Division, under James S. Wadsworth, while Abner Doubleday brought up the other two divisions.

Heth didn't wait for Dorsey Pender to come up, or send back for instructions from Hill. Instead, he attacked straight ahead, though he moved so slowly that Buford's dismounted cavalry were able to hold on until Wadsworth's infantry arrived and occupied McPherson Ridge.

Thereafter Heth sent in two unsupported attacks—Joseph R. Davis's brigade on both sides of the Cashtown road and James J. Archer's brigade about a quarter mile to the south. Davis drove three Union regiments back into Gettysburg, but allowed two of his regiments to get cornered in a deep railroad cut just north of the road, where hundreds surrendered. Archer was careless and permitted the Michigan–Indiana–Wisconsin Iron Brigade to sweep around his flank, and capture nearly a hundred Rebels, including Archer himself.

The Army of Northern Virginia was finding itself in a billowing fight against an enemy of unknown strength. It was being directed by an inexperienced division commander, Harry Heth, who had been told explicitly not to bring on a general engagement, but was doing just that.

The battle thus came as a surprise to Lee and to Hill. Lee rode to the crest of South Mountain on the morning of July 1, heard the distant rumble of artillery, had no idea what it meant, hurried down to Cashtown at the foot of the mountain, and encountered Hill, who knew only that Heth and Pender had gone ahead with orders not to force an action. Hill rode off to find out what the firing involved.

As Lee waited at Cashtown for news, General Richard Anderson arrived. If the force ahead was the whole Federal army, Lee told Anderson, "we must fight a battle here."[1] Impatient, Lee rode on toward Gettysburg, arriving on the field about 2 P.M. He found that the Confederate generals were responding to the battle as it developed, did not know how many Federals they were facing, and had no plan, except to drive the Union forces back into Gettysburg.

Shortly after arriving on McPherson Heights, Reynolds, sitting astride his horse, was struck dead by a Rebel sharpshooter. Meanwhile Oliver O. Howard arrived on the field, and took command by seniority.

Upon getting word of Reynolds's death, Meade, remembering Howard's poor performance at Chancellorsville and having little confidence in his ability, placed Winfield S. Hancock in charge of the left wing. Hancock, highly admired in the army, was commanding 2d Corps at Taneytown, the location of Meade's headquarters. Meade told him to get to Gettysburg, and move the Federal forces back to Pipe Creek. However, if the ground was suitable, and circumstances made it wise, he authorized Hancock to establish a line of battle at Gettysburg.

Around 12:45 P.M. as the 11th Corps arrived at Gettysburg, General Buford rode up with the disturbing news that Ewell's corps was advancing from Oak Ridge, north of McPherson Ridge, and directly on Doubleday's right flank. Doubleday told Howard he

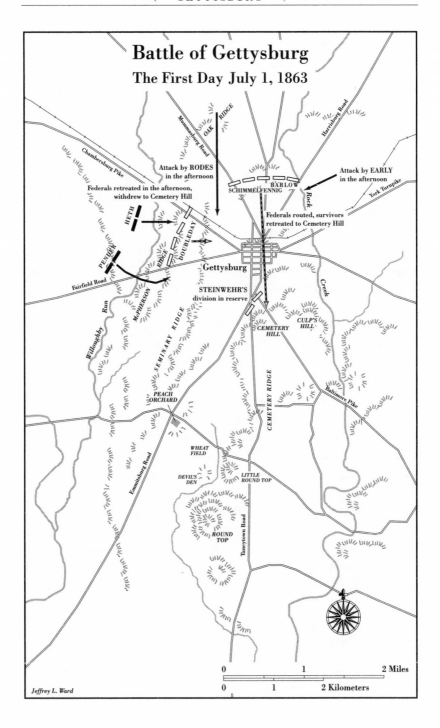

Battle of Gettysburg
The First Day July 1, 1863

OAK RIDGE

Mummasburg Road

Harrisburg Road

Chambersburg Pike

Attack by RODES
in the afternoon

Attack by EARLY
in the afternoon

BARLOW
SCHIMMELFENNIG

York Turnpike

Federals retreated in the afternoon,
withdrew to Cemetery Hill

Rock

HETH

Federals routed, survivors
retreated to Cemetery Hill

DOUBLEDAY

PENDER

RIDGE

Gettysburg

Fairfield Road

Willoughby Run

STEINWEHR'S
division in reserve

Creek

McPHERSON

SEMINARY RIDGE

CEMETERY
HILL

CULP'S
HILL

CEMETERY RIDGE

Baltimore Pike

PEACH
ORCHARD

Emmitsburg Road

WHEAT
FIELD

DEVIL'S
DEN

LITTLE
ROUND TOP

Taneytown Road

ROUND
TOP

| 0 | | 1 | | 2 Miles |
| 0 | | 1 | | 2 Kilometers |

Jeffrey L. Ward

could hold off Hill to the west if Howard could stop Ewell from attacking his right on Oak Ridge.

Howard moved Francis C. Barlow's and Alexander Schimmelfennig's divisions into open, cultivated country just north of town, forming Barlow's division with its right where Rock Creek crossed the Harrisburg road (now U.S. Route 15 Business). To Barlow's east was open country with no sign of the enemy. Schimmelfennig lined up to the west of Barlow, but did not reach all the way to Oak Ridge, leaving nearly half a mile of undefended space between the two corps. Both ends of Howard's line thus were open, and Ewell saw that both could be flanked.

As a reserve, Howard moved his third division, under Adolph von Steinwehr, to Cemetery Hill, just south of Gettysburg, the site of Evergreen Cemetery and a hundred feet above the surrounding countryside.

Robert Rodes sent three North Carolina brigades south down Oak Ridge in the gap between Doubleday's and Howard's corps, evicting Doubleday's reserves but suffering heavy casualties, and finally being stopped at the Cashtown road by a desperate stand of Colonel Roy Stone's Pennsylvania brigade.

From west of McPherson Ridge, Heth had been observing Rodes's attack. As it developed, he rode back to Lee and said: "Rodes is heavily engaged. Had I not better attack?"

"No," Lee had answered, "I am not prepared to bring on a general engagement today—Longstreet is not up."

Now, watching Rodes's difficulties on the Cashtown road, Heth asked again for permission to attack. This time Lee agreed, ordering Heth to make a frontal assault directly into Doubleday's position, while Dorsey Pender's division, which had arrived, advanced on the south, overlapping Doubleday's line for a quarter of a mile.* A bullet

---

* A.P. Hill took little part in the movements of his corps. British lieutenant colonel Arthur J.L. Fremantle, accompanying the Confederate army as an observer, wrote that Hill reported he had been unwell all day. See Fremantle, 203. Hill's sickness was probably psychosomatic, and the first sign that he was unable to handle the responsibility of corps command.

struck Heth in the head almost at once. Though his hat absorbed much of the blow, Heth remained insensible for the next day and a half. Pettigrew took control.

The principal fight developed between Pettigrew's North Carolina brigade and the Iron Brigade on McPherson Ridge. The Tar Heels marched straight into a hellish zone of canister and rifle fire, but forced the Federals back to a reserve line, where a last, desperate charge by Pettigrew broke their resistance. Doubleday ordered 1st Corps back to a last stand around the Lutheran Theological Seminary, on the mostly wooded, long Seminary Ridge a half mile east of McPherson Ridge.

The losses on both sides were appalling. Doubleday lost 5,000 men, half the corps's strength. Heth started the attack with 7,000 men. In twenty-five minutes he lost 2,700 of them. The 26th North Carolina suffered 80 percent casualties. The 24th Michigan, which it challenged, lost 399 of 496 men.

As soon as the Federals became closely engaged on McPherson Ridge, Ewell launched Jubal Early's division east of the Harrisburg road into the right flank of 11th Corps, enveloping Barlow's position. Barlow's and Schimmelfennig's divisions collapsed; many men surrendered; and the remainder ran back into the town, closely followed by Ewell's men. In the town additional 11th Corps men lost their way and were captured.

Ewell's seizure of Gettysburg threatened to cut off 1st Corps at the seminary, and around 4 P.M. Howard ordered both 1st Corps and the 11th Corps survivors to rally on Cemetery Hill.

Cemetery Hill was at the northern end of Cemetery Ridge, an elevation which stretched southward in an arc from the burial ground for two miles to Little Round Top, 480 feet high, with considerable open ground and much exposed rock, and heavily wooded Big Round Top, 600 feet high, just to the south. Half a mile east of the cemetery, forming sort of a fishhook, was Culp's Hill, about a hundred feet higher than Cemetery Hill. Paralleling the ridgeline about a mile to the west across open, mostly cultivated fields was Seminary Ridge, now occupied by the Confederates.

Between the two ridges ran the Emmitsburg road (now U.S. Route 15 Business).

Porter Alexander, who knew it well, called Cemetery Ridge "the most beautiful position for an army which I have ever seen occupied. Good positions were abundant in this section, it being remarkably well cultivated and having numerous extensive ridges, with open rolling lands between."[2]

General Hancock arrived at Cemetery Hill about the time the Union soldiers were fleeing to it. Looking up and down the length of Cemetery Ridge, he told General Howard: "I think this is the strongest position by nature upon which to fight a battle that I ever saw." He concluded that the issue should be decided here, and when Meade got the recommendation, he agreed. To retreat to Pipe Creek would magnify the South's victory. He left Taneytown for Gettysburg, arriving around 11:30 P.M.

By happenstance, the Army of the Potomac concentrated on the ridgeline. Neither Hancock nor Meade had any idea of attacking. Hancock set to work to secure Cemetery Hill, ordering up cannons, placing soldiers behind stone fences, and directing Wadsworth's division to occupy Culp's Hill.

The Union soldiers had been badly handled, had lost half their number, and were demoralized by defeat and retreat. The Confederates also had suffered, but were bolstered by their victory and confident of success. Hill's corps had sustained 3,100 casualties, while Rodes had lost 2,500 of his 8,000 men, and Early about 500.

Edward Johnson's division had been marching to the sounds of the guns all day. As it got close, Johnson sent Kyd Douglas hurrying ahead to tell Ewell that he was near, and ready to go into action. Douglas found Ewell near Cemetery Hill with a group of officers, including John B. Gordon, who was commanding a brigade in Early's division. Gordon said his outfit could join Johnson in carrying Cemetery Hill before dark. Ewell replied: "General Lee told me to come to Gettysburg and gave me no orders to go farther. I do not feel like advancing and making an attack without orders from him."[3]

Sometime afterward, General Lee, on Seminary Ridge, sent Major Walter H. Taylor of his staff to order Ewell to carry Cemetery Hill "if practicable." Soon thereafter, Early and Rodes also urged Ewell to attack.

But Ewell, exhibiting severe command incapacity, could not make up his mind, and Lee did not insist. As the day passed, so did the opportunity. In the disarray of the Union retreat, the Rebels probably could have rolled over the hill before the Federals could establish a solid defensive perimeter. By nightfall, it was too late. Mounting an attack at twilight or darkness would have been difficult and dangerous.

Meantime, Meade's army was rushing toward the battlefield. Of his seven corps, only John Sedgwick's 6th was not nearby by shortly after dark. It was still at Manchester, Maryland, nearly thirty miles away, but began marching for Gettysburg in the early hours of July 2.

Lee had spent July 1, 1863, following precisely the opposite strategy from what he had planned. His purpose going into the North had been to force the Federals to attack him. After Heth stumbled into the fierce engagement west of Gettysburg, Lee should have pulled back to find out Meade's intentions, meanwhile locating a suitable battlefield in case the Federals did attack. Instead, Lee sent Heth into a direct assault, let Ewell join in, and allowed himself to be drawn into an *offensive* battle.

Furthermore, Gettysburg was a terrible battlefield for the Confederates—for the same reason it was a wonderful battlefield for the Federals. Not only was Cemetery Hill and Ridge a superb defensive position, but it was nearly two miles shorter than the line the Confederates, with far fewer men, were taking up.

Longstreet perceived the danger after he rode up on Seminary Ridge. He studied the terrain, and soon came up with a solution: "All we have to do," he told Lee, "is to throw our army around by their left [south], and we shall interpose between the Federal army and Washington. We can get a strong position and wait, and if they fail to attack us we shall have everything in condition to move back tomorrow night in the direction of Washington."

Since the Federal army would be compelled to follow, the Confederates could select a good position where the Army of Northern Virginia could receive battle. "When they attack," Longstreet said, "we shall beat them."

"No," Lee answered, "the enemy is there, and I am going to attack him there." Longstreet responded: "If he is there tomorrow, it will be because he *wants* you to attack him."*

Longstreet's proposal was an alternative both to an assault on Cemetery Hill on the late afternoon of July 1, and to one against Cemetery Ridge on July 2.

Lee didn't like Longstreet's proposal for two reasons: (1) a move on Meade's south—now the Union tactical rear—would be difficult without reconnaissance by Stuart to determine how fully concentrated the Federal army was, and Stuart was still nowhere to be seen, and (2) even if successful, it would only force the Union army back nearer Washington, where the issue would still have to be decided by battle.

Neither argument is convincing. Jenkins's horsemen were nearby and could have reconnoitered ahead. Though the issue had to be decided by battle, a Confederate assault against Cemetery

---

* Johnson and Buel, vol. 3, 339. Longstreet is quoted from Porter Alexander (*Military Memoirs*, 386–87). Freeman, *R.E. Lee*, vol. 3, 75, citing *Annals of the War, Written by Leading Participants North and South* (Philadelphia: Times Publishing Co., 1879), 421, gives this quotation: "If he is there, it is because he is anxious that we should attack him—a reason, in my judgment, for not doing so." Another quotation attributed by Longstreet to Lee was: "They are there in position, and I am going to whip them or they are going to whip me." See Johnson and Buel, vol. 3, 340. However incredible it may appear, it is just possible that Lee did not believe the Union army was concentrating at Gettysburg. In *Annals of War*, 421, he indicated he wanted to attack before the whole enemy army could be brought up. See also Freeman, *Lee's Lieutenants*, vol. 3, 106–10.

Ridge was not the way to resolve it. Longstreet wanted to evict the Union army from Cemetery Ridge without having to attack it, and a strike on the Union rear would have achieved this. General Meade wrote afterward that he would have withdrawn from Cemetery Ridge if Lee had made such a move, since Lee then would have been closer to Washington than he was.

Lee instead fell back into the pattern he had exhibited when he first took command of the army. He decided to attack Cemetery Ridge, despite the virtual certainty that the Federal army would concentrate there the next day.

Stonewall Jackson and Longstreet had seen how attacks almost always failed against prepared positions, and had been pressing for defensive tactics for a year. Jackson was gone, but here on the afternoon of July 1, looking across at the formidable heights of Cemetery Ridge, Longstreet pleaded once more with Lee to shun an attack, to maneuver on the enemy's rear, and force him to take the initiative.

But the Confederates had just crushed two Union corps that day, and Lee's battle lust was up. The "audacity personified" for which Lee had been praised a year earlier was now leading him into a profound error. Lee refused to listen. He intended to attack. In closing his mind, Lee also forgot the *other* way to win the Battle of Gettysburg—simply by not moving an inch from Seminary Ridge!

Porter Alexander later wrote: "It does not seem improbable that we could have faced Meade safely on the 2d at Gettysburg without assaulting him in his wonderfully strong position. We had the prestige of victory with us, having chased him off the field and through the town. We had a fine defensive position on Seminary Ridge ready at our hand to occupy. It was not such a really *wonderful* position as the enemy happened to fall into, but it was no bad one, and it could never have been successfully assaulted."

The onus of attack was on Meade anyhow. Even if he had attacked, and succeeded—a most unlikely outcome—the Confederates could have fallen back to Cashtown and held the mountain passes.[4] Since Meade had no intention of attacking, however, the Confederates could have moved away, ultimately forcing Meade into a direct challenge.

Why did Lee insist on attacking July 2? Lee said in his report that resumption of the battle had become "in a measure unavoidable." Lee's reasons were that to withdraw "would have been difficult and dangerous," and "the country was unfavorable for collecting supplies, in the presence of the enemy."[5]

These reasons were only excuses to hide his stupendous mistake in attacking. Alexander refuted Lee's arguments by pointing out that the army stayed for three days on that very ground, then withdrew with all its trains, and still foraged for a week in extremely restricted territory until it could cross the swollen Potomac.[*]

In the evening, Lee met with Ewell, Early, and Rodes. He wanted Ewell to seize Cemetery Hill and Culp's Hill the next morning. Early, speaking for Ewell and showing a mental dominance over him, argued that Federal forces were concentrating on the heights, and that the best chance for success lay in seizing the Round Tops at the south end of Cemetery Ridge. These elevations dominated the field. If the Rebels could capture them, the Federals would be compelled to evacuate all of Cemetery Ridge.

Lee agreed, and proposed to bring Ewell's corps over to Seminary Ridge, greatly reducing the length of the Rebel line. By facing Cemetery and Culp's Hills, Ewell was forcing the Confederates to take up a concave front five miles long, whereas the

---

[*] Douglas Southall Freeman says (Freeman, *R. E. Lee*, vol. 3, 81) that Lee could not afford to await attack, because the enemy could seize the gaps in South Mountain to the west, "and confine his foraging parties to a very narrow area." See also *Official Records*, vol. 27, pt. 2, 318. This was not true. Albert Jenkins's cavalry brigade of 1,600 men was up and rested and Stuart's cavalry on hand by late July 2, making it possible to shield the passes and spread confusion along the Union supply lines. Also, the Army of Northern Virginia, if actually blocked to the west and south, could simply have moved north, then turned toward Philadelphia or Baltimore. If Meade was unwilling to attack, there was nothing to stop Lee from marching away.

Union army, 25 percent larger than the Confederate army, was occupying a convex front a little over three miles long on high ground, thereby permitting rapid transfer of troops to any point of danger. The exterior lines meant the Confederates could deploy but 13,000 infantry and fifty guns per mile, while the Federals could place 25,000 infantry and a hundred guns per mile.

Early, with Ewell's approval, urged keeping the corps in place, assuring Lee that the enemy would not break through. This was not the point. On Seminary Ridge, Ewell's corps could assist the other two corps, whereas leaving it on the north would neutralize one-third of the army.

At this juncture Lee failed as commander in chief—by not ordering Ewell to Seminary Ridge. "Well," Lee said, "if I attack from my right, Longstreet will have to make the attack. Longstreet is a very good fighter when he gets in position and gets everything ready, but he is so slow."[6]

When Lee got back to Seminary Ridge, he at last received word from Jeb Stuart. He was at Carlisle, was hurrying to the battlefield, but couldn't arrive until late on July 2. Stuart had ridden over a large part of southern Pennsylvania, searching for Confederate forces.

Lee decided it would be better, after all, to bring Ewell's corps around to Seminary Ridge, and to throw all three corps against the south end of Cemetery Ridge. When Ewell got the message, however, he rode to Lee's headquarters and said he believed he could seize Culp's Hill early the next morning. Lee agreed at once. If Ewell could take Culp's, he could evict the Federals from the lower Cemetery Hill, and prevent them from firing enfilade at Longstreet's troops assaulting farther south.

Lee assumed that he could synchronize separate moves at two extreme ends of the battlefield, Ewell on the north and Longstreet on the south. This would require coordination, quick response, and determination from both Ewell and Longstreet. Yet Ewell's failure to attack Cemetery Hill had proved he had little initiative, and Lee himself had complained that Longstreet moved "so slow." In the event, neither general responded at the right time or decisively.

Lee himself virtually foredoomed the attack when he did not insist on it going in at daybreak. If the Confederates were to have any chance of success, they *had* to strike while the Federals were still disorganized and ill-placed. Lee did not order the forces that were to lead the attack to get into position during the night. Rather, Lafayette McLaws's and John Bell Hood's divisions bivouacked four miles away, while E. McIvor Law's Alabama brigade of Hood's force, on guard at New Guilford, twenty-four miles west, couldn't arrive until noon.

Lee turned to Generals Longstreet and Hill sometime around twilight and said: "Gentlemen, we will attack the enemy in the morning as early as practicable." He told them to make the necessary preparations, but named no time and place, and gave no other orders.[7]

The second day at Gettysburg, July 2, 1863, involved inexplicable decisions and failures that have aroused conjecture and controversy ever since. However, the actual events of the day were clear-cut. Three major actions took place:

(1) Longstreet attacked in the south, drove back Daniel Sickles's 3d Corps and reinforcements that came to its aid, but failed to capture Little Round Top.

(2) Ewell waited until almost dark to attack in the north, occupied part of Culp's Hill, but accomplished nothing.

(3) Ambrose R. Wright's Georgia brigade seized the center of Cemetery Ridge. The breakthrough could have ended the war right there with a great Confederate victory if Lee had made adequate preparations, and if Hill had exerted any effort. But neither did, and the Georgians were forced to retreat.

The Army of Northern Virginia had always counted on exhibiting superior leadership. Mistakes had been made, but gross failures

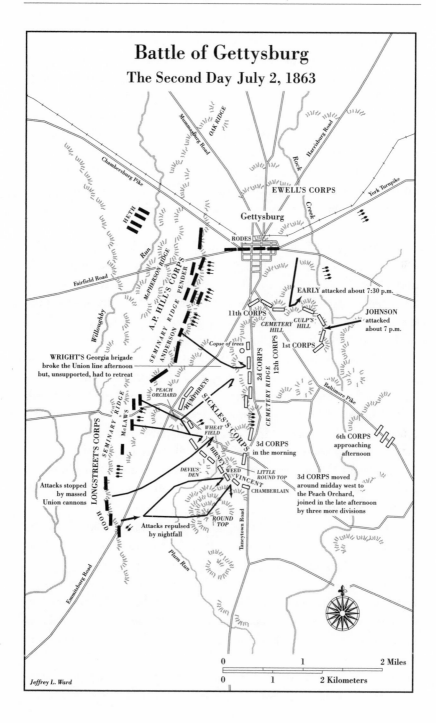

Battle of Gettysburg
The Second Day July 2, 1863

OAK RIDGE

Mummasburg Road

Harrisburg Road

Chambersburg Pike

York Turnpike

Rock Creek

EWELL'S CORPS

HETH

Run

Gettysburg

RODES

Fairfield Road

Willoughby

McPHERSON RIDGE

A. P. HILL'S CORPS

SEMINARY RIDGE PENDER

EARLY attacked about 7:30 p.m.

11th CORPS

CEMETERY HILL

CULP'S HILL

JOHNSON attacked about 7 p.m.

Copse of trees

1st CORPS

ANDERSON

WRIGHT'S Georgia brigade broke the Union line afternoon but, unsupported, had to retreat

2d CORPS

12th CORPS

CEMETERY RIDGE

Baltimore Pike

PEACH ORCHARD

SEMINARY RIDGE

McLAWS

HUMPHREYS

SICKLES'S CORPS

WHEAT FIELD

BIRNEY

6th CORPS approaching afternoon

3d CORPS in the morning

Baltimore Pike

LONGSTREET'S CORPS

DEVIL'S DEN

WEED

VINCENT

LITTLE ROUND TOP

CHAMBERLAIN

3d CORPS moved around midday west to the Peach Orchard, joined in the late afternoon by three more divisions

Attacks stopped by massed Union cannons

HOOD

ROUND TOP

Taneytown Road

Attacks repulsed by nightfall

Plum Run

Emmitsburg Road

0   1   2 Miles

0   1   2 Kilometers

Jeffrey L. Ward

had not occurred, unlike the case with leadership of the Northern army. At Gettysburg, however, leadership by Lee and all three of his corps commanders failed abysmally. On the second day the leaders squandered golden opportunities. In failing they doomed the Confederacy. By the end of the day the battle and the war were lost. What happened on the third day was only a tragic, desperate attempt to reverse the historic decision of the day before.

Around 5 A.M. on July 2 Longstreet met Lee near the seminary building and again proposed to move on Meade's rear. Again Lee rejected the plan, and informed Longstreet he intended to attack on Meade's south.

Meanwhile, Meade arranged his forces in defensive order. He placed the 1st, 11th, and 12th Corps on Cemetery and Culp's Hills, and Hancock's 2d Corps and Daniel E. Sickles's 3d Corps down Cemetery Ridge. George Sykes's 5th Corps went into reserve on the Baltimore pike behind. When 6th Corps came up, it was to be posted in the rear of the Round Tops as a general reserve.

Lee believed that only two Federal corps were occupying the heights and that they were mainly facing north on Cemetery and Culp's Hills. This led him to conclude that he could seize Cemetery Ridge from the south with only two of Longstreet's divisions—Hood's and McLaws's. In fact, the disparity of force between attacker and defender on this wing was about one to three.

Lee told Longstreet to move up the Emmitsburg road from the south, avoid the Round Tops, strike lower Cemetery Ridge at an angle from the southwest, and sweep the Federals from it.

Longstreet's first objective was a short ridge crowned with a peach orchard a mile northwest of Little Round Top and midway between Seminary and Cemetery Ridges, but a bit lower. The Emmitsburg road passed over this ridge and alongside the orchard. If Longstreet could capture the Peach Orchard ridge and plant artillery on it, he could cover an attack on Cemetery Ridge. Lee assumed that the Peach Orchard and both Round Tops would be unoccupied, and that few troops would be deployed on Cemetery Ridge.

Ewell was to strike on the north as soon as he heard Longstreet's cannons, while Hill was to engage the enemy directly ahead on Cemetery Ridge to prevent Meade from massing against Longstreet or Ewell, and to attack if he found the opportunity. Lee thus did not give Ewell and Hill a specific plan to carry out, but relied on their enterprise, which, in the event, was lacking.

Lee's tactical plan was extremely faulty. The two proper choices would have been to follow Longstreet's advice and move on Meade's rear, or to stand on the defensive on Seminary Ridge, trying to induce Meade to attack. Since Lee rejected both these courses, the only reasonable place to attack directly was against Cemetery Hill at a point just southwest of Gettysburg, where the Union lines turned away in both directions (northeast, southwest). And Lee should have used both Ewell's and Hill's corps in the effort.

Ewell's cannons to the north could have delivered punishing enfilade fire against the defending Federals, while assaulting Rebel lines could have approached without being struck by Union enfilade fire from the flanks. The lines would have been exposed to direct fire from only a small portion of the Union line. The aim of such an attack would have been to hold all Union forces in position. Porter Alexander thought this was the only place where a successful direct assault could have been attempted.[*] A two-corps strike here would have drawn most of the Union army to resist. This would have permitted Longstreet to win the actual victory by moving against little opposition on the rear or south, seizing Little Round Top and lower Cemetery Ridge, and rolling up the Federal army from south to north.

Lee sent two engineer officers to determine whether enemy troops were occupying lower Cemetery Ridge and the Round Tops. They reported that some soldiers, but no organized forces, were on Cemetery Ridge, and none on the Round Tops.

Longstreet knew that a direct attack would fail unless he faced little or no opposition. This he could achieve only if he gained

---

[*] On p. 250 of *Fighting for the Confederacy* Porter Alexander's hand-drawn map shows the point he believed the attack should have gone in on the third day. It would have worked even better on the second day, since less of the Union army was up on July 2. See also Freeman, *R. E. Lee*, vol. 3, 152.

surprise. But surprise was impossible unless his troops assaulted before the Federals could react. Lee had already compromised a chance of victory by failing to attack at dawn. Now Longstreet compounded Lee's error by malingering, carrying out the letter of Lee's command with painstaking slowness, but ignoring its spirit.

He thereby gave the Federals time to take over the Peach Orchard, forced the Confederates to expend much of their strength in seizing it, and offered the Federals ample opportunity to occupy Cemetery Ridge to the east. Thus, Longstreet contributed to the devastatingly wrong strategic and tactical decisions Lee had been making since he learned Meade's army was behind him.

Though Lee—exasperated at Longstreet's delay—finally gave him a direct order around 11 A.M. to attack, Longstreet waited to move into position until McIvor Law's brigade arrived around noon. Even after the march got under way around 1 P.M., Longstreet went a longer way after discovering the columns might be visible from Round Top as they crossed a hill, although the soldiers could easily have passed unseen around the shoulder. Alexander estimated Longstreet's detour took a couple hours extra.

Meanwhile on the Union side, General Meade had ordered Sickles to locate his two-division 3d Corps south of Reynolds's 2d Corps and down Cemetery Ridge to Little Round Top, "provided it is practicable to occupy it."[8]

However, Sickles found a soggy depression between the end of Cemetery Ridge and Little Round Top, and decided it would be better to move to the high ground around the Peach Orchard to the west, where his artillery could be deployed to advantage. He also saw that the land directly in front of the Round Tops was broken and full of trees and granite rocks—deserving its name: Devil's Den—and would afford excellent cover for an attacking enemy. Meade, believing a

Confederate attack would come on the north, was not deeply concerned, and sent his artillery chief, General Henry J. Hunt, to examine the Peach Orchard.

Hunt saw that the position was exposed as a salient into the Confederate front, and refused to authorize Sickles to occupy it.

Around noon Sickles dispatched a reconnaissance to Seminary Ridge opposite his position on Cemetery Ridge. There the Federals found Richard Anderson's division of Hill's corps in line of battle. This proved that the Confederate army was not massed on the north, and could advance directly on Sickles's front.

Sickles tarried no longer. He moved his 10,000 infantry off Cemetery Ridge, deploying them and his artillery in an arc, the Peach Orchard forming the westernmost point, with David B. Birney's division spread out thinly to the southeast, and Andrew A. Humphreys's division along the Emmitsburg road to the northeast.

The southeastern anchor of Birney's line was the Devil's Den, separated by a little valley from Little Round Top and Round Top, which he had too few troops to occupy. The deep salient at the Peach Orchard could be approached by the Rebels from north or south, and enfiladed by their artillery fire. At a mile and a half in length, Sickles's line was twice what he had been told to defend on Cemetery Ridge, and he had no reserves.

Neither Lee nor Longstreet had confirmed the reconnaissance of the early morning as to the location of Federal troops. Thus, it was about 3:30 P.M. before Longstreet realized that Sickles had occupied the Peach Orchard and presented an entirely new situation.

Now unable to march up on the Peach Orchard unopposed as planned, Longstreet had to form in line of battle on lower Seminary Ridge. McLaws faced the Peach Orchard, but Hood was obliged to deploy well to the south, directly opposite Round Top, with Law's brigade at the southern end just east of the Emmitsburg road.

No longer could there be a quick seizure of Cemetery Ridge and a prompt roll-up of the Federal line from south to north. The Confederates would have to expend their first fury on Sickles's advanced line, weakening the blow they could deliver against

Cemetery Ridge. Despite this, Longstreet did not inform Lee or consider asking him to rethink his plan. Instead, he stubbornly held to Lee's original concept, as if trying to prove Lee was wrong.

But McIvor Law saw an alternative: Round Top. It rose, he wrote, "like a huge sentinel guarding the Federal left flank, while the spurs and ridges trending off to the north of it afforded unrivaled positions for the use of artillery."

Was it occupied? To find out, he sent six scouts to the summit, with orders to feel down northward to locate the Federal left. Within minutes, Law learned there were no Federals on Round Top, or anywhere near to the north, while on the east side Federal trains stood virtually unguarded.

"There now remained not a shadow of doubt that our true *point d'appui* [base] was Round Top, from which the right wing could be extended toward the Taneytown and Baltimore roads, on the Federal left and rear," Law concluded.[9]

He told Hood that his brigade could seize Round Top, move around its southern flank to the Taneytown road, a quarter of a mile away, then to the Baltimore pike, a couple miles beyond that. Hood agreed, but said his orders were to attack in front. Law answered that a direct assault was unnecessary, and occupation of Round Top would compel the enemy to change front, abandon his strong position on the heights, and attack the Confederates in position. Law was right. His brigade could strike where the enemy was not, and seize the one position that dominated the entire Union line.

Hood sent word to Longstreet endorsing Law's proposal. Longstreet replied that Lee was already fretting over the delay, and he was unwilling to add to it by offering further suggestions. Soon afterward Longstreet rode up, and said: "We must obey the orders of General Lee."[10]

Hood protested, but obediently moved his division in direct assault. "Just here the battle of Gettysburg was lost," Law wrote. "General Lee failed at Gettysburg on the 2d and 3d of July because he made his attack precisely where his enemy wanted him to make it, and was most fully prepared to receive it."[11]

Meade opened a conference of his corps commanders at his head-quarters on the Taneytown road at 4 P.M., about the time Alexander's guns opened on the south, preparatory to Longstreet's attack. Meade's relative position had improved. Lee had not attacked in the morning, and now the 6th Corps was only minutes away. He thus had all seven of his corps up, and leeway to shift troops to meet emergencies.

About 5 P.M. General Sickles arrived, and Meade finally focused on the fact that he had moved entirely off Cemetery Ridge, and had not occupied Little Round Top. Livid with anger, Meade rode over to the Peach Orchard, realized the line couldn't be moved back at this late hour, ordered George Sykes's 5th Corps from reserve to assist Sickles, provided him artillery from the army reserve, and told him he could call on 2d Corps for help if needed.

Before departing Meade told Sickles: "You cannot hold this position, but the enemy will not let you get away without a fight, and it may as well begin now as at any time."[12]

Longstreet having rejected the proper move—sweeping onto and around Round Top—the next-best plan would have been to send both McLaws and Hood in a simultaneous converging attack to squeeze off the Peach Orchard salient. This would have been the shortest line of attack, could have destroyed a large part of Sickles's corps, and might have enabled the Confederates to get on lower Cemetery Ridge before other Federals could arrive in force.

But Longstreet launched Hood first and alone, waiting an hour and a half before he allowed McLaws to attack the Peach Orchard. And he sent Hood against Sickles's entire left flank, instead of con-centrating the division to punch a hole at a single point behind the

Peach Orchard (his third-best plan), thereby threatening the whole Union position. This forced Hood to endure long and desperate individual fights against forces in good defensive positions.

Hood's attack was complicated by the rough nature of the ground, but his actions were as follows: (1) part of his division drove straight ahead and seized the Devil's Den in gruesomely heavy fighting; (2) another part swung over Round Top and up against the southern flank of Little Round Top (which by this time the Federals had occupied); (3) other elements attacked the western face of Little Round Top directly; and (4) one brigade, Tige Anderson's, moved northward against the Union line just southeast of the Peach Orchard. The assaults on Little Round Top failed with heavy casualties, and Anderson's brigade was too weak to break through alone. Hood was severely wounded in the arm twenty minutes after the battle started, and General Law took command.

Four regiments—the 3d Arkansas and 1st Texas of Jerome B. Robertson's brigade, and the 44th and 48th Alabama of Law's brigade—flung themselves against the rocks of the Devil's Den and the narrow "Valley of Death" of Plum Run between the Den and Little Round Top. The Federals had managed to get six cannons in position, protected by J.H. Hobart Ward's brigade. They laid down shattering fire, one shell killing or wounding fifteen Rebels.

The Federals hid behind huge boulders, firing at anything that moved, while the Confederates launched one unsuccessful charge after another. Casualties were heavy on both sides. The 20th Indiana lost its colonel, shot through the head, and 146 of its 268 men in twenty-five minutes. At last, Henry L. Benning's Georgia brigade came up, and drove the Federals northward, capturing 300 prisoners. Benning's and Robertson's Rebels held on grimly to the Devil's Den to the end of the battle.

While the Devil's Den fight was going on, the 15th and 47th Alabama under Colonel William C. Oates swung up the steep western side of Round Top, drove off a few Union skirmishers, and reached the summit. Oates, electrified at seeing the vantage point that Round Top offered, wanted to hold it, drag cannons up, cut down trees to open fields of fire, and shell Little Round Top and Cemetery Ridge ahead. But a staff officer reached Oates and ordered him to advance on Little Round Top to the north.

The astonishing thing about the battle of Little Round Top, about to burst forth in inconceivable violence, is that no senior Confederate leader saw that an attack against Little Round Top was unnecessary—since the Rebels already held Round Top and could dominate Little Round Top and Cemetery Ridge from it. Except for Oates, no Confederate officer recognized the prize that had been gained. Instead, each was intent on attacking and winning Little Round Top by brute force.

As the attack was about to get under way, Meade sent his chief engineer, General Gouverneur K. Warren, to "the little hill off yonder"—Little Round Top—to make sure it had troops protecting it. Warren found the elevation unoccupied except for a signal station, and he saw long enemy lines outflanking the Union position on the south. At once comprehending that the Federals had to hold Little Round Top if they were going to keep Cemetery Ridge, Warren rushed off word to Meade, and began searching for troops to occupy it.

First in position was Strong Vincent's Maine–New York–Pennsylvania–Michigan brigade from James Barnes's 5th Corps division. It formed in an arc facing southwest.

Soon thereafter, Charles E. Hazlett pulled and pushed his six rifled guns to the summit north of Vincent's brigade. Somewhat later, the 140th New York of Stephen H. Weed's New York–Pennsylvania brigade, Romeyn B. Ayres's division, filed in near Hazlett's battery. Hazlett's guns could not be depressed enough to hit the Confederates attacking from the valley. "Never mind that," he said, "the sound of my guns will be encouraging to our troops, and disheartening to the others."[13]

The most critical position went to the 20th Maine, 386 men, commanded by Colonel Joshua L. Chamberlain, a former professor at Bowdoin College. Vincent placed it at the southern end of the arc, covering the wooded saddle between Little Round Top and Round Top. "Hold this ground at all costs!" Vincent told Chamberlain.[14]

The 20th Maine arrived barely in time, for the 47th and 15th Alabama had passed down the northeastern face of Round Top, crossed the saddle, and come charging up the rear of Little Round Top, striking the 20th Maine squarely in front, and opening a murderous fire on its unprotected line. The Federals had no time to throw up breastworks, but resisted with great bravery. Oates said the first Union volley was the most destructive he ever encountered.

Soon afterward, the 83d Pennsylvania on Chamberlain's west fired a heavy volley into the 47th Alabama, wounding Lieutenant Colonel M.J. Bulger, in command, and shaking the regiment. Even so, the 47th struck at the 20th Maine's front, while Oates led the 500 men of the 15th Alabama around to the flank and rear. Chamberlain met this threat by putting the right wing of the regiment into a single rank to resist the 47th, and bent back the five left companies.

Oates's regiment got about halfway to the 20th Maine's position when it was staggered by fire, and fell back. Oates organized another attack. This forced Chamberlain's men uphill. In places fighting became hand-to-hand. Chamberlain wrote that "the edge of the fight swayed backward and forward like a wave."[15] But the line held, and as the Confederate attack lost its impetus and receded, the Federals counterattacked, driving the Alabamians down the hill, some coming so close they had to use their bayonets.

Losses had been tremendous on both sides. Both Chamberlain and Oates believed their forces were losing their capacity for battle. Oates got an exaggerated report that Federals were forming in the low ground east of Round Top. They were only a few skirmishers who presented no danger, but Oates didn't know it, and told his force to retreat back up to Round Top and regroup.

Meanwhile Chamberlain, knowing his men couldn't stand another assault, ordered them to fix bayonets and charge down the hill. The Federals drove the Rebels across the saddle and partway up the slope of Round Top. Here the 20th Maine lost its momentum, and returned to its position on Little Round Top. Oates's men, exhausted and dejected, later moved down and formed at the western foot of Round Top.

That ended the incredible collision between the men from Maine and from Alabama. Chamberlain lost 200 of his 386 soldiers, the 15th and 47th Alabama probably about the same number.

During the night Union junior officers finally recognized the importance of Round Top. The 20th Maine and other Federals climbed to the summit, now unoccupied, built a defensive wall out of loose rocks, and finally secured the left flank of the Union line.

While the battle between Oates and Chamberlain was going on, the 4th and 5th Texas of Robertson's brigade and the 4th Alabama of Law's brigade drove over the lower northern slopes of Round Top and made straight for Vincent's other three regiments, consisting of about 1,000 men, half concealed behind rocks and bushes along Little Round Top. To reach the Federals, the Rebels had to cross the "slaughter pen" of open ground and a steep, rocky slope under intense, short-range fire. The huge boulders forced the men to file

(LIBRARY OF CONGRESS)

View of Little Round Top at Gettysburg.

through narrow gaps, allowing the Federals to channel their fire. Also, the slope was so steep the Rebels couldn't use their weapons. The assault failed. The Confederates held at the bottom for a while, but the fire was so intense they soon retreated. The Rebels regrouped, and for a second time advanced with great courage and boldness, covering the ground with dead and wounded, but again failing to carry the crest.

The 48th Alabama of Law's brigade came up after helping to secure the Devil's Den, and joined in the third assault. However, the 500-man 140th New York of Weed's brigade reinforced Vincent's men just as the Confederates were nearing the Union line. Their fire slowed and finally stopped the Rebels, though many Federals were killed and wounded.

Darkness was coming. The Confederates had done all they could. They pulled back out of range. After the fighting ended, the last three regiments of Weed's brigade arrived, extending the Union defensive arc around the western face of Little Round Top. Confederate artillery and rifle fire continued to come in, however, and General Weed, standing on a bald rock at the summit, was mortally wounded. As Captain Hazlett bent over him, a bullet went through his head, and he fell dead beside him.

～～

While the rest of Hood's division drove toward the Devil's Den and Little Round Top, his last outfit, the Georgia brigade of Tige Anderson, marched eastward across the Emmitsburg road into Rose's Woods, about 500 yards southeast of the Peach Orchard.

Philip Regis de Trobriand deployed his brigade of Birney's division on a stony hill just to the north of the woods and just west of a twenty-acre wheat field. To Trobriand's west was William S. Tilton's brigade of James Barnes's division, and along the edge of the stony hill facing the Peach Orchard was Jacob B. Sweitzer's brigade of the same division.

Anderson's brigade crashed into Trobriand's Federals, causing many casualties, but failing to break through. Seeing he couldn't advance, Anderson called off the attack, and withdrew to the edge of Rose's Woods.

Longstreet at last unleashed McLaws's division at 6:30 P.M., while the struggle for Little Round Top was reaching its zenith.

Joseph B. Kershaw's South Carolina brigade on McLaws's right moved first, crossed the Emmitsburg road, marched through fields of clover "with the precision of a brigade drill," wheeled north, and advanced toward the Peach Orchard and the stony hill. Federal artillery—forty cannons around the Peach Orchard—opened a dreadful barrage. Though distracted by counterfire from Alexander's cannons, the Federal guns cut down hundreds of South Carolinians. But they advanced until the massed Union guns firing canister finally brought them to a halt within yards of the muzzles.

To the right, Trobriand's men and Barnes's two brigades, waiting anxiously, watched the South Carolinians advance, joined on the east by Anderson's Georgians. When the veteran Confederates got within range, they loaded and fired with great deliberation. Dense smoke covered the battlefield. In some cases, the Federals could make out the jets of flame spurting from the muzzles of the Rebel rifles, and they aimed just beneath them.

Trobriand's line was holding, though just barely. But when two of Kershaw's regiments moved on Sweitzer and Tilton on the west, the two Federal brigades melted away, apparently without firing a shot.

Under orders from Barnes, but without approval from any higher officer, Tilton retreated about 500 yards northeast to a stone wall along the western edge of Trostle's Woods, just north of the wheat field. Sweitzer fell back to the southeast of Tilton, to a road along the northern edge of the wheat field. This left a huge hole in the Federal line, and exposed Trobriand to envelopment.*

---

* Barnes's retreat incensed Trobriand and every other Union officer who knew about it. Barnes never got another combat command, and served in an administrative job in Washington until the war was over.

Trobriand withdrew across the wheat field, closely followed by Anderson, while Kershaw pressed across the stony hill. The whole left wing of Sickles's line had been smashed, and the Peach Orchard and the right wing along Emmitsburg road manned by Humphreys's division were in jeopardy.

Birney had been informed that two divisions were on the way—John C. Caldwell's from 2d Corps, and Romeyn B. Ayres's from 5th Corps. To buy time, Birney ordered the 17th Maine and the 5th Michigan of Trobriand's brigade to march into the middle of the wheat field. The South Carolinians, firing from the stony hill, killed or wounded more than a third of the soldiers in minutes.

However, the delay was just enough for Caldwell's division to deploy from Trostle's Woods. Two of Caldwell's brigades drove back Kershaw, while two more stopped Anderson's Georgians. Before they could make any decisive gains, however, William Barksdale's Mississippi brigade and William T. Wofford's Georgia brigade charged Charles K. Graham's Pennsylvania brigade of Birney's division at the Peach Orchard. Alexander moved up twenty cannons directly behind, and opened fire at close range.

This advance cracked the center of Sickles's line. The Federals withdrew, losing hundreds killed or wounded, including General Graham, who was captured along with about a thousand other Federals. General Sickles was wounded, losing a leg.

The Union retreat at first was orderly, but soon became flight. Barksdale pressed up the Emmitsburg road, evicting Humphreys's division, while Wofford drove eastward toward the rear of Caldwell and Birney. These Union forces swiftly extricated themselves, and rushed pell-mell back to Cemetery Ridge.

Sweitzer's brigade held the Rebels in check in the wheat field until Ayres's two brigades came up. They also moved into the wheat field, but collapsed after taking fire from two directions, and retreated to Little Round Top, having lost more than a third of their number in less than half an hour.

As Ayres retreated, darkness, and a gun line established by Federal artillerymen along Plum Run just west of Cemetery Ridge, finally stopped the Rebels.

Meade, making a supreme effort to prevent the Confederates from ascending Cemetery Ridge, sent 50,000 soldiers to oppose the Confederates at the southern end of the line. He left only a single brigade of 12th Corps on Culp's Hill on the northeast.

More than 2,000 men of Hood's division had been killed, wounded, or captured. McLaws's division had suffered nearly as much. Among the killed were Generals Barksdale and Paul Jones Semmes. Among the wounded were Generals Tige Anderson and J.B. Robertson, and about half the field officers of the regiments. Nevertheless, Longstreet's attack, seen solely as a feat of arms, was remarkable, and demonstrated the valor of the Army of Northern Virginia. Two Confederate divisions, 13,000 men and sixty-two guns, had driven back 40,000 Federal infantry and a hundred guns and seized a strong enemy position, the Peach Orchard.

Despite Lee's instructions, Ewell didn't move on the north, and only opened with his cannons against Cemetery Hill and Culp's Hill in the afternoon. Hill likewise only fired his artillery in support of Longstreet. This allowed Meade to shift most of his troops south to contain Longstreet.

When Barksdale advanced northward against Humphreys's division, however, Hill ordered the two southernmost brigades of Richard H. Anderson's division—lined up about 500 yards west of Humphreys's position—to join in Barksdale's attack.

These brigades were Cadmus M. Wilcox's Alabama and David Lang's small 700-man Florida. They assaulted Humphreys's front as Barksdale struck his left and rear. Caught in a pincers, Humphreys fell back to Cemetery Ridge.

The three pursuing Confederate brigades stopped at the gun line along Plum Run at the base of the ridge. Wilcox sent back requests three times for reinforcements to help get onto Cemetery

Ridge, but nothing came forward, and the Confederates were unable to climb onto the ridge.

However, Ambrose R. "Rans" Wright's 1,800-man Georgia brigade did crack the center of the Federal line. Wright's Georgians and Carnot Posey's Mississippi brigade advanced about the same time Lang's and Wilcox's brigades went forward. Posey got involved in a picayune fight with Union skirmishers at a farmstead, and did not contribute otherwise.

Wright's men, however, despite sheets of artillery fire, rushed through the sloping fields toward Cemetery Ridge, 1,400 yards ahead. At the Emmitsburg road, they overran a Federal delaying force with two artillery batteries, and surged onto the crest of Cemetery Ridge just south of a copse of chestnut oak trees, the center of the 2d Corps, and a little more than half a mile south of Cemetery Hill. Parts of Alexander S. Webb's brigade held stubbornly around the copse of trees, but Wright drove south of it on a front of three hundred yards, seized twenty cannons, and pushed back the Massachusetts–Michigan–New York brigade of Norman J. Hall to the eastern side of Cemetery Ridge. Wright had pierced the center of the Federal line!

Although the Rebel assault looked irresistible, it had lost its strength by the time it reached the ridge. Many men were down. One company was being led by a corporal. And Wright was alone. Neither Posey's Mississippians nor Lang's Floridians had advanced—despite urgent requests by Wright.

Meade, however, reacted at once, ordering troops to converge on the break. Abner Doubleday sent the 13th Vermont hurrying to assist Hall's and Webb's brigades. With it and their own men, Hall and Webb attacked from north and south.

"We were in a critical situation," Wright reported. "The enemy's converging lines were rapidly closing upon our rear; a few moments more and we would be completely surrounded; still no support could be seen coming to our assistance, and with painful hearts we abandoned our captured guns, faced about, and prepared to cut our way through the closing lines in our rear. This was effected with tolerable order, but with immense loss."[16]

The Georgians fell back to and beyond the Emmitsburg road, losing more than a third of their number in killed, wounded, and captured.

If Posey or William Mahone's Virginia brigade—in line just north of Posey—had arrived, the Confederates could well have split the Union line asunder, permitting Lee to bring up more troops and press in both directions along Cemetery Ridge.

Anderson and Hill failed abjectly. Anderson refused to advance Posey or Mahone, citing no legitimate reason, while Hill abandoned his post and rode down to the rear of McLaws's division when Anderson's brigades were advancing. Hill made no preparations for possible success along his front. Not only was Anderson's division improperly used, but Hill left his reserve division, Harry Heth's, a mile and a half away from Seminary Ridge and in no position to exploit any success.

Ewell also failed miserably. He did not attack on the north until almost nightfall. Edward Johnson's division got up on Culp's Hill, but stopped in the darkness, and was ripe to be evicted the next morning. Jubal Early's division attacked up the ravine between Cemetery and Culp's Hills, but was stopped by Union artillery and infantry countermoves.

The ultimate failure, of course, was Lee's. He did not require Hill and Ewell to move on time; he didn't snap Anderson and Hill out of their lethargy; and he ignored Heth's improper position. Lee nullified his own plan for a concerted attack by all three corps.

Thus July 2, 1863, ended, the day the scales tilted against the South. There was one chance left to retain some Confederate power: to withdraw the beaten but still powerful Army of Northern Virginia back across the Potomac at once. But this did not happen.

⌇⌇

Pickett's charge was one of the supremely heroic moments in history. The courage, dedication, and resolve of the 13,500 Southerners who crossed three-quarters of a mile of shell-torn, bullet-ridden land-scape to close with the enemy have rarely been equaled and never surpassed. Its magnificent failure has come to represent the tragic valor of the Lost Cause itself.

Yet the public image of the charge is erroneous on several points. It was not made entirely by Pickett's Virginians. His division constituted a little more than a third of the soldiers who assaulted Cemetery Ridge. The traditional "high-water mark of the Confederacy" reached by Pickett's men near the Copse of Trees was not the most forward point attained that day. The farthest advance was by North Carolinians into the orchard about 300 yards to the north.

But the greatest error that popular tradition has affixed to Pickett's charge is that it was a necessary culmination of the mighty confrontation at Gettysburg, the dramatic finale toward which all the fighting of the previous two days had been leading.

In fact, Pickett's charge should be seen as a vastly magnified version of the Charge of the Light Brigade at Balaclava in the Crimean War—as an act of lunacy or perversity by a commander who ignored better counsel and brought on a disaster that could and should have been avoided.

Robert E. Lee insisted upon the charge, and the officers who were party to the decision were unanimous in condemning him for it. Though Lee owned up at its frightful end that it was all his fault, generations after him have tried to take away the blame.

In the South, where a defeated people hunted desperately for symbols of purpose, Lee's undoubted personal bravery, dedication, and high morality made him the beau ideal of the Lost Cause; Southerners glossed over Lee's manifest frailties of judgment, elevated him into a hero without fault, and ignored or explained away every wrong military decision he made.

In the North, Pickett's charge became the crowning event of the war, the climax of the rebellion, the exact moment when the South's tide crested, then began to recede. Pickett's charge seemed to be predestined, and his defeat the inevitable working of fate, brought on by the Union's superior might and its higher moral posture.

Thus, the charge is remembered less for what actually took place, and more as a legend in which each side has inserted its own meaning.

On the night of July 2, Longstreet sent a reconnaissance to his extreme south, still hopeful that Lee might yet move around the Federal left. The morning of July 3, 1863, broke clear, but mists in the valleys betokened a hot and humid day. The battles of the day before had concentrated the Union army from Round Top to Cemetery Hill and Culp's Hill. The Confederates, on the other hand, were stretched out in a long, broken, weak line.

Lee came to Longstreet early in the morning and directed him to attack into the center of the Union line between Cemetery Hill and Round Top.

He thus prescribed an assault at the worst possible location: at the strongest Federal point where the Union artillery had an unobstructed field of fire to the front and could enfilade from Cemetery Hill and Little Round Top any line of battle attacking eastward, and where Meade could reinforce his center rapidly from either wing.

Longstreet protested, said he'd studied the ground on the south, and thought that the army should move in this direction.

"No," Lee replied, "I am going to take them where they are on Cemetery Hill. I want you to take Pickett's division and make the attack. I will reinforce you by two divisions of the 3d Corps."[17] These two 3d Corps divisions were Heth's under Pettigrew, and James Henry Lane's and W. Lee J. Lowrance's North Carolina brigades of Pender's under Isaac Trimble, Pender having been mortally wounded on July 2. Lee also ordered two brigades of Richard H. Anderson's division—Cadmus M. Wilcox's Alabamians and David

Lang's Floridians—to come behind on Pickett's right rear, to guard against an attack on Pickett's flank.[*]

Longstreet said no such body of men "could make that attack successfully."[†] Lee seemed impatient at Longstreet's remarks, and Longstreet went to work to arrange for the attack. Lee personally gave George Pickett directions. He was to cross 1,400 yards of open ground, and attack the Copse of Trees on Cemetery Ridge about half a mile south of Cemetery Hill. Pettigrew and Trimble were to deploy to Pickett's left, or north, and take up the assault at the same time. Wilcox and Lang were to move on Pickett's right after he had advanced.

Pickett was to go forward as soon as Confederate artillery had silenced the enemy batteries. Meanwhile Stuart's cavalry were to ride to Meade's rear to pursue the Federal army in case the Confederates achieved a breakthrough.

At first Lee had hoped that Ewell could also strike Culp's Hill at the same time as Pickett, but the Union 12th Corps assaulted Edward Johnson's division there early on July 3. Though Ewell

---

[*] *Official Records*, vol. 27, pt. 2, 320; Freeman, *R. E. Lee*, vol. 3, 112. Despite claims afterward that Lee intended for Longstreet's and Hill's entire corps to advance with Pickett, Lee never ordered such an advance, nor contemplated it. See Tucker, 337, 343; Johnson and Buel, vol. 3, 356; Long, 294; Taylor, 104, 108. Lee planned at first to use McLaws's and Hood's divisions. Longstreet talked him out of it, pointing out that the Union forces were superior in front of both divisions, and they could not attack where they were, but would have to be withdrawn to strike Cemetery Ridge. This would allow the Federals to pour down from Round Top onto the flank and rear of the Confederate army. See Freeman, *R. E. Lee*, vol. 3, 107–08; Longstreet, 386; William Garrett Piston, in Gallagher, 33–38.

[†] Johnson and Buel, vol. 3, 342–43. When Longstreet protested that Union guns on Little Round Top could enfilade Confederate columns attacking due east toward Cemetery Ridge, Colonel Armistead Long of Lee's staff, an artillerist, replied that the guns could be suppressed. See *Official Records*, vol. 27, pt. 2, 359; Longstreet, 386; Long, 288. Porter Alexander, an artillery officer of true renown, wrote: "It seems remarkable that the assumption of Colonel Long so easily passed unchallenged that Confederate guns in open and inferior positions could 'suppress' Federal artillery fortified upon commanding ridges." Confederate artillery was inferior to Union guns in numbers, calibers, and ammunition. See *Military Memoirs*, 416. In the event, the guns on Little Round Top devastated the Confederate lines of battle.

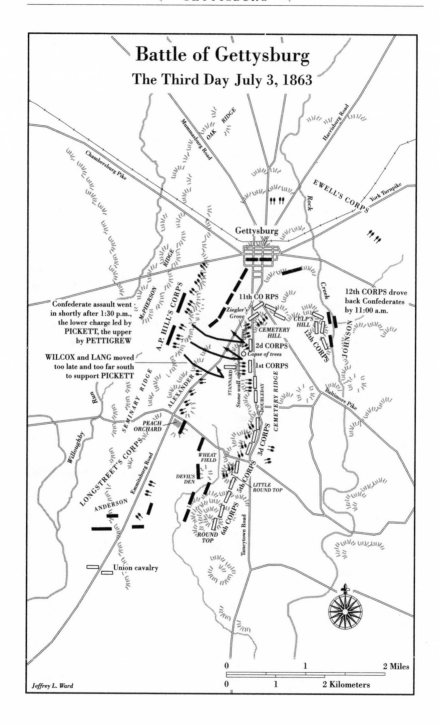

Battle of Gettysburg
The Third Day July 3, 1863

OAK RIDGE

Mummasburg Road

Harrisburg Road

Chambersburg Pike

EWELL'S CORPS

York Turnpike

Rock

Gettysburg

Creek

12th CORPS drove
back Confederates
by 11:00 a.m.

Confederate assault went
in shortly after 1:30 p.m.,
the lower charge led by
PICKETT, the upper
by PETTIGREW

11th CO RPS

Ziegler's
Grove

CULP'S
HILL

12th CORPS

JOHNSON

McPHERSON RIDGE

A.P. HILL'S CORPS

CEMETERY
HILL

2d CORPS

Copse of trees

WILCOX and LANG moved
too late and too far south
to support PICKETT

1st CORPS

STANNARD

Stone wall

Run

SEMINARY RIDGE

ALEXANDER

DOUBLEDAY

CEMETERY RIDGE

Baltimore Pike

Willoughby

PEACH
ORCHARD

3d CORPS

LONGSTREET'S CORPS

Emmitsburg Road

WHEAT
FIELD

DEVIL'S
DEN

5th CORPS

LITTLE
ROUND TOP

ANDERSON

6th CORPS

Taneytown Road

ROUND
TOP

Union cavalry

Baltimore Pike

| 0 | | 1 | | 2 Miles |

| 0 | | 1 | | 2 Kilometers |

Jeffrey L. Ward

threw in reinforcements, and the struggle was close and severe, by 11 A.M. Johnson found the contest hopeless, and retreated to Rock Creek, east of Culp's Hill, where he remained until night.

By 10 A.M. Porter Alexander had seventy-five cannons disposed around the Peach Orchard and along Seminary Ridge. Sixty-three additional guns of Hill's corps were lined up on the ridge to Alexander's left.

But Lee did not call upon Ewell's artillery to play a significant role, despite the fact that his guns were north of Cemetery Hill and could have provided devastating enfilade or flank fire against all of the Union guns and infantry. This, in Porter Alexander's eyes, was a disastrous error.

"A battery established where it can enfilade others need not trouble itself about aim," Alexander later wrote. "It has only to fire in the right direction and the shot finds something to hurt wherever it falls. No troops, infantry or artillery, can long submit to enfilade fire."[18] Only a few of Ewell's batteries fired, couldn't see what the shells were doing, and stopped after a few shots.

About noon, Alexander took a position at a point on Seminary Ridge where he could observe the effects of the cannonade on Cemetery Ridge. Longstreet had ordered him, when he saw that the enemy guns had been silenced or crippled, to give the order to Pickett to attack. Soon a startling note came from Longstreet:

"Colonel: If the artillery does not have the effect to drive off the enemy or greatly demoralize him, so as to make our efforts pretty certain, I would prefer that you should not advise General Pickett to make the charge. I shall rely a great deal on your good judgment to determine the matter, and shall expect you to let General Pickett know when the moment offers."[19]

Alexander was unwilling to order or cancel the attack on his own judgment, and recognized that Longstreet was trying to transfer responsibility from his own shoulders. He wrote Longstreet back:

"General: I will only be able to judge of the effect of our fire on the enemy by his return fire, as his infantry is but little exposed to view and the smoke will obscure the whole field. If, as I infer from your note, there is any alternative to this attack, it should be carefully considered before opening our fire, for it will take all the artillery ammunition we have left to test this one thoroughly, and, if result is unfavorable, we will have none left for another effort, and even if this is entirely successful, it can only be so at a very bloody cost."

Longstreet replied about 12:30 P.M.: "Colonel: The intention is to advance the infantry if the artillery has the desired effect of driving the enemy's off, or having other effect such as to warrant us in making the attack. When the moment arrives advise General Pickett, and of course advance such artillery as you can use in aiding the attack."

General Rans Wright was with Alexander looking at the enemy position during the exchange of notes, and Alexander asked his opinion.

"He has put the responsibility back upon you," Wright told Alexander.

"General," Alexander replied, "tell me exactly what you think of this attack."

"Well, Alexander, it is mostly a question of supports," Wright answered. "It is not so hard to go there as it looks. I was nearly there with my brigade yesterday. The trouble is to stay there. The whole Yankee army is there in a bunch."[20]

Alexander assumed that General Lee surely had given special attention to the supports Pickett and the other attacking forces would require, and, riding back to Pickett, found him "in excellent spirits and sanguine of success." Accordingly, he wrote Longstreet at 12:40 P.M.: "General: When our artillery fire is at its best, I will advise General Pickett to advance."

At 1 P.M. the Confederate signal guns fired, and in another minute 138 Rebel guns were belching forth smoke and shell, the fire converging on approximately one-fourth of a mile of the Federal line along Cemetery Ridge from Ziegler's Grove south to the Copse of Trees. The enemy guns returned the fire, and a fantastic roar of most artillery of both armies burst in on the silence.

The air seemed full of missiles, causing severe casualties on both sides. *New York Times* correspondent Samuel Wilkeson, at Meade's headquarters on the Taneytown road just behind the ridge, wrote that Rebel shells burst and screamed "as many as six a second," making "a very hell of fire." Afterward, Wilkeson found sixteen horses dead at headquarters still fastened by their halters.

Alexander had planned only a fifteen-minute barrage. But he saw that the enemy was generally protected by stone walls and swells of the ground. He couldn't bring himself to give the word to charge. "It seemed madness to launch infantry into that fire, with nearly three-quarters of a mile to go at midday under a July sun. I let the fifteen minutes pass, and twenty, and twenty-five, hoping vainly for something to turn up."[21]

Alexander then wrote Pickett at 1:25 P.M.: "General: If you are to advance at all, you must come at once, or we will not be able to support you as we ought. But the enemy's fire has not slackened materially, and there are still eighteen guns firing from the cemetery."[*]

Five minutes later, Union fire began suddenly to slacken, and the eighteen guns vacated the position. Alexander didn't know it, but Henry J. Hunt, the Federal artillery commander, had sent the pieces to the rear to cool or be replaced.

Since Alexander had never seen the Federals withdraw guns to save for an infantry fight, he concluded it could mean a Confederate victory if they didn't reappear in five minutes. He waited as the minutes passed, with no sign of life on the deserted position, still being swept by Confederate fire, and littered with dead and wounded men and horses, and fragments of disabled vehicles.

At 1:40 P.M. he wrote Pickett: "The eighteen guns have been driven off. For God's sake come on quick, or we cannot support you. Ammunition nearly out."

Meanwhile, Pickett had taken Alexander's 1:25 P.M. note to Longstreet, and asked: "General, shall I advance?" Longstreet wrote

---

[*] Alexander had been told incorrectly that the Copse of Trees was in the cemetery. Thus he was referring to guns at the copse, the focal point of the Confederate attack. See Porter Alexander, *Military Memoirs*, 423.

later: "I was convinced that he would be leading his troops to needless slaughter, and did not speak. He repeated the question, and without opening my lips I bowed in answer. In a determined voice Pickett said: 'Sir, I shall lead my division forward.'"[22] Pickett galloped off, and immediately put the advance in motion.

Longstreet came out alone to Alexander, who told him that he was afraid his ammunition wouldn't hold out.

"Go and halt Pickett right where he is, and replenish your ammunition," Longstreet ordered.

"General, we can't do that," Alexander answered. "We nearly emptied the trains last night. Even if we had it, it would take an hour or two." The only chance "is to follow it up now—to strike while the iron is hot."

"I don't want to make this attack," Longstreet responded. "I believe it will fail. I do not see how it can succeed. I would not make it even now, but that General Lee has ordered and expects it."

Alexander believed that Longstreet was on the verge of stopping the attack, "and that even with slight encouragement he would do it." But Alexander, a colonel who could not take responsibility in so grave a matter, remained silent. Longstreet did nothing.[*]

At this moment, Pickett's division swept out of the wood and showed the full length of its gray ranks and shining bayonets, "as grand a sight as ever a man looked on." Joining in on the left, Pettigrew's line followed by Trimble's stretched farther than Alexander could see.

General Dick Garnett, removed by Stonewall Jackson after ordering a retreat at Kernstown in 1862, passed with his brigade, and saluted Longstreet. Alexander rode with him a short distance. They were close friends, and had served together on the Great Plains before the war. "We wished each other luck and goodbye, which was our last," Alexander wrote. A few minutes later Garnett was dead.

---

[*] Porter Alexander, *Fighting for the Confederacy*, 261; Johnson and Buel, vol. 3, 365. Alexander wrote in *Military Memoirs*, 424: "I was too conscious of my own youth and inexperience to express any opinion not directly asked. So I remained silent while Longstreet fought his battle out alone and obeyed his orders."

Alexander rushed back to select those guns still with ammunition to follow Pickett's advance. He found fifteen, and they started after the infantry, Alexander with them. The guns advanced a few hundred yards across the plain. There Alexander halted, unlimbered, and opened fire.

The Confederate infantry had no sooner debouched on the plain than all the Union line broke out with a thundering barrage. The eighteen guns or replacements were back in place. A storm of shell burst among the advancing infantry, while all the Confederate guns still on Seminary Ridge reopened over the heads of the infantry. Abner Doubleday, watching from Cemetery Ridge, noted that "the Rebels came on magnificently. As fast as the shot and shell tore through their lines, they closed up the gaps and pressed forward."[23]

The assaulting columns consisted of forty-two regiments, nineteen from Virginia, fifteen from North Carolina, three each from Tennessee and Mississippi, and two from Alabama. In addition, Wilcox had five Alabama regiments and Lang three small Florida regiments. In front of Pickett flew the blue banner of the Old Dominion with its motto, *Sic semper tyrannis* ("Thus ever to tyrants"), and the Stars and Bars of the Confederacy.

The Federal center was held by two of Hancock's divisions, John Gibbon's and Alexander Hays's. The Pennsylvania brigade at the Copse of Trees was commanded by Alexander S. Webb. Just to the south was the Massachusetts–Michigan–New York brigade of Norman J. Hall. Ranging down Cemetery Ridge was Abner Doubleday's division of 1st Corps, and beyond Doubleday were remnants of Hancock's other division, John C. Caldwell's, then the 3d, 5th, and 6th Corps.

Lieutenant Colonel Edmund Rice of the 19th Massachusetts of Hall's brigade was south of the Copse of Trees when the attack began. "From the opposite ridge, three-fourths of a mile away," he wrote, "a line of skirmishers sprang lightly forward out of the woods, and with intervals well kept moved rapidly down into the open fields, closely followed by a line of battle, then by another, and by yet a third."

The men of Gibbon's division looked with admiration on the Confederates marching forward with easy, swinging steps. Men exclaimed: "Here they come! Here they come!" "Here comes the infantry!"[24]

Pickett's most sensitive point was on his right, where James L. Kemper's brigade was advancing with its flank in the air. The brigade began to suffer heavy losses from enfilade fire from Union guns on Little Round Top. Pickett sent repeated messages to Wilcox and Lang to come up on Kemper's flank, but they started twenty minutes after Pickett set out, became lost in the gunsmoke that enveloped the field, drifted to the south, and never offered any protection to Kemper.

George J. Stannard's Vermont brigade was the northernmost element in Doubleday's division, just to the left of Gibbon. At first, Kemper made directly for Stannard, but as he crossed the Emmitsburg road, he moved off to his left, to converge on the Copse of Trees. This took the brigade directly across the front of the 14th Vermont, which poured heavy fire into its flank. After marching 300 yards, Kemper changed front to the right. Then the men broke into a wild Rebel yell, and advanced on Hall's brigade just south of the copse.

Stannard saw his chance, threw his brigade forward a hundred or so yards in front of the Union line, faced it at a right angle, and poured deadly fire into Kemper's exposed right flank. Kemper recognized that the assault must go in quick or his brigade would be cut to pieces. He hurried back to Lewis A. Armistead, whose brigade was on Kemper's left rear, and asked it to come forward. Armistead's men immediately broke into a fast charge, and closed up on Garnett's brigade ahead. At this moment Kemper fell from his horse, critically wounded.

Meanwhile Garnett had been pushing straight ahead. At the Emmitsburg road he swept away the Federal skirmish line, and led his men through the hail of Federal artillery fire straight toward the Copse of Trees and a stone wall some fifty yards in front of it running along the front edge of Cemetery Ridge.

When the brigade was halfway up the slope, the Federal line rose from behind the wall, unleashed a devastating blast from polished muskets that witnesses remembered were shining in the sunlight, and many in the Confederate column seemed to disappear.

It was still not close enough for a charge, and Garnett rode along his line, steadying his men. "Don't double-quick. Save your wind and ammunition for the final charge." All at once Garnett and his horse fell, the general hit in several places and never rising again, but the horse struggling to its feet and galloping down the hill.

Stannard's brigade had virtually destroyed Kemper's brigade, which stumbled and advanced no farther. The Vermonters now poured fire into the flanks of Garnett and Armistead as these two brigades, now joined in a confused, tangled mass, rushed the stone wall.

Webb's infantry commenced an irregular, hesitating fire, while shellfire tore gaps through the Virginian lines. Canister and grape whirring over the Rebels sounded to one man like a flock of quail rising in sudden flight. The men of Hall's brigade, their muskets ready, lay in waiting. They could hear their officers: "Steady men, steady! Don't fire!" Not a shot was fired against the Confederate line, whose right was approaching the right of Hall's brigade.

The ground dipped and the Rebels were lost for a moment to view. "An instant after," Rice wrote, "they seemed to rise out of the earth, and so near that the expression on their faces was distinctly seen. Now our men knew that the time had come." Aiming low, they opened a deadly concentrated discharge upon the mass. Nothing human could stand it. Staggered by the storm of lead, the line hesitated, answered with some wild firing which soon increased to a crashing roll, running down the whole length of their front, and then all that portion of Pickett's division which came within the zone of this merciless close musketry fire appeared to melt and drift away.

The surviving Rebels rushed at the stone wall in Webb's sector, using their muskets like clubs and stabbing with their bayonets. No one had time to reload. Canister-shotted Federal cannons fired their last rounds into the faces of the Virginians before the gunners ran away.

At the front of the charge was General Armistead, holding his black hat on his sword point aloft for the brigade to see. Suddenly he was over the wall, and 150 of his men rushed behind him, as Webb's Pennsylvanians ran pell-mell back over the ridgeline. Armistead put his hand on a Federal cannon. At that instant, his hat on his sword, and his hand on the gun, he fell mortally wounded, his body riddled with bullets, some from revolvers fired at arm's length. Half of those who crossed the wall with Armistead were killed as well.

The Virginians' triumph was short-lived, since no one came to their support. If Lee had been bringing forward other brigades, the lodgment might have been transformed into a breakthrough and victory.

The Federals to the north were being pressed at the same instant by Pettigrew's and Trimble's men, and no help came from this direction. But Union troops rushed at once from the south. Hall's brigade came up at a run, and Hancock sent forward part of William Harrow's brigade just south of Hall.

With a cheer, the 19th Massachusetts and the 42d New York of Hall's brigade raced diagonally forward for the Copse of Trees. Many of Webb's men were still lying down in ranks, firing at the Rebels who came after Armistead. The first few men in gray sprang past them toward the cannons, only a few yards away. But the following Confederates piled over the prone Federals, beat them down, and overwhelmed them.

One Confederate battle flag after another appeared along the edge of the Copse of Trees, until the whole clump seemed crammed with men. As the 19th and 42d passed the Rebel line that had formed along the stone wall, Rice "could see the men prone in their places, unshaken, and firing steadily to their front, beating back the enemy. I saw one leader try several times to jump his horse over our line. He was shot by some of the men near me."

The two Union regiments were now almost at right angles with the remainder of the brigade, and men were falling fast from the enfilading fire of Rebels along the stone wall, and from Confederates in the Copse of Trees. The advance stopped, but "as I looked back," Rice recorded, "I could see our men, intermixed with those who were driven out of the clump of trees a few moments before, coming rapidly forward, firing, some trying to shoot through the intervals and past those who were in front."

The crush toward the Rebels in the copse became greater. The men in gray were doing all that was possible to keep off the Federals, but the Union fire was so close and continuous that at last its effects became terrible.

"I could feel the touch of the men to my right and left, as we neared the edge of the copse," Rice wrote. "The grove was fairly jammed with Pickett's men, in all positions, lying and kneeling. Back from the edge were many standing and firing over those in front. By the side of several who were firing, lying down or kneeling, were others with their hands up, in token of surrender. In particular I noticed two men, not a musket-length away, one aiming so that I could look into his musket barrel; the other, lying on his back, coolly ramming home a cartridge. A little farther on was one on his knees waving something white in both hands. Every foot of ground was occupied by men engaged in mortal combat, who were in every possible position which can be taken while under arms, or lying wounded or dead."

A Confederate battery near the Peach Orchard commenced firing at Harrow's men closing upon the Copse of Trees. A shot tore a horrible passage through the men; instantly another shot followed, cutting another road through the mass. Colonel Rice saw it was but a few steps to where the men could extinguish the destructive musketry and be out of the line of the deadly artillery fire. He determined to bring them forward.

"Voices were lost in the uproar," Rice reported, "so I turned partly toward them, raised my sword to attract their attention, and motioned to advance. They surged forward, and just then, as I was stepping backward with my face to the men, urging them on, I felt a sharp blow as a shot struck me, then another; I whirled round, my sword torn from my hand by a bullet or shell splinter. My visor saved my face, but the shock stunned me. As I went down our men rushed forward past me, capturing battle flags and making prisoners."

Pickett's division lost the vast majority of its officers and men. Gibbon's division, its leader wounded, and only half its men remaining, still held the crest.

Hancock was with Stannard when a bullet passed through his saddle into his right thigh. He reeled, bleeding profusely. Stannard made a tourniquet with his handkerchief and pistol barrel. With the flow of blood checked, Hancock refused to go to rear until he could determine the outcome.

Meantime part of Harrow's brigade joined Stannard in an attack on Kemper. With virtually all its field officers gone, the remnant of this splendid brigade ran flying to the bottom of the hill.

When Wilcox and Lang finally approached the Federal line, Stannard's brigade repeated the maneuver, pouring fire into their flank while canister and Caldwell's men shattered their front. The two brigades retired rapidly from this crossfire, leaving many prisoners. Stannard was wounded soon after Hancock, but he also refused to leave the field.

Critical fighting now moved to the Confederate left, as Pettigrew and Trimble assaulted just to the north of Pickett. The march of these two divisions across the open fields was as magnificent as the advance of Pickett's Virginians. The whole assaulting front was three-quarters of a mile wide, and Pettigrew's front was longer than Pickett's.

Pettigrew had to travel farther than Pickett, and move diagonally across the field to converge on the Copse of Trees. The ground offered no protection at all, being less undulating than that traversed by Pickett. The men were particularly exposed to oblique fire from batteries in the cemetery and in Ziegler's Grove. When this fire first struck Pettigrew's men, the line reeled, halted briefly, then moved on steadily ahead, leaving the ground behind covered with the fallen. When Pettigrew reached the Emmitsburg road, the men came directly under fire of the Union line behind the stone wall. As the lines advanced, men dropped steadily.

A couple hundred yards north of the Copse of Trees, the north-south stone wall turned in an east-west direction for eighty yards, then turned back north-south along the crest of the ridge. To the immediate east of the wall in this sector was an orchard. Thus from "the angle" where the stone wall made its turn, the Federal line was eighty yards farther away and higher up the slope than where Pickett struck around the Copse of Trees.

The gap between Pickett and Pettigrew was closed by Colonel Birkett Davenport Fry's Alabama-Tennessee brigade, which advanced to the left of Garnett and suffered the same staggering losses. To Fry's left was Pettigrew's own North Carolina brigade, now led by Colonel James K. Marshall. To Marshall's left was Joseph R. Davis's Mississippi–North Carolina brigade, then J.M. Brocken-brough's Virginia brigade, now commanded by Colonel Robert M. Mayo, but which never closed with the enemy. Directly behind Pettigrew leading two North Carolina brigades—Lee Lowrance's on the right and James Lane's on the left—was Trimble, with enough fight in him, so Kyd Douglas wrote, "to satisfy a herd of tigers."[25]

As the men neared the crest, they let out a shout, and ran toward the wall, being defended here by Alexander Hays's division. Fry's brigade hit the wall just at the angle, but the remainder of Pettigrew's and Trimble's soldiers pressed on to the stone wall eighty yards farther east. Fry's men menaced the flank of Webb, but they in turn were exposed to destructive fire from Union reinforcements rushing up from the south.

The 14th Tennessee started the war with 960 men, had 365 the first day at Gettysburg, but only 60, commanded by Captain B.L. Phillips, in the charge. Here where the wall turned, at what came to be known as the "bloody angle" of Gettysburg, all but three of these sixty fell.

Fry took the rest of his brigade, the 1st and 7th Tennessee and the 5th and 13th Alabama, over the angle, then fell wounded and was captured. Fry's men fought desperately, but they, as Pettigrew's other men elsewhere along the stone wall, were slaughtered or forced back. In front of the wall Colonel Marshall fell from his horse, dead. Pettigrew's hand was shattered, but he ignored the wound.

As Trimble's men came up, someone cried, "Three cheers for the Old North State!" Both brigades let out a shout, and struck the wall.

Lane's and Lowrance's Tar Heels were met by volleys from Hays's line, but some of them jumped over the wall and charged into the orchard. Trimble was wounded near the wall, and fell into enemy hands. The two brigades were now fighting virtually alone. Lane looked to the right and saw that Pickett's line of battle had disappeared. He realized it was hopeless, and ordered the brigades to retreat.

They retired in fair formation, in no disorder. Trimble said: "If the troops I had the honor to command today couldn't take that position, all hell can't take it."

At the wall, he said, "the exposure was dreadful. The incessant discharge of canister, shell, and musketry was more than any troops could endure."[26] The dead and wounded of Pettigrew's and Trimble's divisions were found in the orchard. The troops who advanced the farthest were Captain E. Fletcher Satterfield's company of the 55th North Carolina, part of Davis's brigade. Here in the orchard, the real high tide of the Confederacy, Satterfield and other North Carolinians died.[27]

As soon as he saw the assault had failed, Alexander, still in an advanced position ahead of Seminary Ridge, ceased firing to save his ammunition. But, afraid Meade might launch a counterattack, he held his ground boldly, though his guns were entirely without support. Longstreet also realized the army would be in peril if the Federals attacked, and hurried to get other guns forward to join Alexander. But Meade was grateful that the charge had failed, and was in no mood for aggression.

As the survivors walked or hobbled back, Lee, entirely alone, rode out to Alexander's position and remained for a long time, soon joined by the visiting British colonel Arthur Fremantle. Lee spoke to all the wounded, and urged the fit and the lesser hurt to re-form. A number of badly wounded men took off their hats and cheered him.

General Wilcox came up, almost crying about the state of his brigade. "Never mind, General," Lee said, "all this has been my fault—it is I that have lost this fight, and you must help me out of it in the best way you can."[28]

Confederate guns held their advanced positions all along the line until about 10 P.M., when they withdrew behind Seminary Ridge.

⌇ ⌇

Pickett's charge was doomed before it started. Sending massed bodies of men across nearly a mile of open ground against emplaced riflemen and banked cannons was simply an invitation for destruction. Only a third of the men in the charge even got to Cemetery Ridge. Lee should have learned this lesson at Malvern Hill, a year before.

But Lee made additional errors at Gettysburg. The correct point of an attack was not against the Copse of Trees but against Cemetery Hill, just southwest of Gettysburg, where the Union line bent. Lee allowed the attack to proceed with both flanks in the air—inviting enfilade fire, a flanking attack, and devastating fire directly from the front. He did not require Wilcox's and Lang's brigades to go in at once to support Pickett's right, an omission that gave Stannard time to strike Kemper's flank. Lee did not insist on Longstreet committing the last three brigades of Dick Anderson's division when it was clear Pickett and Pettigrew would reach Cemetery Ridge. Rather he specifically ordered Hill not to send the rest of his corps to aid the advance. Finally, Lee did not recognize the potential of enfilade fire from Ewell's guns on the north.

About half the 13,500 Confederates who made the attack were killed, wounded, or captured. Pickett's division suffered staggering losses, and the survivors actually abandoned the field, a sight never before witnessed in the Army of Northern Virginia.

⌇ ⌇

On the night of July 3, General John D. Imboden went to Lee's quarters and talked for a while about the battle and its results. At the end, Lee said in a loud voice: "Too bad! Too bad! Oh, too bad!"[29]

Until the night of July 4, the Union and Confederate armies remained in position. Then Lee took up the retreat to Virginia.

On the night of July 4 as they were standing around a little fire, Lee said again to Longstreet the defeat was all his fault. He also said to Longstreet at another time: "You ought not to have made that last attack." Longstreet replied: "I had my orders, and they were of such a nature there was no escape from them."[30]

The three-day Battle of Gettysburg was the most sanguinary in American history—50,000 Americans killed, wounded, captured, or missing. The Confederates suffered irreparable losses, 27,000 men, the Federals 23,000. Lee, by his insistence upon fighting at Gettysburg, and especially by demanding Pickett's charge, had lost well over a third of his army and had destroyed the last offensive power of the Confederacy. From this point on, the Army of Northern Virginia was a wounded lion. It could only hold on grimly, exacting grievous damage when attacked, but unable to effect a decision on its own. Its only hope now was to make the war so painful that the North would finally grow weary and stop. The days of the great offensives, of brilliant strikes into the rear of the Union army, of campaigns that could defeat the enemy in battle, were past.

✳ 12 ✳

DEFIANCE

After Pickett's charge had been repulsed, Lee was determined to withdraw immediately to Virginia. The next day, July 4, 1863, the retreat started in a blinding rainstorm. On the same day General John C. Pemberton surrendered the Confederate garrison at Vicksburg.

Heavy rains continued for days, flooding the Potomac River. Lee's army gathered around Williamsport and Falling Waters, five miles downstream, expecting a massive attack. But Meade held off, and the Confederates crossed to safety on the night and early morning of July 13–14.

By August 4, Lee had withdrawn to the south bank of the Rapidan, a few miles north of Orange, and Meade's army came to rest opposite it.

Few Southerners at first believed that Gettysburg foreshadowed eventual failure in the East. Nevertheless, criticism of Lee, though muted, was widespread, and there was a strong undertone of censure.

On August 8, Lee wrote President Davis: "The general remedy for the want of success in a military commander is his removal. . . . I have been prompted by these reflections more than once since my return from Pennsylvania to propose to your excellency the propriety of selecting another commander for this army."

President Davis replied: "Where am I to find that new commander who is to possess the greater ability which you believe to be required?" Someone more fit to command than Lee, Davis wrote, was nonexistent.[1]

Davis was correct. No other senior officer possessed the strength of character, the skill, and the determination of Robert E. Lee. By comparison with the other senior officers of the Confederacy, Lee was indeed a great commander.

Lee did not accept the fact that his army's capacity for decisive offensive campaigns had vanished. He wanted to continue active operations, and resisted the verdict of Gettysburg that he must entrench and fortify, not march and maneuver.

By the end of August 1863 the army had barely attained 60,000 men, and Jefferson Davis told Lee there was no prospect of increasing it. While Meade made no menacing gestures, a grievous threat appeared in the West. In July Union general William S. Rosecrans had moved around Braxton Bragg's flank at Tullahoma, Tennessee, causing Bragg to fall back eighty miles on Chattanooga. If it fell, not only would the best east-west railroad line of the Confederacy be severed, but a way would be opened through the mountains of northern Georgia to Atlanta. This would cut the last major east-west rail connection, and split the Carolinas and Virginia from the rest of the Confederacy.

Davis sought to induce Lee to go to Tennessee and take command, but Lee wanted nothing to do with the war in the West, and convinced Davis to send Longstreet with two divisions—McLaws's and Hood's—to join Bragg, attack Rosecrans, then return to Virginia.

However, Bragg abandoned Chattanooga, and retreated south. On September 19–20, before all of Longstreet's troops had arrived, he defeated Rosecrans at Chickamauga Creek, about twelve miles below Chattanooga, in a gruesomely bloody battle that cost the South 18,000 men and the North 16,000. Rosecrans fell back to Chattanooga, and Bragg, instead of crossing the Tennessee River

(NATIONAL ARCHIVES)

(NATIONAL ARCHIVES)

Ulysses S. Grant

William Tecumseh Sherman

and attacking Rosecrans's supply line, which would have forced the Federals to withdraw, commenced a siege of the city.

Rosecrans stalled while his army, supplied only by a sixty-mile wagon road, began to starve. On October 16, 1863, Lincoln ousted Rosecrans and named Ulysses S. Grant in command in the West. Grant opened a much shorter supply line, raised the siege, and called up his old Army of the Tennessee, now under William Tecumseh Sherman, to secure Chattanooga.

Bragg did nothing. Between November 21 and 25, 1863, Grant and Sherman seized Lookout Mountain and Missionary Ridge, three and a half miles east of Chattanooga, and sent Bragg's army reeling. The Battle of Chattanooga opened the door to north Georgia and a strike at Atlanta, and at last brought down Braxton Bragg, who had contributed much to Confederate defeat in the West.

Late in September 1863 Lee learned through spies that Halleck had sent Meade's 11th and 12th Corps to reinforce Rosecrans, reducing his army to about 80,000 men. Though Lee had fewer than 50,000 men, he decided to strike around the Union army's flank.*

Preceded by Stuart's cavalry, Hill's and Ewell's corps crossed the upper Rapidan on October 9. Meade obligingly retreated, permitting Lee to drive to Bristoe Station on the Orange and Alexandria Railroad, four miles south of Manassas, in hopes of blocking Union forces moving up the rail line.

When Hill approached the station, he saw a large enemy force on the near side of Broad Run, and a larger force on the far side. Without looking further, Hill sent two North Carolina brigades of Henry Heth's division—John R. Cooke's and William W. Kirkland's—in a direct attack. As the Tar Heels moved forward, they met devastating rifle and artillery fire from a long line of Federals behind the railroad embankment on their right flank. Hill had fallen into a sucker's trap. The Rebels fell back in disorder, losing 1,360 men, whereas the Federals lost about 500.

A.P. Hill had demonstrated anew that he was unqualified for senior command. Men in the army were indignant, and Lee, when Hill told him the story, silenced him with a rebuke: "Well, well, General, bury these poor men and let us say no more about it."[2]

The Federals had destroyed the railroad bridge foundation at Rappahannock Station (now Remington). It would take a long time to rebuild it, and, unable to ensure supplies beyond, Lee pulled the army back to the river. But early in November, Jubal Early lost seven regiments in a Union attack on a bridgehead north of the station, while Robert Rodes lost two more in a Federal assault at Kelly's Ford, a few miles downstream. With his bridgeheads gone, Lee couldn't chance being driven against the Rapidan twenty to thirty miles south. He withdrew behind the Rapidan on November 10, and began fortifying a defensive line.

In late November Meade moved around Lee's eastern flank, in an attempt to envelop the Confederate army. Lee met the threat by

---

* Around September 20 Lee began to have violent back pains. Although attributed to various causes, they most probably were symptoms of angina pectoris. See Freeman, *R.E. Lee*, vol. 3, 170.

entrenching behind Mine Run, a bold, south-flowing stream thirteen miles east of Orange and twelve miles west of Chancellorsville. Seeing the strong breastworks that the Rebels threw up in hours, Meade declined to attack, and withdrew back to the Rapidan.

Mine Run demonstrated Lee's skill in defense, though this sort of warfare was not to his liking. Backed against the Rapidan with an army only a shadow of its former strength and with decidedly inferior senior commanders, Lee had no choice but to fight a defensive war. He was superb at it. He had a sure sense of where to draw a defensive line to block the enemy. He now exploited the immense stopping power of breastworks, trenches, dirt-covered log embrasures, cleared fields of fire in front of entrenchments, and abatis of felled trees to slow the approach of attacking infantry.[*]

Lee at last embraced Jackson's and Longstreet's methods of defensive warfare. This explains the Army of Northern Virginia's astounding holding operations of 1864 and the continuance of the war into 1865. Nevertheless, Lee never gave up his preference for the offensive, and always sought ways to resume it.

As winter came on the Confederates suffered great shortages of supplies, especially shoes, blankets, and food. There was food available, but the commissary-general, Lucius B. Northrop, remained incompetent though still protected by his friend, President Davis. Meanwhile, rails and rolling stock were deteriorating greatly, making prompt delivery difficult.

By the beginning of 1864, the war had become an immense burden to the people of the South. Vicksburg and Chattanooga had fallen.

---

[*] William Tecumseh Sherman described the new art of field-fortification building as follows: "Troops, halting for the night or for a battle, faced the enemy; moved forward to ground with a good outlook to the front; stacked arms; gathered logs, stumps, fence rails, anything which would stop a bullet; piled these to their front, and, digging a ditch behind, threw the dirt forward, and made a parapet which covered their persons as perfectly as a granite wall." See Johnson and Buel, vol. 4, 248.

Strength had declined so drastically that Confederate armies everywhere were on the defensive, with no hope of resuming the initiative.

Nevertheless, to many Northerners the prospects seemed equally dismal. After two and a half years of intensive war, the Union had only just gained the outer ramparts of the gateway to Atlanta, while, in Virginia, the Army of the Potomac seemed no closer to Richmond than in the first days of the war.

Though the trans-Mississippi states of the Confederacy were isolated and only parts of Mississippi and Alabama south of the Tennessee River remained unoccupied, the South still retained a bastion of great strength—the four old eastern states where Southern culture had originated, Georgia, North and South Carolina, and Virginia.

If Joseph E. Johnston, the new Confederate commander in the West, could keep Federal forces from advancing down the single-track railroad from Chattanooga to Atlanta, and if Robert E. Lee could prevent the Union army from seizing Richmond, the South might hold out long enough for the Northern people to weary of war and demand a negotiated peace.

There was a strong peace movement building in the North, led by the Democratic Party, and fed by the appalling losses and the seeming impossibility of subduing Southern resistance.

Abraham Lincoln knew a wave of pacifism was sweeping the North. Unless Union armies achieved decisive advances before the presidential election in November 1864, he was sure to be defeated. The Democrats then would make peace with the South.

Lincoln had finally come to realize his greatest failure had been his choices of commander in the East. While Federal generals in the West had generally been superior to the Confederate chiefs there, the Union leaders in Virginia had been outthought, outmaneuvered, and outfought by Lee and Jackson. Once they had emerged from collisions with the Army of Northern Virginia, the Federal commanders retreated, never wanting again to get within the jaws of those terrible Confederate lions.

In the early months of 1864, President Lincoln resolved to find a general who would continue to advance in the East, no matter what the losses, no matter how humiliating the defeat. He found such a general in Ulysses S. Grant. With his chief lieutenant, William Tecumseh Sherman, Grant had fought doggedly to seize Vicksburg and open the Mississippi in 1862–63, and had driven relentlessly against Braxton Bragg to capture Chattanooga and thrust the Rebels into northern Georgia.

On March 4, 1864, Lincoln conferred on Grant command of all Federal armies, directed him to supervise the campaign in Virginia, and promised he would supply men and arms until the South collapsed.

Grant named Sherman to command in the West, and developed a grand strategy to win the war. He realized that the Confederate army was the real objective in Virginia, not Richmond. He told Meade to go after Lee, not territory. Sherman's job was different: he was to capture Atlanta. This city was the focal point of the last major east-west railroad of the Confederacy, and site of vital foundries, machine shops, and munitions factories. Grant recognized that the keys to victory were capture of Atlanta and destruction of the Army of Northern Virginia.

As a distraction to Johnston, Grant ordered Nathaniel P. Banks to seize the port of Mobile, Alabama, and open an alternate route into Georgia from the extreme south. As a rear threat to Lee, Grant directed Benjamin F. "Beast" Butler to advance westward along the south bank of the James River toward Richmond with about 37,000 men. In the event, neither flanking movement succeeded. A Confederate force of 24,000 men under Pierre Beauregard bottled Butler up against the James east of Petersburg, while Banks was so slow that his threat against southern Georgia never materialized.

Lee did not know the details of Grant's strategic plan, but he saw signs of an imminent advance by Meade, a Federal diversion in the

Shenandoah Valley, and Butler's move up the James. Lee girded the Army of Northern Virginia against Grant's four corps (2d, 5th, 6th, 9th), 144,000 men, and 16,000 cavalry armed entirely with breech-loading magazine Spencer repeating carbines, doubling their efficiency.

Lee had about 62,000 men: 10,000 in Longstreet's two-division 1st Corps, just released from service in the West;[*] 17,000 in Ewell's three-division 2d Corps; 22,000 in A.P. Hill's three-division 3d Corps; 8,000 cavalry; and 4,500 artillery.

Lee conferred with his generals on May 2, 1864, and told them he believed Grant would turn the Confederate right flank, and try to march through the Wilderness again. A move in this direction was logical, because a march west would throw the Union army against the Blue Ridge, and far from Richmond.

This offered Lee a great opportunity, provided he moved fast. If he could challenge the Federals in the Wilderness with his full strength on the first day, Grant's soldiers would have no time to build strong breastworks or use their superior artillery. They might suffer the same fate as Hooker's army.

But Lee did not move fast. He left Ewell's and Hill's corps along the Rapidan, and Longstreet's corps near Gordonsville, thirty-three air miles from the Wilderness—too far from the probable battlefield.[†] And when he did move, he sent in his forces piecemeal.

As Porter Alexander later wrote: "What proved a drawn battle when begun by three divisions reinforced by two more after six hours and by three more eighteen hours later might have proved a decisive victory if fought by all eight from the beginning."[3]

On the morning of May 4, 1864, Rebel observers reported that the Union army was crossing Germanna and Ely's Fords of the Rapidan, about twenty miles downstream from the main Union line north of Orange.

---

[*] Charles W. Field of Kentucky and Joseph B. Kershaw of South Carolina had replaced Hood and McLaws as division commanders.

[†] Lee left Longstreet near Gordonsville in case Beauregard needed him against Butler east of Richmond. However, it should have been apparent that the real danger was Meade's army, not Butler's.

Lee ordered the army to head the Federals off. Ewell, taking the Orange Turnpike (now Virginia Route 20), had eighteen miles to go. Hill, leaving Richard Anderson's division on the Rapidan under orders from Lee, followed the Orange Plank Road (now Virginia Route 621) two miles south, and had twenty-eight miles to go. Longstreet should have been moved already to Todds Tavern, five miles south of Chancellorsville, where he could have come up on the north-south Brock Road (now Virginia Route 613), and taken in flank the forces fighting Hill and Ewell. But Longstreet had forty-three miles to travel by road, and no chance of wrapping around behind the Union army.

Grant's aim was to pass Lee's flank, get through the Wilderness, and place his army between Lee and Richmond. His men might have made five or six miles more, but, on Meade's orders, the leading elements bivouacked deep within the Wilderness on the night of May 4—Winfield S. Hancock's 2d Corps at Chancellorsville, and Gouverneur K. Warren's 5th Corps five miles west at Wilderness Tavern.

Ewell, being on the shorter road, might have struck the Federals before nightfall at Wilderness Tavern, junction of the turnpike and the Germanna Plank Road. But Lee had told him to go slowly, to permit Hill to get abreast of him on the Orange Plank Road. And Lee instructed both not to get in general engagement before Longstreet was up.

Consequently, Ewell camped the night of May 4 at Locust Grove, five miles from Wilderness Tavern, and three miles from his battlefield of the next day. Hill's advanced division, Heth's, bivouacked at Mine Run, seven miles west of Parkers Store, and ten miles from the battlefield. Longstreet was still thirty miles away at sundown.

Both armies were in motion early on May 5. At 7 A.M. Warren's 5th Corps collided with Ewell within two miles of Wilderness Tavern. Ewell had two of his divisions up, and Grant realized that the rest of the Confederate army was still not on the field. He determined to overwhelm Ewell before the Rebels could concentrate, turning on Ewell the whole of 5th Corps, 26,000 men, plus half of

John Sedgwick's 6th Corps, 13,000 men. Though Ewell still had one division on the march, the troops in place industriously entrenched between attacks, and stopped every one of numerous Union assaults, with immense Federal casualties.

Meanwhile, Hill found enemy cavalry at Parkers Store, which he drove on ahead, following them down the road toward Brock Road. This road was the only feasible north-south connection between Hancock and the rest of the army. If Hill could seize the junction of Brock Road and the Plank Road, he could isolate Hancock's corps. Grant, seeing the danger, recalled Hancock, now marching toward Todds Tavern, to protect the intersection.

Since Hancock would take hours to arrive, Meade hurried George W. Getty's division of Sedgwick's corps to hold the junction. Getty's men arrived just as the Federal cavalry bolted for the rear, and hastily built a defensive line along Brock Road.

Hill did not press Getty because he was under orders from Lee not to encourage a fight until Longstreet arrived. Accordingly, he stopped Heth's force of 7,000 men, formed a line of battle, and waited, while Cadmus M. Wilcox's division, of about the same size, came up behind.

Grant knew that Longstreet could not possibly reach the field on May 5, and resolved to destroy Hill and Ewell before nightfall. He ordered all of Hancock's corps, 28,000 men, and Getty's division of the 6th Corps, about 8,000, to attack Hill's 14,000. But Hancock delayed a couple hours to complete the entrenchments already started by Getty. This delay enabled Heth to deploy his division, partially select his ground, and build rudimentary field fortifications in a few places. Meanwhile, Hill posted Wilcox's division on his left flank, extending toward Ewell's line, but still leaving a gap of nearly a mile.

Heth's line of battle was squarely across the Plank Road, one brigade on the north, three on the south. On the north side of the road, just behind Heth, was a small house, Widow Tapp's, in a forty-acre clearing. Here William T. Poague's artillery battalion took up a position, and here Lee and Hill made their headquarters.

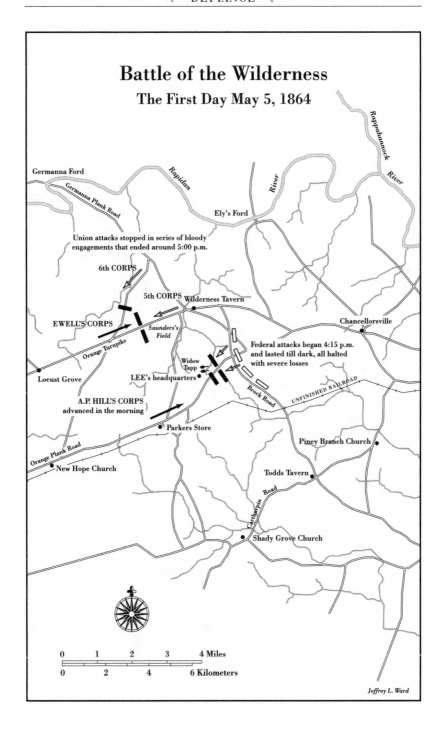

Battle of the Wilderness
The First Day May 5, 1864

Rappahannock

Germanna Ford

Rapidan

River

River

Germanna Plank Road

Ely's Ford

Union attacks stopped in series of bloody
engagements that ended around 5:00 p.m.

6th CORPS

5th CORPS Wilderness Tavern

EWELL'S CORPS

Chancellorsville

Saunders's
Field

Orange Turnpike

Federal attacks began 4:15 p.m.
and lasted till dark, all halted
with severe losses

Widow
Tapp

Locust Grove

LEE's headquarters

Brock Road

UNFINISHED RAILROAD

A.P. HILL'S CORPS
advanced in the morning

Parkers Store

Piney Branch Church

Orange Plank Road

New Hope Church

Todds Tavern

Catharpin Road

Shady Grove Church

| 0 | 1 | 2 | 3 | 4 Miles |
| 0 | 2 | 4 | 6 Kilometers |

Jeffrey L. Ward

At 4:15 P.M. Hancock attacked, but his assaults, all frontal, went in piecemeal. Getty assaulted first, and Heth threw him back with terrible losses. Then David B. Birney's and Gershom Mott's divisions of Hancock's corps launched separate, unconcerted attacks. Heth's troops repulsed them, too, with heavy losses in what one Confederate described as "butchery pure and simple." This permitted Heth to press almost to Brock Road. Only the arrival of John Gibbon's division prevented a breakthrough.

Hancock's last division, Francis C. Barlow's, also came up, making the odds five to one. Lee, seeing the danger, ordered Wilcox to move back and reinforce Heth. But when Wilcox arrived, he and Heth attacked—the wrong thing to do. The two divisions charged on a front of only half a mile. This led only to more slaughter, and weakened the Confederates almost to the breaking point, though Hancock did not recognize it. As the day ended, Barlow's division launched a final piecemeal attack, causing more casualties on both sides, but accomplished nothing.

Hill's men were exhausted, their ammunition low, and their lines disarranged and disconnected.

Grant, exasperated with Meade's inability to concentrate his troops, ordered all four corps to attack in unison at daybreak on May 6. Warren and Sedgwick were to assault Ewell as a diversion; Hancock was to drive west on the Plank Road; and first James S. Wadsworth's division, then two divisions of Ambrose Burnside's 9th Corps, were to move between the two Confederate wings and strike Hill's northern flank.

Lee realized that Hill would be unable to hold, and at 5 P.M. sent a message to Longstreet, who had arrived at Richard's Shop, ten miles southwest of the battlefield, to come up on the Plank Road to support Hill. Longstreet replied that he would move at 1 A.M. May 6.

Lee made plans for Ewell to attack at 4:30 A.M., with the aim of routing Warren and Sedgwick, and snapping Grant's supply line at Wilderness Tavern. He expected Longstreet to take over Hill's positions before daylight, allowing him to shift Hill's corps northward to help Ewell.

On the Plank Road, the exhausted Confederates had dropped in their tracks. No coherent defense system existed. The vulnerability of the troops to an attack terrified Heth and Wilcox, and they asked Hill for permission to set the men to work during the night building field fortifications. Hill told them to let the men alone. Longstreet would be up before daylight, he said, and the troops could fall back behind Longstreet's line.

Wilcox, dissatisfied, carried his petition to Lee, who agreed with Hill. But Lee was probably unaware of the disarray on Hill's front. It was Hill's job, not Lee's, to make sure his corps was safe. The next day Hill became so sick that he had to give up his command, raising the suspicion that his illness—like a similar mysterious malady that had appeared at Gettysburg—was due to his inability to take on the responsibilities his job required.

Longstreet's corps was held up by narrow woods roads, and had not arrived on the Plank Road by daylight. And at 5 A.M. May 6 Hancock launched his assault. Hill's soldiers, knowing it was impossible to hold, withdrew westward, in fair order. From the north, Wadsworth's division rolled up the Confederate positions and broke into the Plank Road. The only force left to protect Lee and his head-quarters was Poague's twelve-gun battalion in Widow Tapp's field.

Behind Wadsworth, Burnside's two divisions were late starting, ran into Stephen Dodson Ramseur's North Carolina brigade north of Hill's corps, and remained useless the whole morning. He at last launched his attack around 2 P.M., but two small Confederate brigades stopped it.

Meanwhile two Maine regiments reached Widow Tapp's field. As the soldiers emerged into the open, Poague's guns opened fire, forcing them to retreat. Almost at the last minute, as more Federals pressed to the edge of the field, John Gregg's Arkansas-Texas brigade, the leading element of Charles W. Field's division, reached the field and prepared to attack. Lee was so excited that he resolved to lead the assault, but was at last persuaded to withdraw.

Gregg's 800 men drove forward on a narrow front, encountering blistering fire, but pressing on. In twenty-five minutes of desperate fighting the Texans and Arkansans lost all but 250 of their number, but, with the assistance of Henry L. Benning's Georgia brigade, split Hancock's attack in two and caused both disconnected parts to rush to the rear. Meanwhile William F. Perry's Alabama brigade advanced just north of the road and sent Wadsworth's division reeling. Union reinforcements finally stopped Longstreet's advance, but his two divisions had stymied Hancock's attack. By 8 A.M. the two sides dropped down, in stalemate, only a few yards apart.

Meanwhile, on the Orange Turnpike, Ewell had attacked at 4:30 A.M., but made no impression. Warren refused to send his men to counterattack, because he was certain they would fail. But Sedgwick ordered his troops forward six times, and six times they were thrown back with heavy losses.

Lee meanwhile was trying to regain the initiative. He had discovered an unfinished railroad line about half a mile south of the Plank Road. His chief engineer, Martin Luther Smith, realized that the Confederates could launch a flank attack from it. Moxley Sorrel, an aide to Longstreet, led the expedition with three brigades—Tige Anderson's Georgians, William Mahone's Virginians, and John Stone's Mississippians and North Carolinians. Hancock had ignored the railway, and his troops were stunned by the unexpected blow, the westward-facing Federal brigades toppling like dominoes as Sorrel struck their southern flanks. In less than an hour Sorrel had evicted all Union forces south of the Plank Road and was driving away the few remaining Federals north of it. Meanwhile Joseph B. Kershaw's division resumed a direct attack on Hancock's front. Upwards of 20,000 Union soldiers fled toward the Union rear, rapidly succumbing to panic.

Longstreet saw a glittering opportunity: he could achieve victory if he drove eastward down the Plank Road and broke the Union line at Brock Road. Micah Jenkins's South Carolina brigade was at hand to do the job.

Longstreet went along with General Jenkins in the lead. But Mahone's Virginians in Sorrel's force had just turned back, and thought the body of troops advancing eastward was Federals. They unleashed a heavy volley, mortally wounded Jenkins, and struck

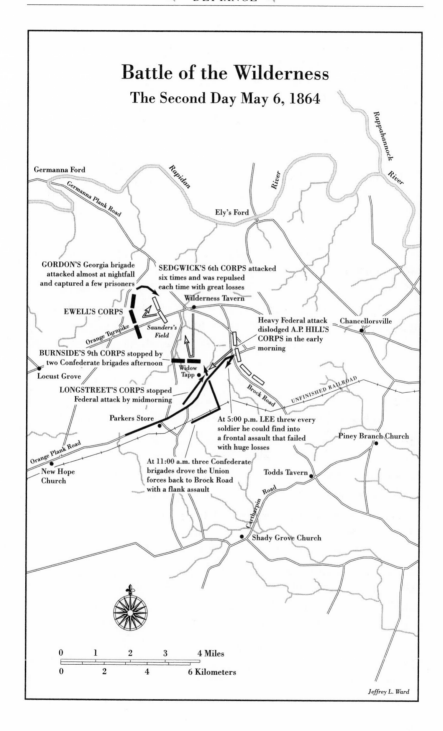

Battle of the Wilderness
The Second Day May 6, 1864

Rappahannock River

Germanna Ford

Rapidan

River

River

Germanna Plank Road

Ely's Ford

GORDON'S Georgia brigade
attacked almost at nightfall
and captured a few prisoners

SEDGWICK'S 6th CORPS attacked
six times and was repulsed
each time with great losses

Wilderness Tavern

EWELL'S CORPS

Orange Turnpike

Saunders's
Field

Chancellorsville

Heavy Federal attack
dislodged A.P. HILL'S
CORPS in the early
morning

BURNSIDE'S 9th CORPS stopped by
two Confederate brigades afternoon

Locust Grove

Widow
Tapp

LONGSTREET'S CORPS stopped
Federal attack by midmorning

Brock Road

UNFINISHED RAILROAD

Parkers Store

At 5:00 p.m. LEE threw every
soldier he could find into
a frontal assault that failed
with huge losses

Piney Branch Church

Orange Plank Road

New Hope
Church

At 11:00 a.m. three Confederate
brigades drove the Union
forces back to Brock Road
with a flank assault

Todds Tavern

Catharpin Road

Shady Grove Church

0   1   2   3   4 Miles

0   2   4   6 Kilometers

Jeffrey L. Ward

Longstreet severely in the neck. The attack at once disintegrated. Lee sent Richard H. Anderson, from Hill's corps, to take over Longstreet's corps. But since Anderson knew nothing of the situation, the attack did not resume.

Taking advantage of his reprieve, Hancock frantically improved the entrenchments on Brock Road.

Stalemate had been achieved. Lee had stopped the threats to both his corps. Sedgwick continued his assaults against Ewell on the Orange Turnpike, but, though bloody, they were fruitless, while Hancock's corps had withdrawn behind the entrenchments along the Brock Road.

A situation strangely similar to that at the dawn of the third day at Gettysburg had come about. Both armies were intact, but sorely wounded, and occupying positions entirely too strong for the other to overrun. Yet Lee reacted at the Wilderness precisely as he had done at Gettysburg. He waited four hours after Longstreet's effort had collapsed, knowing that Hancock was entrenching furiously, then ordered a frontal assault led by Jenkins's brigade on Brock Road. Lee was outnumbered two to one, and his assault went in directly against Hancock's men firing rifles and canister-loaded cannons behind chest-high stacked logs, covered with dirt, abatis of sharpened sticks, and an open, treeless killing zone in front.

The attack lasted half an hour, and was of unprecedented ferocity, but it failed with enormous Confederate losses, while the Federals behind their breastworks were little hurt.

Lee's attack was as mad as Pickett's charge, with even less chance of success. Lee had learned nothing from Gettysburg.

As the day was ending, Lee told Ewell and Jubal Early to allow John B. Gordon to send his Georgia brigade into the Union northern flank, after all hope of a decisive stroke was gone. Gordon captured a few prisoners, but made no other gains. He had been petitioning for the move since morning. Ewell lacked the aggressive spirit essential to success and, without pressure from Lee, waited too long. If Gordon's attack had been made in conjunction with Sorrel's strike on the Union southern flank, the Federal army might have suffered a devastating defeat. But Lee virtually ignored Ewell's front on May 6, and made no attempt at a double envelopment.

Confederate casualties in the Wilderness were severe, about 7,600. Federal losses were much heavier, 17,600, but Grant could replace his losses—Lee could not.[4]

Although beaten, Grant refused to retreat. Instead, he resolved to throw his army once more to the left, forcing Lee to evacuate his entrenchments and place his army between Grant and Richmond.

Stuart informed Lee on the afternoon of May 7, 1864, that Federal trains were moving south along Brock Road. Lee concluded at once that Grant's destination was Spotsylvania Court House, about ten air miles southeast. From there he could approach Hanover Junction (now Doswell), twenty-five air miles south. There the Richmond, Fredericksburg, and Potomac and Virginia Central Railroads intersected. If Grant was seeking to drive Lee's army back on Richmond, and cut supplies, he almost certainly would strike for Hanover Junction.

Lee responded at once, ordering Richard Anderson, now commanding Longstreet's corps, to get his two divisions into blocking position as soon as possible. Anderson's soldiers started on a footrace, moving in a column parallel to the Federals toward their next confrontation.

Although Grant had a slight advantage in road distance— twelve miles to Lee's fifteen—the Rebels had two resolute cavalry divisions blocking the Federals' way. On Brock Road at Todds Tavern was Fitz Lee, and on Catharpin Road (present-day Virginia Route 612) was Wade Hampton. The Rebel horsemen defeated efforts of Union cavalry to break through. Only at daylight, when Federal infantry came up, did the Confederate riders yield slowly in one stubborn delaying action after another.

In this way, Anderson's two divisions arrived at the junction of Block House Road (now Virginia Route 648) and Shady Grove Church Road (now Virginia Route 608) at 8 A.M. on May 8. A mile and a half to the east was Spotsylvania Court House, where Thomas L. Rosser's cavalry brigade was in a heavy fight with James H. Wilson's Union cavalry division coming on the Fredericksburg road (now Virginia Route 208).

But the greatest danger was a mile north at the junction of Block House and Brock Roads. Fitz Lee was being heavily pressed by Warren's 5th Corps infantry. Swelling rifle fire showed the situation was getting critical. Porter Alexander, at the front of Joseph B. Kershaw's division, sent John W. Henagan's South Carolina and Benjamin G. Humphreys's Mississippi brigades to rescue Fitz Lee. He directed the rest of Kershaw's division—the Georgia brigades of William T. Wofford and Goode Bryan—to help Rosser.

Henagan and Humphreys had just fallen into position when three brigades of John C. Robinson's division charged. Warren had promised the soldiers that only Rebel cavalry was ahead, didn't have bayonets, and would run if approached closely. The Union soldiers came right up to a line of rails where the Rebels had emplaced, and were terrified to discover enemy infantry—and bayonets. In the resulting melee the greatly outnumbered Confederates drove back the Federals, leaving the ground blue with fallen soldiers.

Meanwhile, Field's division arrived and went to support Kershaw, while the two brigades sent to help Rosser returned when Wilson's cavalry backed off. Thereafter ensued a day of solid, hard fighting—two weak divisions holding back two full Federal corps, Warren's 5th and Sedgwick's 6th, entrenching as best they could in the intervals between attacks.

The only near disaster occurred when Warren and Sedgwick united near sundown and advanced on a front wider than the two Confederate divisions. This allowed part of Horatio G. Wright's division to overlap the 1st Corps's line on the right. But at that moment Richard Ewell's corps came into line, and Robert Rodes's division

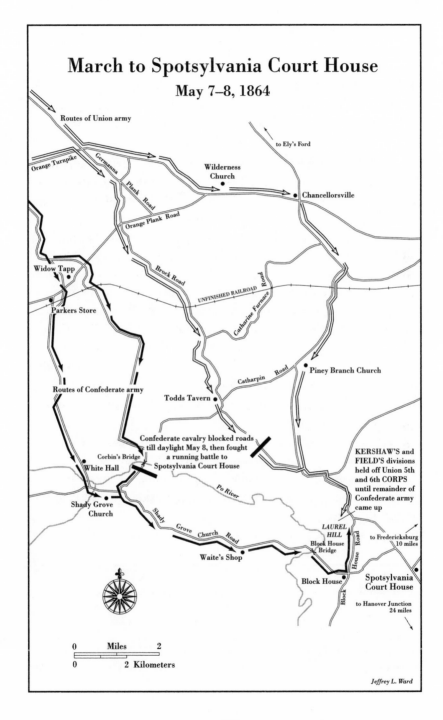

March to Spotsylvania Court House
May 7–8, 1864

Routes of Union army

to Ely's Ford

Orange Turnpike

Germanna

Plank Road

Wilderness Church

Chancellorsville

Orange Plank Road

Widow Tapp

Brock Road

Catharine Furnace Road

UNFINISHED RAILROAD

Parkers Store

Piney Branch Church

Catharpin Road

Routes of Confederate army

Todds Tavern

Confederate cavalry blocked roads till daylight May 8, then fought a running battle to Spotsylvania Court House

Corbin's Bridge

White Hall

KERSHAW'S and FIELD'S divisions held off Union 5th and 6th CORPS until remainder of Confederate army came up

Po River

Shady Grove Church

Shady Grove Church Road

LAUREL HILL

Block House Bridge

to Fredericksburg 10 miles

Waite's Shop

Block House Road

Block House

Spotsylvania Court House

to Hanover Junction 24 miles

0   Miles   2

0   2 Kilometers

Jeffrey L. Ward

drove Wright back. Ewell thereupon extended the line eastward and entrenched.

On May 9 1st Corps reached from the little Po River on the west to the Block House and Brock Roads junction, a mile northeast. To the right and north of the court house was Ewell's corps, and on the east covering the court house and the Fredericksburg road was Hill's corps, now under Jubal Early because of Hill's sickness.

Both sides spent May 9 improving their trenches and parapets.* There was little action, other than sharpshooting. One bullet killed General Sedgwick at a range of about 700 yards. General Wright succeeded him as 6th Corps commander.

A real danger appeared on the west, however. Hancock built three pontoon bridges across the Po River, as Grant planned to send three divisions around the Confederate left flank. Hancock moved too slowly, however, and Lee was able to move Heth's division across the Po to take Hancock in flank on May 10. It was a desperate move, one division against three, and probably would have failed, allowing Grant to get on Lee's rear. But Grant saw what he thought was a better opportunity at a peculiar salient on Ewell's front that the Rebels called the Mule Shoe. He called off the envelopment of Lee's western flank, and brought Hancock back to attack the vulnerable location.

The Mule Shoe came about on the first day when Lee's senior engineer, Martin Luther Smith, discovered open ground where Union cannons could be emplaced to the north of the line Ewell occupied to the right of Anderson's corps. He decided to take this ground into the Confederate defenses, creating a big salient more than a mile wide, pointing north a mile from the main line. This

---

* Field fortifications were constructed to varying degrees of perfection, depending on how much time the soldiers had to build them. A trench, or ditch, was rarely wider than three feet or deeper than two feet. A parapet was usually about two and a half feet high, reinforced, when possible, with logs or other solid objects. Hence the distance from the top of the parapet to the bottom of the ditch was about four and a half feet. Porter Alexander drew a cross-section of works in *Fighting for the Confederacy*, 409.

Battle of Spotsylvania Court House
May 8–20, 1864

Attack by seven Union brigades repulsed May 10.
At dawn on May 12 four Union divisions broke the line.
In hand-to-hand fighting that raged until 10 p.m.,
Confederates pushed back the Federals, then retired to
a new line at the base of the Angle. On May 18 GRANT
attempted a final attack, which failed.

0   .5   1 Mile

0   1   2 Kilometers

Ni River

Brock Road

THE BLOODY ANGLE
(First called the Mule Shoe)

GRANT planned to
send three divisions
around LEE'S flank,
but acted too slowly

GORDON attacked and
restored the line

Pontoon
Bridges

LAUREL
HILL

Confederate
entrenchments

LONGSTREET'S CORPS
(under Richard Anderson)

EWELL'S CORPS

Block House
Bridge

Brock Road

HETH'S division
moved to block
May 10

Shady Grove Church Road

Block House Road

Spotsylvania
Court House

Block House

BURNSIDE'S CORPS attempted to break
through on May 12, but was thrown back

Po

A.P. HILL'S CORPS
(under Jubal Early)

River

Old Court House

Jeffrey L. Ward

Mule Shoe could be enfiladed by Federal gunfire and had large spaces where it could be approached by Union infantry before being seen by defenders. The salient also lengthened the Confederate line by two miles—and Lee was already desperately short of troops.

Grant saw that the Mule Shoe was a great mistake, and recalled Hancock to assault its western face on May 10 with seven brigades. The Federals had only a short distance to go under fire, and advanced about 4 P.M. directly on Rodes's division. But the Confederates had heard them forming, and were waiting. Their response was prompt and bloody. A few Federals reached the parapets, but Dodson Ramseur's North Carolina brigade flung them back with great loss.

At 6 P.M., after a half-hour cannonade, the Federals tried again, this time at the apex of the angle by Emory Upton with three brigades advancing in four lines, while Gershom Mott's two-brigade division approached on Upton's left. Mott's approach was over ground the Confederates could see, and they broke it up almost entirely with artillery fire before Mott's troops got near.

But Upton had only 200 yards to go under fire, and by sheer weight of numbers stormed over the parapet and captured about a thousand men of George Doles's Georgia brigade. However, John B. Gordon's division in reserve fell on Upton's men and drove them out with many killed and wounded.

Hancock made a third attack at 7 P.M., with half a dozen more brigades. Once again Confederate artillery and rifle fire broke up the assault with more losses.

Grant devoted Wednesday, May 11, to planning a better-managed attack on the Mule Shoe. He also wrote General Halleck in Washington that "I propose to fight it out on this line if it takes all summer."[5] As part of his preparations, Grant moved Burnside's corps slightly westward from the court house to take part in the assault the next morning, May 12. He also sent an infantry brigade to scout westward toward Todds Tavern.

Lee got word of these westward movements from Stuart, and took them to be preparations for a Federal footrace around his left flank. To be ready to move at a moment's notice, Lee ordered all artillery close to the enemy to be withdrawn at nightfall. Porter Alexander in 1st Corps knew that the defense of the entrenched lines depended on cannons, and withdrawing them would leave them weakened in case of a surprise attack. He kept his guns in position, but ordered ammunition to be loaded in wagons, and the vehicles placed so they could withdraw easily without noise. The artillery chiefs in the other two corps, however, executed Lee's orders literally, removing twenty pieces from the Mule Shoe.

Thus two errors by Lee contributed to the disaster about to unfold: he allowed the Mule Shoe to be occupied in the first place, and he withdrew the cannons protecting it.

Grant prepared a supreme effort at dawn, May 12. Hancock massed four divisions, eleven brigades, for a direct assault upon the apex of the angle. On his right, 6th Corps was to hold the trenches with one division, while the other two, eight brigades, were to assist Hancock as needed. On Hancock's left three divisions of Burnside's corps, six brigades, were to attack 3d Corps at dawn.

Hancock moved forward on an extremely narrow front over the same ground Mott had advanced through two days previously. In the case of Francis C. Barlow's division advancing on the left in the open, he abandoned the customary wide line of battle two men deep for a formation that resembled nothing so much as an ancient Greek phalanx—four brigades in a huge mass about two hundred yards wide and a hundred deep, or about 300 men abreast by twenty men deep.

On the right David B. Birney's and Mott's divisions marched in traditional formations because they traversed a marsh and a low pine thicket, and could approach close to the Rebel trenches without being seen. John Gibbon's division brought up the rear. Altogether nearly 20,000 men took part in the assault.

The Confederates heard the Federals massing all night, and were alert and waiting. Edward Johnson, whose division held the point of the salient, called for the twenty displaced cannons to be brought back. They were ordered to rejoin Johnson at daylight. But just at that moment the Federals assaulted.

The Rebels heard them coming when they were 400 yards away. If the cannons had been in place and primed with canister, they could have done great execution to the closely packed Union soldiers.

But now the blue wave couldn't be stopped. Barlow's division overran the trench, swarmed over the parapet, overwhelmed the thin lines of Confederate defenders, opened the way for Birney and Mott to follow, and captured the twenty cannons coming in at a gallop. Within minutes a large part of Johnson's division surrendered, 3,000 men, including General Johnson and General George H. Steuart.

Ewell was left with only two divisions, Gordon's and Rodes's, not more than 9,000 men. His line had been breached with at least 20,000 Federals. There were no Rebels to stop the Federals from rushing on and breaking the Confederate line. But the Federals didn't do so because too many men had been brought together in one place. The units got in each other's way when they tried to re-form in lines of battle. The advance stopped while the regiments and brigades tried to sort themselves out.

This gave Gordon time to move his three brigades from reserve and prepare to counterattack into the heart of the Union penetration. As he was forming his troops near the base of the Mule Shoe, General Lee, as he had done in the Wilderness, tried to accompany the charge. He paid no attention to Gordon's remonstrations or to the calls of the men: "General Lee to the rear!" At last, a sergeant took the reins of Lee's horse, Traveller, and turned the general away.

Meanwhile Burnside's attack had a small preliminary success. Robert B. Potter's division captured some entrenchments in James H. Lane's North Carolina brigade, plus two guns. But Lane's men rallied, helped by Alfred M. Scales's North Carolina brigade and Edward L. Thomas's Georgia brigade, and recaptured the guns and the original trench line. Under urgent orders from Grant, Burnside made repeated attacks, but all failed.

A remarkable process now began to unfold. Grant had struck the Confederate line with a stunning force, had actually cracked the line, and had captured virtually an entire Rebel division. But the Confederates had not collapsed. Rather, they gathered their tiny reserves and prepared to attack the attackers.

Grant at once abandoned all thought of maneuver and finesse, and resolved to conquer by main force. Thereupon ensued a struggle more desperate, bloody, and prolonged than any that took place in the war.

Grant brought up every artillery piece he could find to pound the Confederate positions. He ordered Wright to reinforce Hancock with the eight 6th Corps brigades, and directed Warren to send two of his four divisions. He also ordered Warren to assault Anderson's corps, which Grant thought must have been weakened to reinforce Ewell. But when Warren attacked, 1st Corps easily repulsed the effort.

In this press of people, little could be accomplished, making it possible for Gordon's division and the brigades of Daniel and Ramseur to drive the Federals beyond the log parapets of the Mule Shoe. It was a miserable, gruesome process, made worse by heavy rain, which continued to fall into the night. Lee sent in three brigades from the 3d Corps to help—Abner Perrin's Alabama, Nathaniel H. Harris's Mississippi, and Samuel McGowan's South Carolina.

The Federals stopped on one side of the parapet, the Rebels on the other, ten to twelve feet apart, the men standing twenty to forty deep. A desperate hand-to-hand struggle erupted and continued for the remainder of the day and on into the night.

Men in the rear passed rifles to soldiers in front, who fired random shots at the other side. Bullets flew in torrents. Occasionally Union soldiers would try to regain a stretch of the Confederate works. The soldiers of the two armies were so close that sometimes, when a Rebel leaned over the parapet, the Federals grabbed him, pulled him down, and killed him. Many were stabbed or bayoneted through crevices in the logs. Men on both sides mounted the works and fired rifles handed them until they were shot down; then others took their places.

By mid-afternoon the soldiers were so weary they scarcely knew what they were doing. But the Confederates were told to remain until a new line—hurriedly under construction across the base of the Mule Shoe—could be finished. The bitter exchange of fire in the Mule Shoe, now renamed the Bloody Angle, continued until at least 10 P.M.

Philip Sheridan

It was past midnight when the survivors, staggering with fatigue, fell back to the new line.

Grant's supreme effort to crush Lee's army by force had failed. The campaign of 1864 was teaching a dismal lesson, though Grant was not yet heeding. Barricades protected by resolute men firing rifles and canister-armed cannons were virtually impossible to carry by assault. Only when somebody made a mistake, like Lee withdrawing artillery from the Mule Shoe, could gains be made.

Federal losses at Spotsylvania totaled 18,400, Confederate about 9,000, including Johnson's division of 3,000 captured. The Rebel losses included some of the best troops and ablest leaders of the army. Two generals died, Junius Daniel and Abner Perrin, and three were severely wounded: James A. Walker, Robert D. Johnston, and Samuel McGowan. Many lesser-known officers were killed or wounded. And Jeb Stuart died from a wound at Yellow Tavern, a few miles north of Richmond, where he and his troopers were fending off an advance by Philip Sheridan on the capital. Confederate command had been shattered to a degree no one recognized at the time.

Grant allowed his men to rest for a day, then tried to attack Lee's right, but the assault went nowhere in rain and darkness. Early on May 18, he attempted another attack on the Bloody Angle, but the Federal soldiers didn't press it hard, and the Confederates repulsed it easily, primarily with artillery fire. At last giving up, Grant ordered the Army of the Potomac to swing around Lee's right, or east, and turn south.

It was obvious that Grant's objective was Hanover Junction at the North Anna River, twenty-four air miles southeast. But Lee had the inside track this time, and by the night of May 22 his army was on the south side of the stream. On the march, A. P. Hill, his health improved, returned to command of 3d Corps.

Since the start of the 1864 campaign, the Army of Northern Virginia had lost about 17,000 men, the Federal army about twice as many. Grant was getting replacements for his losses, and at Hanover Junction Lee partially replaced his—9,000 men. They came because two Union threats elsewhere had been blunted. John C. Breckinridge defeated a Union force under Franz Sigel at New Market in the Shenandoah Valley on May 15, permitting him to bring 2,500 men to help Lee.* And Beauregard defeated Butler at Drewry's Bluff on the James River on May 16, "bottling" him at Bermuda Hundred against the James, and allowing George Pickett's division of 5,000 men and a brigade to join Lee.

On the afternoon of May 23, Hancock's troops captured most of a Rebel bridgehead over the North Anna at the RF&P Railroad and Telegraph Road (now U.S. Route 1), then seized the land south of the river. Meanwhile, Burnside's corps reached Ox Ford, two miles west, but found the south bank so strongly held that he decided not to cross. However, Warren's corps crossed at Jericho Mill, four miles west. But before he could entrench, Cadmus Wilcox's division of Hill's corps made a frontal assault. Warren brought the attack to a halt, but only after both sides had lost about 1,500 men. Wright's 6th Corps now joined Warren at Jericho Mill.

This engagement demonstrated that Lee—despite his superb defensive stand at Spotsylvania—by no means had abandoned his

---

* At New Market, the Virginia Military Institute cadet corps of 225 boys aged sixteen to eighteen charged and captured a Federal battery, losing eight killed and forty-six wounded. This assault, with that of the 62d Virginia beside it, broke the back of Sigel's defense, forcing his army to retreat.

propensity for direct attack. Indeed, he was angry with Hill for hav-ing failed to push it hard. "Why," he asked Hill, "did you not do as Jackson would have done—thrown your whole force upon these people and driven them back?" And he told his staff: "We must strike them a blow! We must never let them pass us again!"[6]

But the Army of Northern Virginia did not have the power to drive back Grant's army. Once more Lee's genius for defensive war-fare came to the fore. He saw that Grant had divided his army, with 5th and 6th Corps at Jericho Ford, 9th Corps at Ox Ford, and 2d Corps at Hanover Junction. Accordingly, he built a line in the shape of an inverted V, the apex resting on the river at Ox Ford, Hill's corps holding one arm of the V from the ford to Little River, a mile and a half southwest, and Anderson and Ewell holding the other arm from the ford to the railroad, two and a half miles southeast. Lee thus held the river and the point of a wedge between the two wings of Grant's army. Neither could reinforce the other, while Lee readily could transfer troops to any endangered point.

To bring the two wings together, Grant ordered Burnside to attack and carry Ox Ford. But Burnside pronounced the job impos-sible, and did not attempt it. Hancock on the east and Warren on the west felt out the Rebel lines, but also advised against an attack.

Once more baffled by Lee's defenses, Grant gave up, and on the night of May 26, his army began its fourth turning movement since the opening of the campaign. It disappeared from the North Anna front, and began marching down the north bank toward Hanover and the Pamunkey River, eight miles southeast. Lee's army immediately moved to intercept the Federals. During this march Ewell's health finally gave way, and Early replaced him as 2d Corps commander.

On the afternoon of May 28 Sheridan's Union cavalry collided with Wade Hampton's and Fitz Lee's horsemen at Haw's Shop, just west of Hanover, in one of the severest cavalry engagements in war. The Federal cavalry, armed with Spencer magazine repeating car-bines, forced Hampton and Fitz Lee back.

The Union infantry then advanced to Totopotomoy Creek, an east-west stream about seven miles south of Hanover, but by this

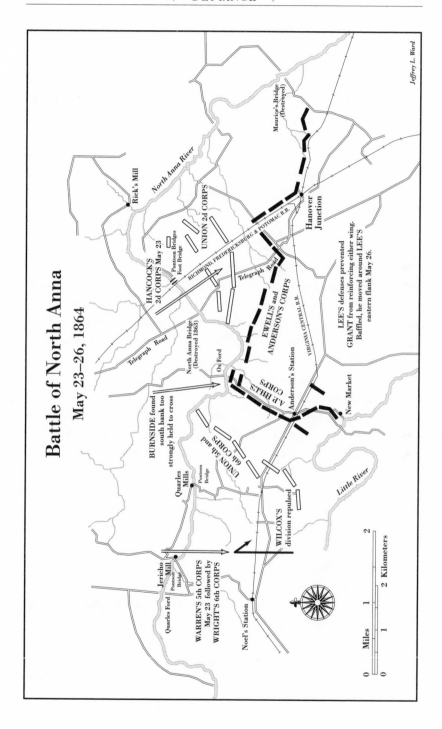

Battle of North Anna
May 23–26, 1864

Jeffrey L. Ward

Rick's Mill

North Anna River

Maurice's Bridge
(Destroyed)

Hanover
Junction

UNION 2d CORPS

Pontoon Bridges
Foot Bridge

HANCOCK'S
2d CORPS May 23

RICHMOND, FREDERICKSBURG & POTOMAC R.R.

Telegraph Road

EWELL'S and
ANDERSON'S CORPS

Telegraph Road

North Anna Bridge
(Destroyed 1863)

Ox Ford

LEE'S defenses prevented
GRANT from reinforcing either wing.
Baffled, he moved around LEE'S
eastern flank May 26.

VIRGINIA CENTRAL R.R.

Anderson's Station

A.P. HILL'S CORPS

New Market

BURNSIDE found
south bank too
strongly held to cross

UNION 5th and
6th CORPS

Little River

Quarles
Mills

Pontoon
Bridge

WILCOX'S
division repulsed

Jericho
Mill

Pontoon
Bridge

Quarles Ford

WARREN'S 5th CORPS
May 23 followed by
WRIGHT'S 6th CORPS

Noel's Station

Miles

2

1

0

2 Kilometers

1

0

time Lee's army had arrived and dug in on the south bank. Lee remained extremely bellicose, trying to shift over to the attack at any moment. For example, he ordered Early to seize a road junction half a mile in front of the Confederate lines, though an enemy brigade already occupied it. Early sent Edward Willis's Georgia brigade. It evicted the Union brigade, but stirred up an enemy division and artillery, which routed the Georgians with heavy loss, and cost Willis and two of his colonels their lives.

Grant decided the Confederate position along Totopotomoy Creek was too strong to attack, and commenced once more what the Rebel soldiers called his "sidling" movements, this time toward Cold Harbor, on the ground of the 1862 Battle of Gaines Mill, only about nine miles from Richmond.

Three brigades of Sheridan's cavalry took possession of Cold Harbor on May 31. Wright's 6th Corps was marching to relieve them, but was spread out along the road. Lee saw an opportunity to clear away the cavalry, and destroy Wright's corps before he could get help. To do the job, he sent Anderson's corps and a 6,000-man division under Robert F. Hoke, brought over from Beauregard's command.

But Anderson did not push an attack against the cavalry, and did not send Hoke's division around their flank. It was a bad job, and the only effect was to solidify a new line of Rebel entrenchments at Cold Harbor.

Grant now resolved on another major frontal assault against the Confederate army on June 1, using Wright's corps and a 16,000-man force, 18th Corps, under William F. Smith, transferred from Butler's army.

It was 6 P.M. before the two corps lined up, in three and four ranks, and attacked. But the fire was so intense that the Federals, except in one place, came nowhere near the Confederates, standing in a single rank behind their quickly dug breastworks. The exception was a fifty-yard gap of a wooded ravine and small stream between the right of Kershaw's division and the left of Hoke's. Federals passed through the ravine, turned the flank of both

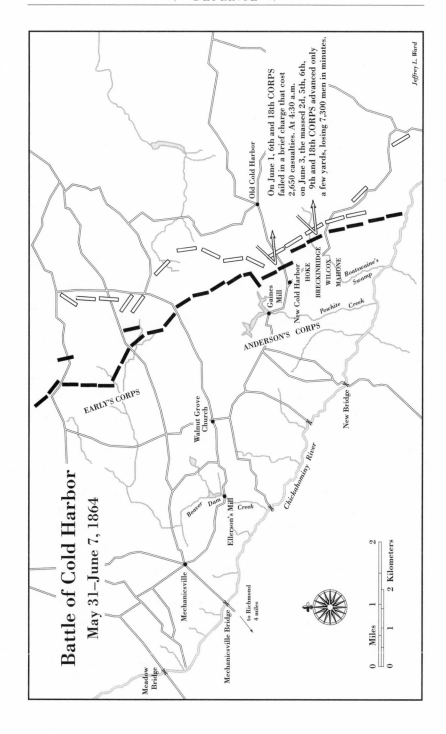

Battle of Cold Harbor
May 31–June 7, 1864

Meadow Bridge

Mechanicsville Bridge

to Richmond 4 miles

Mechanicsville

Ellerson's Mill

Beaver Dam Creek

Walnut Grove Church

EARLY'S CORPS

ANDERSON'S CORPS

Gaines Mill

New Cold Harbor

HOKE

BRECKINRIDGE

WILCOX

MAHONE

Boatswaine's Swamp

Powhite Creek

Chickahominy River

New Bridge

Old Cold Harbor

On June 1, 6th and 18th CORPS failed in a brief charge that cost 2,650 casualties. At 4:30 a.m. on June 3, the massed 2d, 5th, 6th, 9th and 18th CORPS advanced only a few yards, losing 7,300 men in minutes.

Jeffrey L. Ward

0 Miles 1 2

0 1 2 Kilometers

divisions, and captured a few prisoners, but were driven out by troops pulled from Pickett's and Field's divisions on the left.

In this single, brief charge the Federals lost 2,650 men, the Rebels only a few. The mathematics of defensive warfare were inexorable. Frontal attacks were failing. But Grant was not paying attention.

Grant ordered Hancock's 2d Corps and Warren's 5th Corps to join in the attack, with Burnside's 9th Corps massed behind the 5th to give support. Due to delays in getting into position, Grant postponed this massive, army-wide advance till 4:30 A.M. on June 3.

Lee, seeing that a major effort was brewing, moved Breckinridge's, Wilcox's, and Mahone's divisions to his right, extending the Confederate line nearly to the Chickahominy River, a couple miles south of Cold Harbor.* The move also stimulated Lee's offensive spirit: he sent Early around Hancock's abandoned trenches to sweep down the flank of the Union army. It was a quick and bold move, and, if Early had had more troops, might have dislodged the enemy line. But after some hard fighting, Federal guns brought the advance to a halt.

The 1864 campaign had educated soldiers as to what the war had come down to. To attack into the defensive trinity that had been perfected—infantry rifles, artillery canister, and men secure behind field fortifications—was almost a guarantee of death or maiming.

But Ulysses S. Grant was either not convinced or didn't care. As E. McIvor Law, commanding an Alabama brigade, observed: "We were not prepared for the unparalleled stubbornness and tenacity with which he persisted in his attacks under the fearful losses which his army sustained at the Wilderness and at Spotsylvania." The universal verdict of Confederate officers was that "he was no strategist and that he relied almost entirely upon the brute force of numbers for success."[7]

On the night of June 2–3, many Union soldiers, knowing what lay in store for them, pinned signs on their backs giving their

---

* The end of the Rebel line was the same Turkey Hill at Boatswain's Swamp that Fitz John Porter's Union corps had occupied during the Battle of Gaines Mill on June 27, 1862.

names and hometowns, so their families could be notified after they had died.

The Union soldiers had only about a hundred or so yards to cover between their positions and the Confederate trenches. But the Rebels were waiting. For an hour before the assault burst forth the Confederates, crouching in their depressions in the ground, were alert to muffled commands and smothered movements in front of them. The assault commenced with a vast cheering as the Federal lines of battle rushed forward.

They were met by sheets of rifle fire and by cannons pushed up to the firing lines unleashing double-shotted canister directly into the Federal host. The roar of the firing overwhelmed the senses of everyone on the battlefield, and the noise reached Richmond, where people came out on the streets to listen. Both armies were colliding with their whole strength, more fully than ever before. Within seconds, thousands of Union soldiers fell, dead or wounded. Whole ranks of Federal brigades vanished.

The assaults generally reached only about fifty yards from the Rebel lines, though in a few places Federal officers died on or near the Confederate parapets. At only one point did the Federals overrun a Rebel trench, and capture cannons and a few prisoners. This occurred where troops from Francis C. Barlow's division approached unobserved within seventy-five yards of the Rebel lines. But nearby Confederates quickly recaptured the guns, and healed the breach.

Within minutes, 7,300 Union soldiers were killed or wounded. Confederate casualties were extremely small, perhaps not more than a few hundred.

Grant demanded more attacks. But, as William Swinton, a Northern historian, wrote, every man believed that further effort was hopeless. When Meade sent orders to renew the assaults, "no man stirred, and the immobile lines pronounced a verdict, silent, yet emphatic, against further slaughter."[8]

Grant, refusing to admit he had been defeated, would not ask for a flag of truce until the evening of June 7. By then the most seriously wounded Union soldiers had died.

As word of the massacre at Cold Harbor seeped into the North, a deep gloom that had been sweeping the Union intensified. Faith in Grant eroded. Families everywhere were mourning dead sons and husbands. Enlisting had almost ceased, despite huge bounties. Politicians were predicting that Lincoln would lose reelection in November.

During this period, the Federal lines at Cold Harbor remained still.* Grant's direct-attack plan had failed. He was being forced to see the futility of frontal assaults, and come up with an entire change in plan of campaign. He resolved to cross the James ten miles below City Point (now Hopewell) with most of his army, swing around Butler's bottled-up force at Bermuda Hundred, seize Petersburg, and cut the main railroad connection of Richmond with the rest of the Confederacy.

Grant's envelopment of Lee's army took place over three days, June 15–17, 1864. During this period Lee refused to believe it, and was extremely slow in moving his army to meet the threat. Petersburg was at first defended only by 2,500 men under Beauregard.

On June 15, troops of William F. Smith's 18th Corps seized part of a thinly manned outer line of Confederate entrenchments, forcing Beauregard to a new defensive line a half mile closer to the city, occupied by Hoke's division of 5,000 men, which arrived during the evening. Beauregard brought up Bushrod Johnson's division (7,000 men) from Bermuda Hundred on June 16, and doggedly held off attacks by the gathering Union army until the night of June 17, when he pulled his troops back to a third line half a mile behind the second. There the men began to dig in.

---

* But the horrible nature of trench warfare was being thrust upon military leaders. During the period of June 3–12, 1864, John Gibbon's single Union division reported 280 men killed or wounded by sharpshooter fire. Porter Alexander told of a twelve-pounder Napoleon in Henry Colter Cabell's artillery battalion that, when being tipped to replace wheels that had been shot to pieces, thirty-seven Minié balls fell out of the barrel. See Porter Alexander, *Fighting for the Confederacy*, 412.

Beauregard was able finally, at 3 A.M. on June 18, to convince Lee that Grant's army was at Petersburg. Lee then acted with alacrity, directing Anderson's corps to march at once for Petersburg.

At 4 A.M. on the 18th 50,000 Federals assaulted the second line, finding, to their surprise, that it was empty. Grant now had a great opportunity to sweep the Confederates out of their new and still rudimentary third line, and end the war in a day. Beauregard probably had no more than 10,000 men remaining, and Kershaw's 5,000-man division of Anderson's corps couldn't arrive until 7:30 A.M., and Field's, about the same size, until 9 A.M.

Grant had achieved a coup in getting the Army of the Potomac across the James. But the officers and men felt little elation. They remembered more the 62,000 men the army had lost from the Wilderness to Petersburg. Demoralized and utterly exhausted, like their Rebel counterparts, the Union soldiers did not press the attack, but pulled back and began building entrenchments of their own. The investment of Petersburg began. The lines established remained substantially in the same position to the last days of the war.

★ 13 ★

STALEMATE

Although Lee had frustrated Grant every time he tried to turn the corner on the Confederate army and had inflicted almost unimaginable casualties, the Federal commander nevertheless had moved steadily southward. He had crossed the James and invested Petersburg, not as the final achievement of a carefully executed plan, but because Lee had blocked his direct strike at Richmond from the north. However, the move on Petersburg, though opportunistic, was the culminating act that strategically nullified all Lee's tactical gains.

Grant had achieved what no other Union general had been able to accomplish. He had penetrated to the very heart of Lee's stronghold. By getting on Lee's flank, and threatening to cut the railways, Grant had placed Lee in an impossible position. Though Lee had wounded the Army of the Potomac to the point that it was momentarily incapable of decisive movement, the blows would heal. The immensely superior North could replace its losses. While Grant's army would grow into an overwhelming force, Lee's army, if it remained at Petersburg, would be slowly eaten away.

Lee could hold Richmond and throw the war into a stalemate—but only for a while. Defending Petersburg was a strategy of defeat. Grant would not win the war at Petersburg, but Lee could lose it there.

On the other hand, Lee could abandon Richmond and restore a war of movement. This choice offered real chances for success, in one of two ways: a semiguerrilla struggle, or a strategy that exchanged territory for maneuvering room. Either would capitalize on Confederate advantages and at least partially neutralize Union advantages.

The South was an ideal region for guerrilla warfare. The Confederates possessed an army whose members were filled with a sense of rightness in their cause and a friendly population that would hide, feed, and clothe partisans and spy on Federals. The South itself was large, with wide rivers, deep forests, mountains impossible to conquer, and a communications system inadequate to begin with, greatly damaged by the war, and imposing severe limitations on the movement of Union armies. Sometime in the spring of 1864 Lee told President Davis that, "with my army in the mountains of Virginia, I could carry on this war for twenty years longer."[*]

The alternative—a defensive strategy combined with movement and offensive strikes—offered at least as attractive possibilities. In

---

[*] J. William Jones, *Life and Letters of Robert Edward Lee, Soldier and Man* (Washington, 1906), 295; Freeman, *R.E. Lee*, vol. 3, 496 n. A guerrilla strategy implied breaking up Confederate field armies into small units operating out of safe bases in mountains, forests, or swamps, or submerging like "fish" in the "water" of the civilian population. Guerrillas could strike at enemy railways, convoys, occupied cities, depots, and isolated units, then retreat to their bases or take off their uniforms and return temporarily to civilian pursuits. Although the Federals could have occupied the entire South, they would have had to disperse forces widely to protect supply lines and bases. Guerrillas could have decided when, where, how, and in what strength to attack, giving them the initiative, and turning the Union army into a passive occupying force that could only respond to the actions of the guerrillas, not take decisive action on its own. So long as the South remained defiant, the Federals could never have won, yet would have suffered continuous losses in manpower and goods. In time the Northern people would have become disillusioned, and required the government to end the war, thus giving the South its independence. A guerrilla strategy required the support of the civilian population, who would feed, clothe, and hide guerrillas. In the Napoleonic wars in the early years of the nineteenth century, Spain neutralized a large French army by such guerrilla tactics. A third of a century after the Civil War, the Afrikaans-speaking Boers of South Africa gained practical independence from Britain by carrying out a similar guerrilla war. Alexander the Great of Macedonia believed that a country could not be held in subjection by a foreign army. J.F.C. Fuller said that Alexander's first claim to greatness lies in this idea. See Fuller, *The Generalship of Alexander the Great* (New Brunswick, N.J.: Rutgers University Press, 1960; New York: Da Capo Press, 1989), 271–72.

addition to the Army of Northern Virginia, the South possessed a strong army under Joe Johnston at Atlanta, while other, smaller, detachments were scattered throughout the South, inefficiently employed in local defenses. If Lee abandoned Richmond, marched his army southward, and swelled his numbers by picking up isolated units, Grant would be presented with a daunting task.

The British strategist J. F. C. Fuller argued that Northern forces might have occupied Virginia, but would have been unable to move far into central or Piedmont North Carolina because of dependence on a single railroad, running through central North Carolina to Charlotte and beyond.[*] Confederate forces operating on the flanks could have constantly cut the railway, crippling the Northern army obliged to protect this vital supply line.[†]

---

[*] J. F. C. Fuller, *Military History of the Western World* (New York: Funk and Wagnalls, 1954–57; New York: Da Capo, 1987), vol. 3, 15. In 1863, the Confederate government built a line joining Danville, Virginia, and Greensboro, North Carolina. Until then, the main line through central North Carolina went from Greensboro through Raleigh, connecting by the Weldon Railroad with Richmond. See Porter Alexander, *Fighting for the Confederacy*, 124; Freeman, *R. E. Lee*, vol. 3, 168; *Official Reports*, vol. 29, pt. 2, 736.

[†] William T. Sherman wrote that "railroads are the weakest things in war; a single man with a match can destroy and cut off communications." Wooden bridges and water tanks could be burned, trains attacked from ambush, and tracks torn up. Sherman wrote that, with a Federal advance, "the war closes in behind and leaves the same enemy behind." Because of that, he said it would be necessary to reconquer the South "as we did from the Indians," presumably by driving all Southerners out of their homes, leaving a desert behind. In 1864 he wrote: "I am satisfied, and have been all the time, that the problem of the war consists in the awful fact that the present class of men who rule the South must be killed outright rather than in the conquest of territory." The Confederacy already had a brilliant record of the effects of strikes on Union communications. From December 1862 to early January 1863, Nathan Bedford Forrest killed or captured 2,500 Federals, seized 10,000 rifles, burned fifty railroad bridges, and severely damaged the Mobile and Ohio Railroad in a raid into western Tennessee. This ruined an overland advance by Ulysses S. Grant. Early in 1863, 13,000 Rebel cavalry and guerrillas threatened north Mississippi and west Tennessee. To defend against them, the North deployed 51,000 men. In the spring of 1863, Grant's army before Vicksburg numbered 36,000 men, while the forces guarding his lines of communication northward amounted to 62,000. See Hattaway and Jones, 250, 300, 317, 357; Earl Schenck Miers, *The General Who Marched to Hell* (New York: Dorset, 1990), 218.

(NATIONAL ARCHIVES)

Joseph E. Johnston

Grant's difficulty in pursuing the Army of Northern Virginia might have given Lee time to reinforce Johnston and destroy Sherman's army. Even if this had failed, the remaining strength of the Confederacy could have been concentrated into one army or two cooperating armies that, operating on interior lines, could have exploited the wide expanses of Georgia, the Carolinas, and Virginia, kept contact with Alabama and Mississippi, and very likely surrounded and defeated enemy columns that might have penetrated into the region.*

Half a year later, Sherman recognized the danger. Prior to the Carolinas campaign early in 1865, Sherman questioned whether Lee "would permit us, almost unopposed, to pass through the states of South and North Carolina, cutting off and consuming the very supplies on which he depended to feed his army," and remarking that "if Lee is a soldier of genius, he will seek to transfer his army to

---

* Neither the Tredegar Iron Works in Richmond nor the port of Wilmington, North Carolina, was vital to the Confederacy. The ironworks made cannons, but the Rebels had sufficient artillery, and could capture more from the Union army. By moving into the interior, Confederate forces could exploit local food and other resources, replacing the limited supplies coming to Petersburg by way of blockade-runners into Wilmington. The one great need was gunpowder, and the South possessed the world's largest powder factory at Augusta, Georgia. Lee might have followed a strategy similar to that of Frederick the Great of Prussia in the Seven Years War of 1756–63. Frederick did not have enough strength to destroy his enemies, but won partial victories, kept his own army in existence, and waited for an opportunity that would give him victory. This occurred in 1762, when Peter III became czar of Russia, and withdrew from the war.

Raleigh or Columbia; if he is a man simply of detail, he will remain where he is, and his speedy defeat is sure."[1]

The evidence is that Lee was a man of detail. Despite his comment about fighting in the mountains, Lee was uninterested either in a guerrilla struggle or in conducting a wide-open campaign of movement in the interior. He refused to consider the abandonment of Richmond. When an aide, Charles S. Venable, asked him why he didn't give up the city, Lee responded sharply that, if he did so, he would be a traitor to his government.[2] By this decision, he ensured that the Confederacy would die.

A remarkable fact about the last nine months of the war is that Lee stood immobile until actually evicted by Grant. The only possible way Lee's strategy could have resulted in a Southern victory was for the people of the North to become weary of the war, and give it up. Thus, Lee depended, not on his own actions or those of his army, but on the reaction of his enemy—not on the offensive spirit that had inspired his army till now, but on despair overtaking his enemy.

For a policy of despair to succeed, the news from the battlefronts had to be uniformly bad.

Even in Virginia this was not so, because Grant, in besieging Petersburg, was able to tinge with a bit of success a campaign that otherwise had been a disaster.

But the news coming from Georgia was lifting Northern morale. Since May, Sherman's army had pushed Joe Johnston's Confederates relentlessly back through north Georgia, primarily by *not* following the tactics Grant was practicing in Virginia. Grant attacked frontally the blocking positions Lee took up, suffering staggering casualties. Sherman, faced with the same sort of barricades by Johnston, acted far more wisely than Grant. He simply swung around the Rebel defenses, forcing Johnston to retreat. Sherman's losses were tiny, and by July 1864—when Petersburg was settling into a deadlock— Sherman was at the gates of Atlanta threatening to break in.

Johnston's strategy was utterly wrong. Instead of setting up defensive blocking positions with his whole army, Johnston should have divided most of it into numerous detached forces in the rough mountains of north Georgia, and sent them to cut repeatedly the single-track railroad leading back to Chattanooga. This was Sherman's Achilles' heel, his only means of supplying his 100,000-man army. Breaks on this railroad—as well as cavalry strikes on the line running back to Louisville, Kentucky—would have forced Sherman to use most of his strength to reopen his supply line, and prevented him from moving on Atlanta at all.

Johnston did not see this, always challenged Sherman head-on, and ignored the railroad. As Porter Alexander observed: "It is a fact that Johnston had never fought but one aggressive battle, the battle of Seven Pines, which was phenomenally mismanaged."[3]

Sherman's success relieved to a considerable degree the black mood brought on by Grant's failures. It also suggested that more good news might rekindle the North's determination to win. By becoming passive, by responding only to their enemy's actions and abandoning positive actions of their own, Lee and Johnston left in the hands of the Northern people—and their generals—the decision as to whether the North would continue the war.

In making this choice for passivity, Lee and Johnston disregarded the still-awesome strengths of the Confederate army. These were the morale, élan, and dedication of the soldiers and their skill as fighters. This was especially true of the Army of Northern Virginia, which could move fast and decisively, and whose veteran units possessed a strong cohesion and sense of mutual confidence and loyalty. All of these assets were wasted in the trenches of Petersburg.

Though Lee became idle at Petersburg, he did not give up his desire to return to the offensive. But the strikes he authorized were only delaying tactics. These efforts were seen by many later writers as evidence of Lee's irrepressible effort to win the war by offensive campaigns. They were nothing of the sort. They were limited, indecisive efforts, designed only to prolong the conflict.

In fact, they reflected the offensive policy Lee had followed throughout the war. Lee had never gone for the jugular. He did not have a true killer's instinct, as, for example, Stonewall Jackson had.

While Jackson wanted to strike into the North and destroy factories, railways, and people's livelihoods, Lee wanted only to win victories over Northern armies on the field of battle, not fight the Northern people. For example, while Jackson sought to drive John Pope's army against the Rapidan in August 1862 and destroy it, Lee desired only to push it out of Virginia.*

Thus, Lee's decision immediately after Cold Harbor to send Jubal Early on a dramatic strike directly against Washington was not an effort to seize the Union capital, and win the war by force. In 1888 Early wrote: "General Lee did not expect me to enter Washington. His orders were merely to threaten the city, and when I suggested to him the idea of capturing it he said it would be impossible."[4]

The last nine months of the war, therefore, were a slow decline to surrender. The Confederacy had no other senior commander who could reverse this slide. Of the full generals besides Lee and Johnston, Braxton Bragg was incompetent and Beauregard had wonderful theories that evaporated when responsibility fell on his shoulders. When Beauregard was being pressed by Halleck after Shiloh in the spring of 1862, for example, he could think of nothing to do but retreat. None of Lee's or Johnston's corps commanders was a superior field commander. Early came closest, but he mostly attacked the enemy directly in front of him, and did not know, as Stonewall Jackson did, how to strike at his opponent's weakness.

⁓ ⁓

Early's march on Washington was a response to a conception of Grant to send Philip Sheridan's cavalry corps west from around Hanover Junction, destroying the Virginia Central Railroad, and

---

* Lee apparently had as much compassion for his enemy as for his own men. On August 16, 1864, in the midst of an engagement north of the James, a group of Federal prisoners came up boldly to Lee and complained that a Rebel private had taken one Union soldier's hat. Lee at once stopped what he was doing, sought out the Confederate soldier, and ordered him to return the hat. See *Southern Historical Society Papers*, vol. 17, 242; Freeman, *R.E. Lee*, vol. 3, 484–85.

linking up with David Hunter, Sigel's successor, who was marching up the Shenandoah Valley with 18,000 men, burning public and private property as he went, including the Virginia Military Institute.

The idea was for Sheridan and Hunter to unite at Lynchburg, and destroy anything that could provide the Confederacy with food and supplies—railroads, farms, private homes, public buildings, factories, and depots. However, Wade Hampton stopped Sheridan on June 11–12 at Trevillians, near Gordonsville.

Consequently, Lee saw a chance both to dispose of Hunter and to use Early's corps and Breckinridge's division to frighten the North, and hopefully relieve pressure on Petersburg by diverting troops to protect the Federal capital.

Gathering a force about half the size of Hunter's army, including convalescents from hospitals, militia, and the VMI cadet corps, Early stopped a modest attack by Hunter west of Lynchburg on June 18. He was preparing to move against Hunter on the 19th but found that the Union general had already turned tail and started running. Early pursued him across the Blue Ridge, through Salem, and only stopped when Hunter retreated toward Lewisburg, West Virginia, deep in the Appalachians.

Hunter was a great embarrassment to the Union army. Grant, trying to put as good a face on his flight as possible, reported that Hunter had retreated "owing to a want of ammunition." Early scoffed that "this is a little remarkable," since the expedition was a long-planned, prominent feature of the 1864 campaign, and he'd done little fighting to expend ammunition anyway.[5]

Early now turned north and drove down the Shenandoah Valley with 10,000 infantry and 2,000 cavalry. On July 5, he crossed the Potomac at Shepherdstown, moved over South Mountain, and occupied Frederick. He sent Bradley T. Johnson's cavalry brigade eastward on July 9 with orders to break the railroad on the Gunpowder River between Baltimore and Wilmington, and between Baltimore and Washington.

Meanwhile Early's infantry came up on about 6,000 Federals along the Monocacy River, a couple miles southeast of Frederick.

About half the Union troops were green recruits under Lew Wallace, the rest part of James B. Ricketts's division of Horatio Wright's 6th Corps, rushed northward from Petersburg by Grant. Early dislodged the Federals by sending John McCausland's cavalry brigade, dismounted, onto their left flank. The Federals retreated, after losing about 1,900 men, mostly captured. Early lost about 700.

Early now marched straight for Washington, arriving July 11 at Fort Stevens—one of the ring of bastions around Washington—two and a half miles south of Silver Spring on the Seventh Street Turnpike in the District of Columbia. As Early's infantry approached over ground cleared within cannon range, troops of the 6th and 19th Corps, sent up from Petersburg and Fort Monroe, began filing into the fortress and opened fire with artillery already emplaced there.

Early thought about attacking on the morning of July 12, but, seeing that the trenches and ramparts of Fort Stevens were heavily manned, backed off, withdrawing during the night. Meanwhile Bradley Johnson's cavalry burned railroad bridges around Baltimore, and withdrew as well.

Pursued by the 6th and 19th Corps, Early crossed the Potomac at White's Ferry near Leesburg on July 14, retired through Snicker's Gap into the Shenandoah Valley, and stopped on July 22 at Strasburg.

Early's whole effort was little more than a raid, and not effective. He had used little imagination striking straight for Washington. The forts surrounding the city made it immune to direct assaults. He would have caused much more difficulty by descending with his whole force on the railroads north and south of Baltimore, where he sent only Bradley Johnson's small cavalry brigade. This would have shut off the food supply to Washington. With such a small force, Early's only hope was to reduce the pressure on Petersburg, not reach a decision in Maryland.

If Early had been a resourceful commander, he could have created such chaos in Maryland and such fear of starvation in Washington that a large part of Grant's army might have been diverted to evict him. This might have given Lee an opportunity to strike at the reduced force remaining at Petersburg. In the event, Early was more concerned about his line of retreat than his avenue of advance. Thus his march on Washington had no chance of achieving lasting gain.

Rather, the advance precipitated a decision by Grant to carry out one of the most damaging campaigns of the war: he sent Philip Sheridan to the Shenandoah Valley with instructions to defeat Early and destroy crops, granaries, houses, shops, animals, farm equipment, and anything else that could provide food or goods for the Confederacy. The comment attributed to Sheridan after his depredations—that a crow crossing the valley would have to carry its own rations—sums up Grant's intention and Sheridan's achievement.

Sheridan received more than 50,000 troops. During most of the campaign Early commanded no more than 13,000 men.

On September 19, Sheridan and Early collided in a face-to-face battle at Winchester, both sides fighting without cover, with one frontal assault after another. Sheridan drove the Confederates from the field, but lost 5,000 men to Early's 3,600, including division commander Robert Rodes, killed.

Early retreated to Fisher's Hill, just south of Strasburg, but on September 22 was easily thrown into retreat by the surprise movement of two divisions under George Crook around Early's western flank. Sheridan lost only about 500 men, Early 1,200, most of them captured. Early fled past Harrisonburg, and turned toward Port Republic, nearly fifty miles south, where Lee had hurried Joseph B. Kershaw's division to join him.[*]

This opened most of the Shenandoah Valley to destruction. Union cavalry moved to Staunton and Waynesboro, tore up railway track and bridges and demolished large quantities of army stores. The horsemen then turned back north and burned, ruined, or carried away everything of use from Staunton to Winchester. All supplies for the Confederate army vanished, but also most of the food, animals,

---

[*] Lee did not believe Sheridan had more than 12,000 infantry, when in fact he had almost 33,000 in the field, plus a garrison at Harpers Ferry and about 6,500 cavalry. See *Official Records*, vol. 43, pt. 1, 61; Freeman, *R.E. Lee*, vol. 3, 495.

and tools for the sustenance of the civilian population, which was thrown into destitution.

Sheridan withdrew his army of about 40,000 men to Cedar Creek, just north of Strasburg and a mile and a half south of Middletown.

On October 19, 1864, Early secretly moved up his 9,000 infantry and 1,200 of his 3,000 cavalry, and attacked Sheridan's left, or eastern, flank. He achieved complete surprise, threw Crook's corps and William H. Emory's 19th Corps into headlong flight, dislodged Horatio Wright's 6th Corps, and seized eighteen cannons. The Federals rallied tentatively just west of Middletown, but the Confederates pushed them north, where Wright's corps re-formed about a mile and a half above the village. It looked like a devastating Union defeat.

However, the Union cavalry gathered on both flanks of Early's army, and two brigades on the east charged and checked the Confederates. Also many of the hungry Rebels left ranks and plundered the abandoned camps of the Federals. In addition, 6th Corps remained in line of battle, but Early concluded that it would retreat shortly. General John Gordon disagreed.

"This is the 6th Corps, General," Gordon said. "It will not go unless we drive it from the field."

"Yes, it will go directly," Early answered.[6]

But Wright's corps did not go, and Early decided to chance nothing more, trying to hold what he had gained.

Sheridan had not been on the field when the battle opened. He arrived around 10:30 A.M. and, rallying his hugely superior army, ordered a general advance in the late afternoon. Though Rebels on the east repulsed a Federal cavalry charge, the Confederates knew they were greatly outnumbered. When a Union infantry force penetrated their line on the extreme west and began rolling it up, the entire Confederate line broke and ran, many surrendering as they fled.

It was a complete rout, though the Federals lost nearly 6,000 killed, wounded, or captured to Early's 4,200, and most of his artillery and trains. One of the Confederate dead was Dodson Ramseur, the outstanding division commander from North Carolina.

Early withdrew the remnants of his force to New Market, and remained on the defensive for the remainder of the war, his infantry going back to Lee. Most of Sheridan's infantry also went back to Petersburg or to other posts.

When Early sent his report to General Lee, by way of his engineer, Jedediah Hotchkiss, he admonished Hotchkiss "not to tell General Lee that we ought to have advanced in the morning at Middletown, for . . . we ought to have done so."[7]

Why did Early attack an army three times the size of his own at Cedar Creek? It is not remarkable that he lost. It is more remarkable that he gained as much as he did. Early answered the question: "It was of the utmost consequence that Sheridan should be prevented from sending troops to Grant, and General Lee, in a letter received a day or two before, had expressed an earnest desire that a victory should be gained in the valley if possible, and it could not be gained without fighting for it."[8]

Once more, Lee was willing to risk battle to prolong the war, but not to win it. Sheridan's victory lifted Northern spirits. Stonewall Jackson had been able to transform some of Lee's limited aims into spectacular victories. The lesser generals now serving Lee, with lesser means at their disposal, were unable to do so.

⌒⌒ ⌒⌒

In June 1864, the Army of the Potomac lay stymied before the works at Petersburg. In theory Grant could have continued his flanking movements, swinging around Petersburg to the south. But Grant's army was unwilling to undertake such efforts with the enthusiasm it had exhibited earlier. Since the Wilderness, it had lost as many men as Lee counted in his whole army. Casualties were twice Lee's. Officers and men no longer had faith in the bludgeoning tactics of Grant. Cold Harbor had convinced the rank and file that he was a

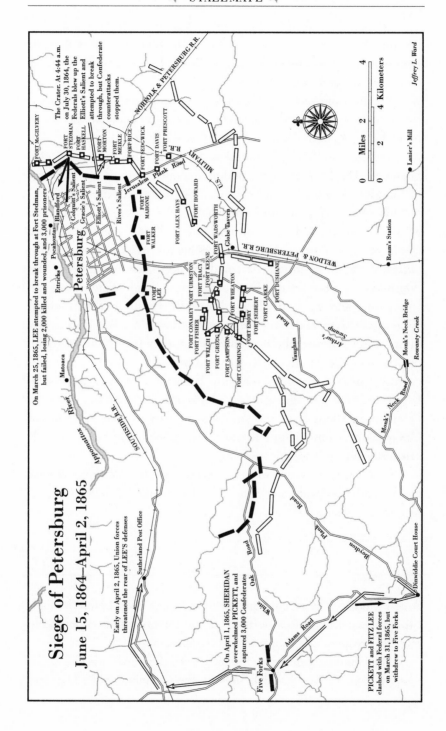

Siege of Petersburg
June 15, 1864–April 2, 1865

On March 25, 1865, LEE attempted to break through at Fort Stedman, but failed, losing 2,000 killed and wounded, and 3,000 prisoners

The Crater: At 4:44 a.m. on July 30, 1864, the Federals blew up the Elliott's Salient and attempted to break through, but Confederate counterattacks stopped them.

Early on April 2, 1865, Union forces threatened the rear of LEE'S defenses

On April 1, 1865, SHERIDAN overwhelmed PICKETT, and captured 3,000 Confederates

PICKETT and FITZ LEE clashed with Federal forces on March 31, 1865, but withdrew to Five Forks

Jeffrey L. Ward

butcher. As they demonstrated on June 18, 1864, in front of the still weakly manned and incomplete defenses at Petersburg, the soldiers no longer pressed their attacks.

When Grant ordered a flanking move around Lee's right or south on June 22 by the 2d and 6th Corps, the commanders carelessly left a gap between their forces, and William Mahone's division rushed into it, rolled up two Union divisions, and captured 1,600 prisoners. The Federals' poor performance was due as much to low morale as to Mahone's quickness in exploiting a weakness.

Another swing around the southern flank resulted in few gains. Grant wanted to destroy Lee's railroad connections by means of cavalry strikes. Federal horsemen broke up several miles of track on the Weldon Railroad, leading south, tore up the Southside (Lynchburg) Railroad from near Petersburg to Burkeville, and the Danville road from Burkeville to the Staunton (Roanoke) River, a distance of about forty miles. But a tiny, raw militia force stopped the horsemen when they tried to destroy the bridge over the Staunton River. And when Rooney Lee's Rebel cavalry came up on their rear, the Federals retreated at once to Reams Station on the Weldon Railroad, eight miles south of Petersburg. There they ran into an ambush by two brigades of Mahone's division on June 28, and lost about 1,500 men, all their artillery, and their wagon train.

It took weeks to repair the damaged lines, but Grant concluded he did not have cavalry superiority, and suspended strikes by horsemen on Lee's supply lines.

⌒⌒ ⌒⌒

A new kind of warfare emerged at Petersburg. Never before had the two armies settled into a permanent confrontation that appeared to offer no prospect of a return to mobile operations.

The Petersburg defenses foreshadowed the trench warfare of the western front in World War I. Indeed, the commanders in Flanders and France virtually copied the techniques the Confederates and Federals pioneered at Petersburg, modifying them only to accommodate the different weapons developed in the interim.

The essential elements of the Petersburg defenses were numerous bulwarked citadels or individual redoubts where artillery was mounted, and infantry trenches and parapets with ditches and abatis in front connecting the citadels. Troops reached this main line of resistance from the rear by a maze of deep, narrow cross-trenches, or traverses. In places, both sides built pits, with "head logs" or sandbags above loopholes through which rifles could be fired without exposing the soldiers greatly.

High-velocity rifled artillery and smoothbore cannons firing canister were of little use against troops protected by entrenchments, though they were necessary to break up assaults across the "killing ground" between the lines. To reach the enemy in the trenches, both sides resorted to mortars. These were weapons with short barrels that could lob a shell a limited distance on a high trajectory directly down on the heads of men in trenches. They were not very accurate, but dangerous enough to force soldiers to build "bombproofs," or deep holes covered with logs, rocks, and earth. The greatest danger came not from artillery or mortars, but from sharpshooters, who became so proficient that the slightest exposure of a person was likely to result in his wounding or death.

Though Lee saw no way to extricate his army, Grant became exasperated quickly. However, the failed flanking movement to the south on June 22 gave him pause. Then Henry Pleasants, a mining engineer commanding a regiment of miners from the Schuylkill coal region of Pennsylvania, came up with a radical idea. He proposed that his men dig a tunnel 500 feet long to reach under the most exposed Confederate salient, Elliott's, "protruding," as one Federal officer wrote, "like the ugly horn of a rhinoceros,"[9] a quarter of a mile southeast of Blandford Cemetery on the eastern side of Petersburg. The miners proposed to fill the hole with gunpowder, blow it up, and create a huge gap through which the Union army could rush and achieve almost instant victory.

Pleasants had a hard time convincing the senior generals, but Ambrose Burnside liked the idea, and he authorized the start of digging on June 25. The Confederates quickly suspected the threat. Porter Alexander, going on a short leave July 1 because of a wound, told Lee he was convinced the Federals were mining. Rebel diggers sank countershafts, but found nothing.

To divert attention, Grant sent 2d Corps north of the James on July 27 to threaten Richmond. Lee rushed up four infantry divisions and about half his cavalry, thinning the forces at Petersburg to only 18,000 men—Robert Hoke's and Bushrod Johnson's divisions of Beauregard's command, and Billy Mahone's division and part of Cadmus M. Wilcox's division of 3d Corps.

By the night of July 29–30, Lee was satisfied that the Federals were merely feinting toward Richmond, and were preparing to attack Petersburg. At 2 A.M. on July 30, he issued a general warning. Hoke, on the left, was defending from the northern edge of Petersburg at the Appomattox River to a point nearly a mile south. On Hoke's right was Johnson's division containing the salient of Stephen Elliott Jr.'s South Carolina brigade, where evidence of mining was strongest.

At 4:44 A.M. on July 30, 1864, a mighty explosion of 8,000 pounds of gunpowder threw men, earth, guns, carriages, and timbers high into the air, destroyed 135 feet of Elliott's front line, and left a crater thirty feet deep, and extending 97 feet front to rear. The blast killed nearly everyone in nine South Carolina companies, as well as the men of R. G. Pegram's Virginia battery, emplaced nearby.

As soon as Lee got word of the catastrophe, he ordered the line restored at once. A. P. Hill rushed off to bring up Mahone's division on the south, and it moved quickly.

Meanwhile James H. Ledlie's 1st Division of Burnside's 9th Corps rushed into the crater, with orders to push on and seize Cemetery Hill or Blandford Cemetery, about 400 yards to the northwest. Ledlie himself remained for the whole action well to the rear in a bombproof. The press of men created a huge traffic jam, and when some soldiers climbed the steep far slope to move on to the cemetery, survivors of Elliott's brigade and Virginians of Henry A. Wise's brigade to the south shot them down. This sent Ledlie's entire division back into the crater, where it milled about helplessly.

Confederate artillery sprang into action. On Wise's front, one gun, pointed directly at the crater, fired canister into the mass of Federals with deadly precision. On a rise a couple hundred yards northwest, four twelve-pounder Napoleons had a clear line of fire at virtually point-blank range. The gunners fired as fast as they could serve the pieces. Guns and mortars located farther away also got the range and plastered the hole with round after round.

Meanwhile, Robert B. Potter's 2d Division of Burnside's corps, supposed to advance on Ledlie's right, failed to negotiate the labyrinth of Confederate trenches, cross-trenches, and bombproofs there, and, stung by heavy Rebel canister and rifle fire, also pressed into the crater—creating an even denser mob of leaderless soldiers.

As Major William H. Powell, an aide to Ledlie, wrote: "Every organization melted away, as soon as it entered this hole in the ground, into a mass of human beings clinging by toes and heels to the almost perpendicular sides. If a man was shot on the crest, he fell and rolled to the bottom of the pit."[10]

General Potter organized a small undertaking with two regiments that seized about 200 yards of Rebel trenches to the north, but got no farther. When Orlando B. Willcox came up with his 3d Division of 9th Corps, he realized no more troops could be squeezed into the crater, and carried Rebel entrenchments for a few dozen yards to the left or south of the crater. However, he was unable to hold them long.

The final act of Federal command madness took place at 7 A.M.: General Burnside ordered his fourth division, 4,300 black soldiers, mostly former slaves, commanded by white officers and under Edward Ferrero, to press forward at all hazards to Cemetery Hill. The two-brigade division, under galling fire, moved bravely around the crest of the crater. But Rebel fire was so intense that the soldiers sought cover in trenches and below the crest. General Ferrero, safe in a bombproof in the rear, sent orders to the division to attack Cemetery Hill at once.

Though Henry G. Thomas, commanding one of the black brigades, wrote that "I thought not a man would live to reach the crest," the soldiers obediently moved forward.[11] John C. Haskell's sixteen-gun battalion on the Jerusalem Plank Road 600 yards west of the mine quickly broke up this attack.

Meanwhile, Mahone was forming his division in a ravine about 200 yards behind the crater, though J.C.C. Sanders's Alabama brigade had not arrived. Seeing Ferrero's troops moving beyond the crater, Mahone ordered his men to charge. The Confederate line swept up the hill, and shattered the black division—killing or wounding 900 men in Thomas's brigade, about 150 in the other. But the Rebels were stopped short of the crater's edge by murderous Union fire.

Sanders's Alabamians arrived at 11 A.M., the last uncommitted force Lee possessed. The rest of his line was almost stripped bare. On Mahone's old front, only one man every twenty paces remained. Knowing they had to win the crater's edge or all was lost, Sanders's men stopped for nothing, and rushed to the edge, though many men fell on the way. Some Alabamians lifted their caps on ramrods just over the rim. Hundreds of bullets tore the caps to tatters. At once the Alabamians sprang into the crater, followed by the other brigades. A bloody melee ensued. One captain fell dead with eleven bayonet thrusts.

Bewildered, Federals who could do so fell back into a smaller pit in the crater. The Rebels were about to follow when wild cries, shouts, uplifted hands, and frantic appeals showed that the Union soldiers in the front were trying to surrender. Meantime thousands of Federals behind scurried across the open ground to their trenches.

The battle of the crater was over. Rebels quickly ran an earthwork around the edge of the pit, and restored the line. The Federals lost 4,000 men, about half killed or wounded, the rest prisoners. The Confederates suffered about 1,500 casualties—278 killed when the mine exploded.

The crater had emphasized the gruesome reality of trench warfare. Lee had won a tactical victory, but nothing else. Strategically, Grant still held the Confederate army in a tight battle embrace, limiting Lee's mobility, but not his own.

For Lee to continue this sort of warfare was a guarantee of defeat, but he remained obdurately in place. Indeed, he concentrated on small tasks to achieve small gains. For example, the Federals were digging a canal across Dutch Gap on the James, about five miles southeast of Drewry's Bluff. They wanted to get their boats beyond range of cannon fire from the Rebel line a few miles west. Lee decided to interrupt the canal digging.

Grant stopped this effort with a counterattack north of the James on August 14. Federal forces advanced directly on Richmond over the terrain of the Seven Days battles of 1862. Lee sent up much of his army from Petersburg to contain the threat.

It ended on August 17 as quickly as it began, but Lee had been made victim of a ploy: Grant had used the opportunity to draw off most of Lee's army to shield Richmond, and he struck on August 18 south of Petersburg to cut the Weldon Railroad into North Carolina, Lee's primary line of supply.

On the morning of August 19, three Federal divisions seized Globe Tavern on the railway three and a half miles south of the Confederate right. Later in the day, A. P. Hill's corps struck near the tavern, and captured 2,700 Federals. But Grant had too much force, and kept his grip on the railroad.

Lee was obliged to abandon the railroad to Rowanty Creek, fifteen miles south of Petersburg, and subsequently had to depend on the Southside road and the Richmond and Danville Railroad.

Wade Hampton found Hancock's 2d Corps isolated from the rest of the army, as it was tearing up the railroad south of Globe Tavern. Seeing an opportunity, Lee hurried down infantry, and, on August 25, Hampton sent three brigades around Hancock's northern flank at Reams Station, while moving his dismounted cavalry around the left or southern flank. Most of Hancock's troops were raw and inexperienced, and they collapsed at once. Hampton captured 2,000 men, and Grant abandoned any further effort to tear up the railroad.

All these engagements looked like Confederate victories, but Grant was tightening the noose. The seizure of Globe Tavern placed Grant where he could extend his left, or southern, flank farther, and bring Lee one step closer to a formal siege. Lee had only about 50,000 men now, fewer than half the army Grant commanded. He plainly saw that Grant was trying to starve him out—yet throughout this period he could have withdrawn with impunity. A carefully managed evacuation, in stages to maintain secrecy, could have preserved the whole army, and kept Grant from getting on his tail and destroying his forces piece by piece.

Meanwhile, disaster was visited on the Confederacy at Atlanta. On July 17, Jefferson Davis, dissatisfied with Joseph E. Johnston's policy of retreating before Sherman, replaced him with John Bell Hood, a general known for his willingness to fight but not for strategic insight.

The outcome was as might have been expected: Hood launched frontal attacks against Sherman's well-entrenched army, suffered stupendous casualties, shattered his soldiers' morale, and abandoned Atlanta on September 1. On September 2, Sherman telegraphed Washington: "So Atlanta is ours and fairly won." The news—combined with David G. Farragut's seizure of the port of Mobile, Alabama, on August 23—electrified the North, revived hope of victory, ensured Lincoln's reelection, and sealed the fate of the Confederacy.

As gloom enveloped the South, Hood made another irretrievable mistake. Instead of blocking Sherman at Atlanta, he took off on a wild-goose chase to cut Sherman's supply lines, aiming primarily at capturing Nashville. But Sherman, realizing that Atlanta was 450 miles from his real base of supplies, Louisville, Kentucky, saw that he had an alternative. He could march straight to Savannah, 220 air miles away, and get all the supplies he needed by sea! To guard Nashville, however, he sent back his best general, George H. Thomas, with an army more than twice the size of Hood's.

Hood's army was entirely useless in influencing the outcome of the war. Hood obstinately went on to fight and lose a frontal battle at Franklin, Tennessee, on November 30, then march to Nashville, where Thomas struck him on December 15, and virtually destroyed his army.

Meanwhile, Sherman marched against feeble opposition on Savannah, creating a path of destruction sixty miles wide and two hundred miles long from Atlanta to the sea, splitting the South in two, gravely damaging the Southern people's faith in the Confederate government, and capturing the port city on December 20. Sherman previously had set his men to plunder, burn, and destroy farms in northern Georgia, had evicted the entire population of Atlanta, and had burned the business section just before setting off for Savannah. His policy of destroying the property of all the Southerners who came within his reach was even worse than Sheridan's plundering of the Shenandoah Valley, and had no parallel in modern history. He left a lasting legacy of hate. He struck, not at the Confederate army, but at the will of the Southern people to pursue the war, and ultimately broke it.

Between the fiasco of the crater and March 1865, Grant contented himself with movements north and south of Petersburg. He abandoned attacks upon Confederate lines in favor of feints, first upon one flank and then upon the other. These threats forced Lee to extend his entrenchments to a distance of thirty-seven miles from White Oak Swamp east of Richmond to the southernmost point below Petersburg. To man this long front Lee had 50,000 men, Grant 124,000.

The safest course for Lee would have been to avoid fights and preserve his army. But Grant's moves stirred Lee's aggressiveness. On September 30, 1864, he sent two divisions into three frontal attacks to recapture a fort seized by the Federals a couple miles east of Chaffin's Bluff, on the James about nine miles downstream from Richmond. The attacks failed with heavy casualties, and showed that Lee had not learned from the disastrous direct assaults he had ordered at Gettysburg and the Wilderness.

Morale in the Confederate army sank as a result of the steady losses, the bad news from Georgia, and a sense of hopelessness among the men manning the Richmond–Petersburg lines. Numbers of Rebels deserted, most going home, but a few crossing over to the Union line.

On October 19, General Longstreet returned after recovering from the severe wound he had suffered at the Wilderness. He had lost use of his right arm, but was fit for duty, and Lee put him in command of the north side of the James River.

In December, a naval expedition badly led by Benjamin Butler failed to seize Fort Fisher, guarding Wilmington. Grant fired Butler, and in mid-January 1865 another expedition under General Alfred H. Terry and Admiral David Dixon Porter captured the fort, and closed the Confederacy's last outlet to the sea.

The winter of 1864–65 was unusually severe, and the Confederates in the trenches before Petersburg suffered greatly from insufficient clothing and food. The repeated failures of the commissary-general, Lucius B. Northrop, finally induced his close friend, President Davis, to dismiss him in February 1865, replacing him with Brigadier General I. M. St. John, who had done well in securing nitre and other minerals. On February 6, James A. Seddon, Davis's yes-man secretary of war, also resigned, replaced by General John C. Breckinridge.

On February 1, 1865, Sherman marched northward into the Carolinas with his 60,000-man army. This march into the last bastion of the Confederacy brought dismay to the people of the South, and finally forced Jefferson Davis to appoint Lee as commander in chief of all Confederate armies on February 6. While at Petersburg, however, Lee could not hinder Sherman's advance, and Sherman seized South Carolina's capital, Columbia, on February 17, forcing the evacuation of Augusta and Charleston, and precipitating Lee to recall Joseph E. Johnston on February 22 to command Confederate forces facing Sherman.

Lee told Johnston to collect the scattered troops in the Carolinas, and attack Sherman on the march, before he could join a 21,000-man Union army under John M. Schofield, which had landed at New Bern, North Carolina, and was moving west to Goldsboro.

Even at this late hour Lee was unrealistic about the situation facing him. He concluded on February 22 that his army would have to leave the trenches once Sherman reached the Roanoke River, about seventy air miles south of Petersburg. Yet this would be much too late. Between them, Grant and Sherman could grind Lee's army to pieces on the Roanoke. Their combined armies would total at least 180,000 men, and would be invincible.

The only strategic move that made any sense now was to attempt as a desperate move what Lee could have ventured with every likelihood of success the previous summer: abandon Richmond-Petersburg, steal at least one day's march on Grant, hopefully two or three, unite with Johnston, try to smash Sherman, then turn back on Grant.

But Lee cited the poor condition of his horses and mules and the muddy state of the roads. Yet to delay meant that Grant would drive him out under great duress. At the very least Lee should have deposited rations at railway stations along his expected line of retreat. This would have guaranteed food for the army.

Johnston found that his army was suffering heavily from desertion. Instead of 29,000 men, as estimated, it had only 15,000, a measure of the despair being felt everywhere. From Lee's failure to join Johnston in the summer of 1864—while the Confederacy still had great strength, high morale, and an enormous arena for maneuver—had issued the disasters that had engulfed the South since. Many people realized that their leaders had no program to stop the invading Northerners, and their faith in the government lessened with every mile that Sherman advanced.

Colonel Walter H. Taylor, Lee's adjutant-general, wrote regarding the last thirty days at Petersburg: "The loss to the army by desertion averaged a hundred a day. . . . The condition of affairs throughout the South at that period was truly deplorable. Hundreds of letters addressed to soldiers were intercepted and sent to army headquarters, in which mothers, wives, and sisters told of their inability to respond to the appeals of hungry children for bread, or to provide proper care and remedies for the sick, and in the name of all that was dear appealed to the men to come home and rescue them from the ills which they suffered and the starvation which threatened them. Surely never was devotion to one's country and to one's duty more sorely tested than was the case with the soldiers of Lee's army during the last year of the war."[12]

Belatedly and with extreme slowness, Lee began to contemplate abandoning Richmond-Petersburg, marching southwest, and uniting with Johnston at Danville, Virginia, on the North Carolina border.[13] A move in this direction implied giving up any attempt to keep Grant and Sherman apart. It offered no dividends other than uniting the two last armies of the Confederacy. At Danville, the Rebels would have only one viable strategic option: to move into the mountains of Virginia or North Carolina and embark on a guerrilla war.

Despite the threat front and rear, Lee refused to make the decision to save his army until Sheridan's troopers destroyed Jubal Early's tiny observation force at Waynesboro on March 2, 1865. Sheridan's 20,000 cavalry now rode unhindered across central Virginia, wrecking property as they went, to rejoin Grant at Petersburg.

Confederate depots at Lynchburg, Danville, and Greensboro, North Carolina, had food and ammunition, and Lee ordered plans to be made to deliver food along the retreat route when the time came. But he sent none in advance—for Lee still intended to remain in the entrenchments.

He had come up with the most bizarre and impractical plan he contrived in the war. It was precipitated by a March 11 wire from

Johnston proposing that Lee, instead of leaving the trenches, should "hold one of the inner lines of Richmond with one part of your army, and meet Sherman with the other, returning to Richmond after fighting."[14]

The idea was senseless on its face. Even if the attack were successful, the most men that Lee might have sent south was 25,000, giving Johnston only half the troops of the combined Union army he would be expected to defeat, while leaving Lee with an army only a quarter the size of Grant's.

Nevertheless, Lee ordered John B. Gordon to seize Fort Stedman in a frontal strike with half the army. Stedman was a strongpoint on high ground just east of Petersburg and three-quarters of a mile southeast of the Appomattox River. If the blow was successful, Lee thought, Grant would abandon the left of his line or shorten his front. Lee could then hold the shorter line with fewer men, and send the remainder to Johnston.

Throughout the war, Lee had opted for a direct assault to retrieve every tactical impasse. These attacks had cost enormous casualties, and, except in a few cases, had failed. Yet once more Lee chose a bloody, frontal confrontation against a superior enemy that, moreover, was deeply entrenched.

The assault on Fort Stedman went in on March 25, 1865. Despite extreme valor on the part of the Rebel attackers, it failed miserably against overwhelming fire. Lee lost nearly 3,000 prisoners and about 2,000 men killed and wounded—one-tenth of his army. Six days previously Johnston likewise had been defeated by Sherman at Bentonville, North Carolina, permitting Sherman to join Schofield at Goldsboro. Between battle losses and desertions, Johnston's army was down to 13,500 men.

On March 26, Lee admitted to President Davis that he could not prevent a junction of Grant and Sherman and must move his army out of their way. It was much too late, but even now he was reluctant to go. The survivors of the attack on Stedman needed to rest. Davis's administration was not ready to evacuate Richmond, as the roads were still bad.

Grant forced Lee's hand. On March 28, intelligence reports showed that Grant was moving around Lee's extreme right flank, below Petersburg, with the aim of cutting the last two rail lines serving Lee—to Lynchburg and Danville.

Fitz Lee reported that Sheridan was near Dinwiddie Court House, sixteen miles southwest of Petersburg, and moving on Five Forks, five miles northwest, en route to the Southside Railroad, about three miles farther on.

On March 31, Fitz Lee, with about 1,800 horsemen, and George Pickett, with 6,400 infantry, got into a lively fight north of Dinwiddie Court House, but withdrew at daybreak on April 1, closely followed by Federal cavalry. The Confederates halted and formed a line of battle at Five Forks. But the position Fitz Lee and Pickett selected was poor. The troops faced into a forest, limiting visibility. Fitz Lee and Pickett thought their advance had broken up the Federal movement, and, expecting nothing to happen the rest of the day, sent out

(NATIONAL ARCHIVES)

Ruins of Richmond below the capitol.

no patrols, and went off to a fish fry some distance away. This permitted Sheridan to advance unobserved right up to the Rebel line. Shortly before 3 P.M., while Union cavalry demonstrated on the front, Gouverneur Warren's Union 5th Corps swung around the Rebel left, or eastern, flank, routed the whole Rebel force, and captured more than 3,000 of Pickett's infantry.

It was a disastrous defeat, due in part to the superior forces of the enemy, but caused primarily by the irresponsibility of the two Confederate generals. In two hours, the force Lee had established to protect his right flank had been swept away. Now there was nothing to prevent Grant from driving entirely around Lee's army on the south. If Lee remained at Petersburg, his army was certain to be surrounded and destroyed.

At 4:45 A.M. on April 2, 1865, the Federals commenced a bombardment along the whole line, followed by infantry assaults. In places the Rebels held doggedly, but below Petersburg Union forces broke through.

A.P. Hill, hearing the heavy artillery fire, rode off to check his line, ran into two Federals who had gotten behind the lines, called on them to surrender, and was shot dead. When Lee got the news, his eyes filled with tears. "He is at rest now," Lee murmured. "And we who are left are the ones to suffer."[15]

Union forces began to penetrate into the Confederate rear, setting off pandemonium. As Lee made frantic efforts to contain the incursions, his obligation became clear: he had to get his troops out of the line during the night and on the road toward Danville. At 10:40 A.M. Sunday, April 2, Lee wired Secretary of War Breckinridge: "I advise that all preparations be made for leaving Richmond tonight. I will advise you later, according to circumstances."[16] President Davis received the message in St. Paul's Episcopal Church, opposite the capitol, during the morning service. He got up and left the building.

✳ 14 ✳

SURRENDER

Lee hurriedly arranged details of the evacuation. Columns were to advance on a number of roads from Richmond and Petersburg. The point of reconcentration was to be Amelia Court House, forty miles west of Petersburg, on the railroad to Danville.

At 3 P.M. Lee issued formal orders for retreat that night. Some of Porter Alexander's artillery battalions were defending Richmond, and he rode up to the Richmond and Danville Railroad station just south of the Mayo Bridge to superintend their departure.

There he found a long train that had come up from Danville loaded with rations. Knowing that the army would have to be fed at Amelia Court House, Lee had ordered this train to drop its provisions at Amelia. But the train commander had also received orders to come to Richmond to take off personnel and property of the government. Instead of leaving the food cars at Amelia, he had brought them to Richmond. Here they were destroyed in the retreat. The commander's disobedience meant that Lee's army would find no food at Amelia. This, and Lee's failure to lay in food supplies along the route in advance, were the principal reasons why the army could not get away and join Johnston's army in North Carolina.

While at the station, Alexander heard a terrific explosion of the arsenal at Richmond. These and explosions of other magazines set off fires that consumed a wide section of the downtown along the river and below the capitol. On the morning of April 3, as his last battalion passed, Alexander took a final look at the city. Everything along the riverfront appeared to be in flames. Many citizens

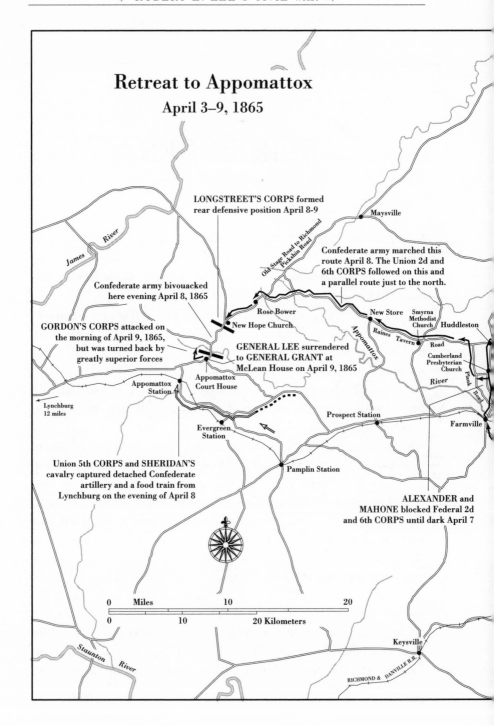

Retreat to Appomattox
April 3–9, 1865

LONGSTREET'S CORPS formed
rear defensive position April 8-9

Maysville

James   *River*

Confederate army marched this
route April 8. The Union 2d and
6th CORPS followed on this and
a parallel route just to the north.

Confederate army bivouacked
here evening April 8, 1865

Old Stage Road to Richmond
Pickshin Road

Rose Bower

New Store   Smyrna
Methodist
Church   Huddleston

GORDON'S CORPS attacked on
the morning of April 9, 1865,
but was turned back by
greatly superior forces

New Hope Church

Appomattox

Raines   Tavern   Road

GENERAL LEE surrendered
to GENERAL GRANT at
McLean House on April 9, 1865

Cumberland
Presbyterian
Church

Appomattox
Court House

River

Plank   Road

Appomattox
Station

Lynchburg
12 miles

Prospect Station

Farmville

Evergreen
Station

Union 5th CORPS and SHERIDAN'S
cavalry captured detached Confederate
artillery and a food train from
Lynchburg on the evening of April 8

Pamplin Station

ALEXANDER and
MAHONE blocked Federal 2d
and 6th CORPS until dark April 7

0	Miles	10		20

0		10		20 Kilometers

Keysville

Staunton   *River*

RICHMOND &   DANVILLE R.R.

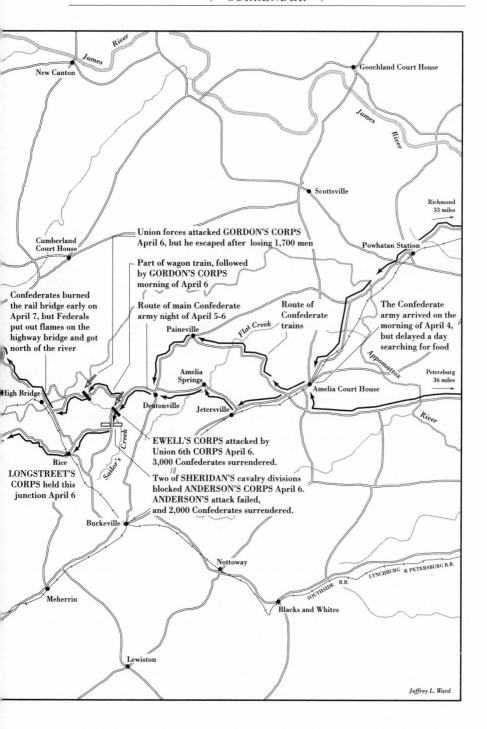

New Canton

James River

Goochland Court House

James River

Scottsville

Richmond
33 miles

Cumberland
Court House

Union forces attacked GORDON'S CORPS
April 6, but he escaped after losing 1,700 men

Powhatan Station

Part of wagon train, followed
by GORDON'S CORPS
morning of April 6

Confederates burned
the rail bridge early on
April 7, but Federals
put out flames on the
highway bridge and got
north of the river

Route of main Confederate
army night of April 5-6

Paineville

Flat Creek

Route of
Confederate
trains

The Confederate
army arrived on the
morning of April 4,
but delayed a day
searching for food

Appomattox

Petersburg
36 miles

High Bridge

Amelia
Springs

Amelia Court House

Dentonville

Jetersville

River

EWELL'S CORPS attacked by
Union 6th CORPS April 6.
3,000 Confederates surrendered.

Rice

LONGSTREET'S
CORPS held this
junction April 6

Sailor's Creek

Two of SHERIDAN'S cavalry divisions
blocked ANDERSON'S CORPS April 6.
ANDERSON'S attack failed,
and 2,000 Confederates surrendered.

Burkeville

Nottoway

LYNCHBURG & PETERSBURG R.R.

SOUTHSIDE R.R.

Meherrin

Blacks and Whites

Lewiston

Jeffrey L. Ward

frantically removed food from a huge army commissary at Fourteenth and Cary Streets just north of Mayo Bridge before the fire consumed the building.

Union officers were unaware that the Confederate army had got clean away during the night of April 2–3, and made no effort to pursue. Thus Lee gained a full day's head start. But when he found no food at Amelia on the morning of April 4, he realized he would have to scour the countryside for supplies, losing at least his day's advantage.

Lee disencumbered his army of everything not absolutely necessary, ordering only the best artillery battalions to remain, and the other guns and many of the supply wagons to take the road to Lynchburg. From this point on, the army would have to march lean, hoping food could be delivered at the railway stations along the way.

Although Grant's cavalry was reported beyond Amelia, Lee believed he could continue down the railroad toward Danville. The Staunton (Roanoke) River was four days distant by forced marches, and would make a strong line, while in Danville were 1.5 million rations.

Lee's wagons came in from the countryside on April 5, but were almost empty. The farmers had little to offer because they already had been stripped of food. Hungry, and in deep gloom, the men marched off.

They didn't get far. Around Jetersville, seven miles down the road (present-day U.S. Route 360), the Rebels came upon Sheridan's cavalry, entrenched in a well-chosen position, with Union infantry coming up. Because of the delay at Amelia, the Federals had overtaken Lee.

Lee decided he could not attack with his weakened, famished troops. The hope evaporated of marching along the railroad to Danville, picking up food delivered by trains. Lee ordered the army to turn in the only direction remaining, westward toward Farmville, about eighteen miles away, where 80,000 rations had been delivered on the Southside Railroad. From Farmville, Lee intended to turn south once more toward the Staunton River.

A forced march on the night of April 5–6 now was Lee's only chance of escape. But the exhausted, disillusioned soldiers stumbled slowly over the crowded roads, prey to any sound or rumor, many deserting, others throwing away their arms.

Longstreet's corps moved off first, followed by Anderson's corps, a mixed force under Ewell, and Gordon's small corps serving as rear guard. Their course was north to Amelia Springs, west to Deatonville, and southwest to Rice, six miles east of Farmville (now Virginia Routes 642, 617, 600). The trains followed a more northerly route through Paineville, but Federal cavalry raided the column, burned 200 wagons, and captured more than 600 soldiers and teamsters, forcing the wagons into the main line of march, mostly between Anderson's and Ewell's forces.

Despite the strike on the north, most of Sheridan's horsemen were moving on Lee's southern flank, parallel to the line of march. Lee sent his cavalry to help protect the front and back of the army,

(NATIONAL ARCHIVES)

Park of captured guns at Richmond dock.

and left the task of guarding the southern flank to the infantry. To prevent cavalry from breaking in and dividing the army, Lee directed all commanders to allow no separation between units on the march.

But on the morning of April 6, when Longstreet's corps reached Rice, Anderson's corps was not behind. Union cavalry had come up from the south and stabbed at the wagon train. Anderson's infantry drove them off, but his corps stopped to allow part of the wagon train and guns to pass ahead, in the event Gordon needed help defending the rear.

This was a great mistake and directly against orders, explainable only because Anderson was exhausted. When the train segment moved ahead toward Rice, the Federal cavalry rushed back in, and set some vehicles afire. By the time Anderson could drive away the enemy and get started again, Sheridan had deployed two full divisions of cavalry in a strong position on his front, about four and a half miles east of Rice.

Meanwhile, Ewell had made a fatal error. Fitz Lee had told him of the cavalry barricade, and he had sent the remainder of the wagon train and all the rest of the artillery about three miles to the north and west. He hadn't told Gordon what he was doing, however, and Gordon's corps followed the rear of the wagon train—leaving Ewell at the rear without a single piece of artillery and with his and Anderson's advance blocked ahead!

Anderson rode back to talk with Ewell. Ewell thought the best idea was to strike out northwestward through the woods and find a road around the enemy. But Anderson, trained in Robert E. Lee's school of direct attack, decided on a frontal assault. Ewell agreed, and started his men up the road to help. But he got word that the 2d and 6th Federal corps were on his rear a little over a mile away on a hill just east of Sailor's Creek, and were making ready to attack.

Anderson turned to assault alone the Union cavalry on his front, while Ewell drew up his 3,000 men on the western side of Sailor's Creek. But with no artillery opposing them, the Federal guns pounded the Rebel line with impunity. Casualties mounted quickly. Ewell then did a strange thing: he abandoned his post and rode back to see how Anderson's attempted attack was faring.

While Ewell was gone, the Union brigades attacked, their line so long it overlapped both Confederate flanks. The Rebels waited until the Federals were close, unleashed a heavy volley, and sent the Federals recoiling. But the Union brigades made another assault, this time wrapping around the right flank, and breaking into the rear. Overwhelmingly outnumbered, with nowhere to retreat, its leader absent from the field, the entire Confederate line collapsed, and nearly all of the men surrendered.

Meanwhile, Anderson's attack was a disaster. Perhaps the men were discouraged by the threat on their rear. More likely they realized a frontal assault against entrenchments and a superior force firing Spencer repeating rifles would be a bloodbath. They made only a feeble attempt, and the great majority surrendered, though a few hardy men escaped through the woods, as did Anderson himself. Ewell rode back toward his own force, and was captured by a cavalry officer.

Perhaps 5,000 Confederates lay down their arms at Sailor's Creek, and another thousand were killed or wounded. It was a deplorable end to two of Lee's four corps, caused by poor judgment and an unbelievable lack of initiative on the part of two lieutenant generals. Lee removed Anderson from the army at once.

Meanwhile, other Union forces attacked Gordon at a lower crossing of Sailor's Creek (on present-day Virginia Route 619). Gordon put up a valiant defense, and saved the wagon train. But when Anderson's and Ewell's corps were gone, the Federals were able to concentrate against him. He lost 1,700 men before withdrawing.

Also during the day, Confederate cavalry destroyed a Union cavalry and infantry force that tried to capture the wagon road and High Bridge of the Southside Railroad over the Appomattox, four and a half miles north of Rice. This prevented the Union army from crossing the river and approaching Farmville from the north.

Lee pulled back Billy Mahone's division to the ridge above Sailor's Creek, while Longstreet marched on to Farmville. During the night, Mahone withdrew through woods to the High Bridge, which he had orders to hold until Gordon's corps and any stragglers had crossed. Then he was to burn the bridge and the lower wagon road to prevent the Federals from moving north of the Appomattox. Meanwhile, Lee ordered Porter Alexander to burn the railroad and highway bridges over the river at Farmville as soon as the army passed.

By keeping the Federals temporarily south of the river, Lee hoped to steal a day's march on them by proceeding on the north side of the river to Appomattox Station, on the Southside Railroad about twenty-five direct miles west of Farmville. There Lee had ordered rations to be delivered from Lynchburg.

However, Mahone reported early on April 7 that, though he had burned High Bridge, the Federals had beaten out the flames on the wagon bridge, and were streaming over it and marching north of Farmville.

This meant failure of Lee's plan. Nevertheless, he resolved to carry out his retreat by a circuitous route north of the river, about thirty-three miles long, despite the fact the enemy would be on his tail—and despite the fact there was no food anywhere along the march. Yet the direct road to Appomattox (present-day U.S. Route 460) was about eight miles shorter, and paralleled the route of the Southside Railroad, which might have brought rations closer than Appomattox.

On the morning of April 7 at Farmville, Porter Alexander pointed out the direct, shorter route on Lee's map. But Lee ignored him. "Saying there would be time enough to look after that, the general folded up his map," Alexander wrote.[*]

Thus, while two corps pursued the tail of Lee's army, Sheridan's cavalry, Meade's 5th Corps, and much of Edward O.C. Ord's Army of the James marched on the direct road to Appomattox—certain to

---

[*] Porter Alexander, *Military Memoirs*, 598. Lee's roundabout approach to Appomattox has never been satisfactorily explained. Lee's biographer, Douglas Freeman, wrote (*R.E. Lee*, vol. 4, p. 99) that Lee did not stop "to explain [to Alexander] that he had no choice of route because he had to keep close to the railroad in order to meet his supply trains and to feed his men." This is incorrect, of course, because Lee's march route was well *away* from the railroad.

arrive at this vital intersection before Lee, and certain to intercept all food delivered on the railroad.

Although Lee had about 30,000 men left, only about 12,000 still carried their rifles. The Army of Northern Virginia was dying. Lee was opposed by 100,000 Union soldiers within striking distance, thousands more within a few days' travel. While Grant's army had food in plenty, Lee's men and animals were beginning to starve. One gunner wrote: "Horses and mules dead or dying in the mud. . . . The constant marching and fighting without sleep or food are rapidly thinning the ranks of this grand old army. Men who have stood by their flags since the beginning of the war fall out of their ranks and are captured, simply because it is beyond their power of physical endurance to go any farther."[1]

As the army, Gordon in the vanguard, marched north out of Farmville on the Plank Road (present-day Virginia Route 600), Lee ordered Porter Alexander's guns and Mahone's division to block the Federal advance at Cumberland Presbyterian Church, about three miles north on a parallel road (now Virginia Route 45). The Rebels held their position all day, allowing the rest of the army to turn west on the Raines Tavern Road (present-day Virginia Route 636). Mahone repulsed a 2d Corps attack in the afternoon, and Fitz Lee's horsemen turned back a Federal cavalry strike.

After sundown, the Federals passed a flag of truce with a message from Grant that further resistance was hopeless and asking Lee to surrender. Lee sent back a request for terms. When Longstreet read Grant's message, he handed it back to Lee with two words: "Not yet."[2]

April 8 was a quiet day of marching. Though 2d Corps followed closely, trailed by 6th Corps, it made no effort to strike, while Sheridan and the rest of the army took the more direct route to Appomattox.

In the afternoon, Gordon's lead force reached the old stage road to Richmond (now Virginia Route 24), and turned southwest for five miles to the Appomattox River, here only a small stream. One mile ahead lay Appomattox Court House, and two miles beyond it lay Appomattox Station.

Pendleton rode down toward the station and found parked the artillery Lee had declared surplus at Amelia and directed to move ahead of the army. While there Federal cavalry attacked the guns, but were driven off. This was an ominous sign. The presence of Union cavalry at the station showed they were south and west of Appomattox. This meant they not only were in possession of the railroad, but had cut off further retreat of the Confederate army. That night Union cavalry stormed the batteries and captured them. Campfires cast up a red glow onto the clouds around the station, revealing that Federal forces were blocking the Confederates in nearly every direction.

Gordon bivouacked where he had stopped, the rest of the army stopping up the road to the north. By flag of truce, Lee received an answer to his request for terms. Grant wrote that all men who surrendered would be paroled until exchanged. Lee responded with a query as to terms he might expect if he surrendered all Confederate forces, not just the Army of Northern Virginia, and said he would be glad to meet with Grant at the rear of his army at 10 A.M. the next day, Palm Sunday, April 9, 1865.

That night Lee held a council of war with Longstreet, Fitz Lee, and Gordon. They resolved that one more effort must be made early on April 9 to break through the Union cordon and reach Johnston. Gordon's infantry, supported by Fitz Lee's cavalry, were to attack along the stage road. If successful, they would wheel to the left to shield the passage of the wagons and Longstreet's corps; then the army would press on toward Danville. If they failed, they acknowledged somberly that the end would have come.

Lee dressed faultlessly, with his most handsome sword and a sash of deep, red silk. He told Pendleton he expected to be Grant's prisoner, and wanted to appear in his best attire.

At 3 A.M. Lee started to the front. What was left of the Army of Northern Virginia was alongside a single road, the vanguard not more than four miles from the rear guard. Fewer than 8,000 infantry still carried rifles. Gordon's corps, 7,500 men on March 25, was down to 1,600. Field's division had 11,000 on March 25, now fewer than 4,000.

At daybreak, Gordon spread his tiny corps in line of battle half a mile west of Appomattox Court House, on either side of the road. To the right were all of the remaining Confederate cavalry, 2,400 troopers.

In hope and with a spark of the army's old élan, Gordon's men swept forward, quickly overran hastily built enemy breastworks a short distance beyond, seized two new fieldpieces, and drove out the defenders—fortunately cavalry, who hurried back to their horses and ran away. Gordon had opened the road for the army.

Scarcely had he achieved this gain, however, when he discovered that heavy bodies of Union infantry were in a wood to his right, facing the Confederate cavalry. Within a short time, this infantry—from Ord's Army of the James—attacked Fitz Lee and drove him back on Gordon's right flank. Other infantry emerged from woods to the right rear of Gordon's position, and moved as if to get between Gordon and Longstreet, whose corps had pulled up behind. Soon thereafter, Union cavalry began pressing Gordon's left. Threatened on three sides, Gordon saw there was no hope of a breakthrough.

Colonel Charles Venable of Lee's staff rode up for a report. "Tell General Lee," Gordon said, "I have fought my corps to a frazzle, and I fear I can do nothing unless I am heavily supported by Longstreet's corps."[3]

Gordon was one of the most daring commanders in Lee's army. If he couldn't advance, no one could. When Lee got the report, he told his staff officers: "There is nothing left me to do but to go and see General Grant, and I would rather die a thousand deaths."[4]

Lee looked out over the field. "How easily I could be rid of this, and be at rest!" he exclaimed. "I have only to ride along the line and all will be over." Then, with a deep sigh, he said: "But it is our duty to live. What will become of the women and children of the South if we are not here to protect them?"[5]

Lee sent for Longstreet, and recited the situation: Gordon couldn't open the road, and the food train from Lynchburg doubtless had not arrived or had been captured. What were they to do? Longstreet asked whether sacrifice of the army would help the cause elsewhere. "I think not," Lee responded. "Then your situation speaks for itself," Longstreet replied.[6]

Porter Alexander thought entirely otherwise. He tried to convince Lee to order the men to take to the woods, and make their way either to Johnston or to their states' governors. It was a thinly veiled proposal to embark on a guerrilla war. Alexander said two-thirds of the army would get away. "We would be like rabbits and partridges in the bushes and they could not scatter to follow us," he said.

But Lee answered that not all the men who got away would continue resisting. Many would go home. Also, he protested, the men, no longer under the control of their officers, would be compelled to rob and steal to live. "They would become mere bands of marauders," Lee said. This was not the sort of war Lee wanted to fight. He concluded: "The only dignified course for me would be to go to General Grant and surrender myself and take the consequences of my acts."[7]

Soon after, Lee rode under a flag of truce to a point midway between the rear of his army and 2d Corps, expecting to meet Grant. But a Union officer delivered a message from Grant that he had no authority to discuss general peace terms, and could only deal with the surrender of the Army of Northern Virginia. Lee at once proposed a meeting for that purpose. After asking for a temporary armistice, granted by Meade after some delay, Lee went back to his headquarters.

Unknown to Lee, Fitz Lee went off with the cavalry, determined not to share in the surrender. Gordon's troops withdrew to the north side of the Appomattox River. Gordon faced no attack, however, because the Federal commanders to his front also had agreed to an informal truce.

Lee was very tired, and sat down under an apple tree on some blankets on fence rails that Alexander had arranged for him. Longstreet came up and sat down with Lee. At 12:15 P.M. under another flag of truce, a Union officer rode up, escorted by a Confederate officer. Everyone guessed his mission.

As the rider approached, Longstreet said to Lee: "General, unless he offers us honorable terms, come back and let us fight it out."[8]

The messenger, Grant's aide, Lieutenant Colonel Orville E. Babcock, delivered a letter from Grant saying he was riding for Appomattox and would meet wherever Lee wished. Lee rode toward the village with Colonel Babcock, and two orderlies, one Union, one Confederate, while Colonel Charles Marshall, Lee's secretary, rode ahead to find a suitable place to hold the meeting.[9]

Marshall accepted the invitation of Major Wilmer McLean to use his own brick home. McLean had owned a farm on Bull Run, and his house had been General Beauregard's headquarters on July 18, 1861, just before the First Battle of Manassas. To get away from war, he moved his family to Appomattox and bought the house, where, by strange irony, the closing scene of the war was to be acted out.

Lee sat down in a corner of the front parlor, and waited half an hour until Grant arrived, directed to the spot by Babcock's orderly. Grant wore a mud-spattered uniform and no sword. The two generals shook hands quietly, and spoke a few words. Lee sat down, while Grant left briefly, and returned with a dozen officers, including Sheridan and Ord, all of whom stood behind Grant.

There was easy conversation for a while between Grant and Lee, much of it centered on mutual memories of the Mexican War. Soon, however, Lee brought the meeting back to the matter at hand: "I suppose, General Grant, that the object of our present meeting is fully understood. I asked to see you to ascertain upon what terms you would receive the surrender of my army."

Grant answered without changing expression: "The terms I propose are those stated substantially in my letter of yesterday— that is, the officers and men surrendered to be paroled and disqualified from taking up arms again until properly exchanged, and all arms, ammunitions and supplies to be delivered up as captured property."

Grant talked for a while of peace and its prospects. Lee waited, then suggested that Grant commit his terms to writing so they could be acted upon formally. Grant agreed and commenced writing in his order book. When he finished he rose and took the book to Lee.

Grant had added a sentence that the Confederate officers could keep their sidearms, private horses, and baggage. "This will have a very happy effect on my army," Lee told Grant.

"There is one thing I would like to mention," Lee went on. "The cavalrymen and artillerists own their own horses in our army. Its organization in this respect differs from that of the United States. I

(LIBRARY OF CONGRESS)

The Appomattox Court House shortly after the surrender.

would like to understand whether these men will be permitted to retain their horses."

Lee knew what horses and mules would mean to the South, stripped of its draft animals. Lee wanted the animals for spring plowing, but was unwilling to ask for them directly.

Grant caught Lee's meaning, and at once announced that he would instruct the officers receiving paroles to let all men who claimed horses or mules to take the animals home with them.

Lee, in relief, said: "This will have the best possible effect upon the men. It will be very gratifying and will do much toward conciliating our people."

As Marshall drafted a reply of acceptance, Grant introduced the officers, who, until then, had remained silent in the background.

Lee told Grant he had a thousand or more Union prisoners, whom he would send to Federal lines as soon as possible, as he had no provisions to feed them. Indeed, he said, he had no food for his own men or forage for the animals. He said he had wired Lynchburg for rations. When they arrived, he said he would be glad to have the wants of men supplied.

There was a stir among the Federal officers. Unknown to Lee, Sheridan had captured the rations train the previous night at Appomattox Station. Grant told Lee he would like his men released, and he would supply Lee's army with rations immediately. Lee gratefully acknowledged Grant's generosity, signed the letter accepting the surrender, shook hands with Grant, bowed to the spectators, walked outside, returned the salutes of several Federal officers on the front porch who jumped to their feet, climbed on Traveller, and rode back in defeat to his surrendered army—but also to his finest hour.

By no means all of the officers and men of the Army of Northern Virginia were prepared for surrender. The circle of fire reflected on the clouds the night of April 8–9 had shown that the army was virtually surrounded, and the relays of officers under flags of truce had given hints of the nature of affairs. But such was the faith of the army in its invincibility and its leadership that many of the men were unbelieving that the end had come.

Lee rode erect, staring straight ahead, down from the village, across the little Appomattox River, through the pickets, and into the line. A number of men were waiting in formation for him. They started to cheer, but something about Lee's somber countenance stopped them. They hesitated briefly, then, without a word of command, broke ranks and rushed toward him.

"General, are we surrendered?" The question was on a thousand lips, as the soldiers crowded about him, bareheaded. Lee took off his own hat. Emotion welled up in him. He tried to hide it and ride on, but the road was too full of dedicated, honorable, steadfast men with upturned faces and questioning eyes.

At last he was able to speak: "Men, we have fought the war together, and I have done the best I could for you. You will all be paroled and go to your homes until exchanged." Tears came into his eyes. "Be as good citizens," he told them, "as you have been good soldiers." He tried to say more, but could bring forth nothing more than a choking "Good-bye" as he rode on to the orchard.

The news rushed through the men like wildfire. A low wail of grief spread across the hillside.

At the orchard, a group of officers was waiting. Lee told them the terms, and that rations soon would be delivered. Now overcome, Lee withdrew a short distance into the orchard. He was distracted as groups of Federal officers arrived, their hats off, eager to meet this man who had done more than anyone else to keep the Confederacy alive. Lee received them politely, but with great reserve.

Lee waited at the orchard until the Federal supply wagons began to arrive, then he got back on Traveller and started toward his headquarters, about a mile to the rear. On each side of the road two solid walls of men—the soldiers who had done their duty to the end—formed along the whole distance. As he entered this avenue, Lee took off his hat and held it in his hand. His eyes filled, and the tears trickled down his cheeks. All along the way the scene repeated itself over and over: the men started with cheers, but seeing this man who embodied their ideals and the cause they had lost, they began to sob, many falling to the ground and weeping like children.

Robert E. Lee

The next day, Lee issued his farewell address:

After four years of arduous service marked by unsurpassed courage and fortitude, the Army of Northern Virginia has been compelled to yield to overwhelming numbers and resources. I need not tell the brave survivors of so many hard-fought battles, who have remained steadfast to the last, that I have consented to this result from no distrust of them; but feeling that valor and devotion could accomplish nothing that could compensate for the loss that must have attended the continuance of the contest, I determined to avoid the useless sacrifice of those whose past services have endeared them to their countrymen. By the terms of the agreement, officers and men can return to their homes and remain until exchanged. You will take with you the satisfaction that proceeds from the consciousness of duty faithfully performed; and I earnestly pray that a Merciful God will extend to you His blessing and protection. With an unceasing admiration of your constancy and devotion to your country, and a grateful remembrance of your kind and generous consideration for myself, I bid you all an affectionate farewell.

  R. E. Lee, Genl.

People do not always act in their own interests. Indeed, the whole Civil War can be seen as a parable proving this. The South spent infinitely more in lives and treasure keeping slavery than the institution was worth in economic terms. The North spent infinitely more forcing and punishing the South than it would have cost to pay slaveowners for their chattels many times over. People by and large are guided by leaders. When their leaders march off into folly, the people often follow.

The greatest gift that Robert E. Lee gave his nation was to stand up at Appomattox and call for an end to folly. The most remarkable and uplifting event that took place at Appomattox was the way Lee acted just before and just after he surrendered to General Grant at McLean house.

Just prior to the surrender Lee forcefully and finally rejected a proposal by the South's great artillery commander, Porter Alexander, to turn the war into a guerrilla struggle. Many other Confederates felt as did Alexander, and, except for the refusal of Lee, would have avidly pursued hostilities.

When Lee rode back from McLean house, and his devastated, weeping troops clustered around him, he told them to return to their homes and be as good citizens of a united nation as they had been good soldiers in war. By turning his people's thoughts from continuing the struggle to a peaceful, united future, Lee changed the course of history.

By April 1865 Lee virtually *was* the Confederacy. He embodied the final flickering hopes of the Southern people for independence. All during the retreat from Petersburg, the people had waited with fear and foreboding for news. They expected the worst. Jefferson Davis and his government had proved to be incapable of defending the South and had become fugitives, fleeing from the advancing Federal forces. But Lee and his battered army had remained steadfast to the last. While the Confederacy was crumbling everywhere, Lee's army, asking no quarter though it was plain to all that it was dying, had fought bitter, dogged, valiant battles against tremendous odds.

The Army of Northern Virginia was world-famous long before the retreat to Appomattox. But it was during this march toward surrender and defeat that the legend was born that this had been one of the greatest armies of all time. Its early victories had been stupendous, but the army's behavior in those final days aroused a new understanding of how far beyond arms and power that heroism and dedication can carry a body of men.

Lee, as commander of this army, personified the army's renown. The Southern people added to this fame a feeling of deep respect and honor for the man himself, a feeling that also expressed their gratitude for his efforts. Lee could never be accused of having failed to fight for Southern independence to the last inch. Therefore, when Lee urged his soldiers to be as good citizens of a united nation as they had been good soldiers in war, his admonition had immense and lasting power. It turned many Southerners away from their feelings of hate and revenge toward cooperation with the North and peace.

By 1865, slavery could not be reinstituted, not only because the rest of the civilized world had rejected it, but because the people of the South no longer wanted it either. The war had taught them that it was too expensive. The day after the surrender, Lee told General Grant that the South now was as opposed to human bondage as the North.[10]

Though this meant that the Southern ruling class was impoverished, Lee realized that it also meant that the *only* real issue dividing North and South had been settled.

Lee saw there was no reason remaining, except pride, to keep the South from returning to the Union. Pride is often another word for folly, and Lee understood that he—and perhaps he alone—had the trust of the Southern people sufficient to show them that it was in their interests to forget their pride, recognize that the Civil War had been a tragic dispute among brothers, not a war to the death between enemies, and that they and the soldiers of the North shared common ideals, a common hope for the future, and a common patriotism.

If Lee had advised otherwise, a solid core of dedicated men like Porter Alexander would have followed him—and American history would have recorded additional pages of killings, maimings, destruction, and division. From Appomattox until he died in 1870, Lee devoted himself to the reconciliation of the two sections of the country. He rejected many offers by industrialists to become a wealthy executive. Instead, he took a low-paying job as president of Washington College in Lexington, Virginia, now Washington and Lee University. There he commenced a deliberate program of educating a new generation of Southerners to be patriotic, loyal citizens of a united nation. Lee's program and his example did more than any-thing else to end rancor and to reconcile the Southern people.

Lee failed to win Southern independence. But more than any other American, he made it possible for the North and South to come back together in friendship and unity. More than any other American, he made it possible for the North and South together to create the greatest and most prosperous nation in history. Surely this is a finer legacy than to be remembered as a great general.

SELECTED BIBLIOGRAPHY

Alexander, Bevin. *Lost Victories: The Military Genius of Stonewall Jackson*. New York: Henry Holt, 1992; Edison, N.J.: Blue & Grey Press, 1996.

Alexander, Edward Porter. *Military Memoirs of a Confederate: A Critical Narrative*. New York: Charles Scribner's Sons, 1907.

———. *Fighting for the Confederacy: The Personal Recollections of General Edward Porter Alexander*. Ed. Gary W. Gallagher. Chapel Hill: University of North Carolina Press, 1989.

Allan, William. *The Army of Northern Virginia in 1862*. Boston: Houghton Mifflin & Co., 1892.

———. *History and Campaign of Gen. T.J. (Stonewall) Jackson in the Shenandoah Valley of Virginia*. Philadelphia: J.B. Lippincott, 1880.

Beringer, Richard E., Herman Hattaway, Archer Jones, and William N. Still, Jr. *Why the South Lost the Civil War*. Athens: University of Georgia Press, 1986.

Bigelow, John, Jr. *The Campaign of Chancellorsville*. New Haven, Conn.: Yale University Press, 1910.

Boggs, Marion Alexander, ed. *The Alexander Letters: 1787–1900*. Athens: University of Georgia Press, 1980. Originally printed Savannah, Georgia, in private edition 1910.

Bridges, Hal. *Lee's Maverick General: Daniel Harvey Hill*. New York: McGraw-Hill Book Co., Inc., 1961.

Chambers, Lenoir. *Stonewall Jackson*. 2 vols. New York: William Morrow & Co., 1959.

Cooke, John Esten. *Stonewall Jackson: A Military Biography*. New York: D. Appleton and Co., 1876.

Dabney, Robert Lewis. *Life and Campaigns of Lieut.-Gen. Thomas J. (Stonewall) Jackson*. New York: Blelock & Co., 1866.

Donald, David Herbert. *Lincoln*. London: Jonathan Cape Random House, 1995.

Doubleday, Abner. *Chancellorsville and Gettysburg*. New York: Charles Scribner's Sons, 1882.

Douglas, Henry Kyd. *I Rode with Stonewall*. Chapel Hill: University of North Carolina Press, 1940, 1968.

Farwell, Byron. *Stonewall: A Biography of General Thomas J. Jackson*. New York: W.W. Norton, 1992.

Freeman, Douglas Southall. *R.E. Lee, A Biography*. 4 vols. New York and London: Charles Scribner's Sons, 1934–35.

———. *Lee's Lieutenants: A Study in Command*. 3 vols. New York: Scribner's, 1942–46.

Fremantle, Arthur James Lyon. *The Fremantle Diary*. Edited by Walter Lord. Boston: Little Brown and Co., 1954.

Fuller, Major General J.F.C. *Grant and Lee: A Study in Personality and Generalship*. Bloomington: Indiana University Press, 1957, second edition. First edition 1932.

———. *The Generalship of Ulysses S. Grant*. Bloomington: Indiana University Press, 1958.

Gallagher, Gary W., ed. *The Third Day of Gettysburg and Beyond*. Chapel Hill: University of North Carolina Press, 1994.

Gordon, John B. *Reminiscences of the Civil War*. New York: Charles Scribner's Sons, 1903; Baton Rouge: Louisiana State University Press, 1993.

Griffith, Paddy. *Battle Tactics of the Civil War*. New Haven: Yale University Press, 1989.

Hattaway, Herman and Archer Jones. *How the North Won*. Urbana: University of Illinois Press, 1991.

Henderson, Colonel G.F.R. *Stonewall Jackson and the American Civil War*. 2 vols. New York: Longmans, Green and Co., 1898; reprint, 1 vol. New York: Longmans, Green and Co., 1936, 1937, 1943, 1949; reprint, 2 vols. New York: Konecky & Konecky, 1993.

Hood, John B. *Advance and Retreat: Personal Experiences in the United States and Confederate States Armies*. New Orleans, 1880. Reprint, Bloomington: Indiana University Press, 1959.

Humphreys, Andrew A. *The Virginia Campaign 1864 and 1865*. New York: 1883; Da Capo Press, 1995.

Jackson, Mary Anna. *Memoirs of Stonewall Jackson*. Louisville, Ky.: Prentice Press, 1895.

Johnson, Robert U., and C.C. Buel, eds. *Battles and Leaders of the Civil War*. 4 vols. New York: Century magazine, 1887–88; reprint, Secaucus, N.J.: Castle, n.d.

Johnston, Joseph E. *Narrative of Military Operations*. Bloomington: Indiana University Press, 1959; New York, Kraus, 1969.

Jones, Archer. *Civil War Command and Strategy: The Process of Victory and Defeat*. New York: Free Press, 1992.

Lee, Robert E. *Lee's Dispatches, Unpublished Letters of General Robert E. Lee, C.S.A., to Jefferson Davis and the War Department of the Confederate States of America 1862–65*. Ed. by Douglas Southall Freeman. New York: G.P. Putnam's Sons, 1957 (originally published in a limited edition, 1915); Baton Rouge: Louisiana State University Press, 1994.

Long, A.L. *Memoirs of Robert E. Lee*. Secaucus, N.J.: The Blue and Grey Press, 1983 (originally published Charlottesville, Va., 1886).

Longstreet, James. *From Manassas to Appomattox*. Philadelphia: J.B. Lippincott Co., 1903.

Marshall, Charles. *An Aide-de-Camp of Lee*. Ed. Sir Frederick Maurice. Boston: Little, Brown and Co., 1927.

Matter, William D. *If It Takes All Summer: The Battle of Spotsylvania*. Chapel Hill: University of North Carolina Press, 1988.

Maurice, Major General Sir Frederick. *Robert E. Lee the Soldier*. New York: Houghton Mifflin Co., 1925; Bonanza Books, n.d.

McKenzie, John D. *Uncertain Glory: Lee's Generalship Re-Examined*. New York: Hippocrene Books, 1997.

Nolan, Alan T. *Lee Considered: General Robert E. Lee and Civil War History*. Chapel Hill: University of North Carolina Press, 1991.

Palfrey, Francis Winthrop. *The Antietam and Fredericksburg*. New York: Charles Scribner's Sons, 1882.

Pfanz, Harry W. *Gettysburg—the Second Day*. Chapel Hill: University of North Carolina Press, 1987.

———. *Gettysburg—Culp's Hill and Cemetery Hill*. Chapel Hill: University of North Carolina Press, 1993.

Rhea, Gordon C. *The Battle of the Wilderness May 5–6, 1864*. Baton Rouge: Louisiana State University Press, 1994.

Robertson, James I., Jr. *General A.P. Hill, The Story of a Confederate Warrior*. New York: Random House, 1987.

———. *Stonewall Jackson, The Man, the General, the Legend*. New York: Macmillan Publishing USA, 1997.

Ropes, John C. *The Army Under Pope*. New York: Charles Scribner's Sons, 1881.

Scaff, Morris. *The Battle of the Wilderness*. Boston: Houghton Mifflin Co., 1910.

Sears, Stephen W. *Landscape Turned Red: The Battle of Antietam*. New York: Ticknor & Fields, 1983.

———. *To the Gates of Richmond: The Peninsula Campaign*. New York: Ticknor & Fields, 1992.

Selby, John. *Stonewall Jackson as Military Commander*. London: B.T. Batsford Ltd., n.d.; Princeton: D. Van Nostrand Co., Inc., 1968.

Southern Historical Society Papers. 50 vols. Richmond: 1876–1953.

Taylor, Walter H. *Four Years with General Lee*. 1877; reprint New York: Bonanza Books, 1962.

Thomas, Emory M. *Robert E. Lee: A Biography*. New York: W.W. Norton & Co., 1995.

Tucker, Glenn. *High Tide at Gettysburg*. Boston: Bobbs-Merrill Co., 1958; New York: Smithmark Publishers, 1995.

United States Department of War. *Official Records. The War of the Rebellion: A Compilation of the Official Records of the Union and Confederate Armies*. 128 parts in 70 vols. and atlas. Washington: Government Printing Office, 1880–1901. Citations refer to Series I volumes unless specified.

Vandiver, F.E. *The Mighty Stonewall*. New York: McGraw-Hill Book Co., Inc., 1957.

Wiley, Bell Irvin. *The Life of Johnny Reb*. Baton Rouge: Louisiana State University Press, 1943, 1978, 1995.

———. *The Life of Billy Yank*. Baton Rouge: Louisiana State University Press, 1952, 1978, 1995.

Wise, Jennings Cropper. *The Long Arm of Lee: The History of the Artillery of the Army of Northern Virginia*. Lynchburg, Va.: J.P. Bell Co., Inc., 1915. Reprinted by Oxford University Press, New York, 1959.

Wolseley, Field Marshal Viscount. *The American Civil War: An English View*. Charlottesville: University Press of Virginia, 1964.

Woodworth, Steven E. *Davis and Lee at War*. Lawrence: University Press of Kansas, 1995.

NOTES

In the following notes, some references give only the last name(s) of the author(s) or editor(s). Works so referred to are cited in full in the Selected Bibliography. Works not listed in the bibliography are cited in full where they appear in the notes. Numbers at the end of citations refer to pages.

CHAPTER 1
1. Porter Alexander, *Fighting for the Confederacy*, 91.

CHAPTER 2
1. Johnson and Buel, vol. 2, 361.
2. Ibid., 337.
3. Porter Alexander, *Fighting for the Confederacy*, 110.
4. Porter Alexander, *Military Memoirs*, 167–71; Henderson, vol. 2, 70–71; Taylor, 41–44.
5. Johnson and Buel, vol. 2, 390–91.
6. Ibid., 392–94, 416–23.
7. Ibid., 432; Porter Alexander, *Fighting for the Confederacy*, 114; Freeman, *R.E. Lee*, vol. 2, 220.

CHAPTER 3
1. Griffith, 129–30.
2. Freeman, *R.E. Lee*, vol. 2, 102; *Southern Historical Society Papers*, vol. 40, 173–74.
3. Heros von Borcke, *Memoirs of the Confederate War for Independence* (New York: Peter Smith, 1938), vol. 2, 117; Henderson, vol. 2, 341. Later, after the Battle of Chancellorsville, Jackson told his medical officer, Hunter McGuire: "We sometimes fail to drive them from position, but they always fail to drive us." See *Southern Historical Society Papers*, vol. 25, 110; Bigelow, 340 n.
4. *Southern Historical Society Papers*, vol. 25, 119; Bigelow, 340 n. Jackson's close associate, Robert Lewis Dabney, expressed the same idea in somewhat different words. See Dabney, 699–700.
5. Johnson and Buel, vol. 2, 297.

CHAPTER 4
1. Hattaway and Jones, 210.
2. Porter Alexander, *Military Memoirs*, 179.
3. Field Marshal Viscount Wolseley, commander in chief of the British army, wrote in 1887 that Jackson's action at Cedar Mountain "showed how a small army may be superior at the point of contact to the fractions of a larger." See Wolseley, 138.

4   *Official Records*, vol. 12, pt. 2, 185; Henderson, vol. 2, 106–07; Porter Alexander, *Military Memoirs*, 182, 185.

5   Lee, 56–58; Freeman, *R.E. Lee*, vol. 2, 259, 328–29.

6   Thomas, 183, 204.

7   George H. Gordon, *The Army of Virginia* (Boston: Houghton, Osgood and Co., 1880), 9. See also Henderson, vol. 2, 115; Dabney, 511.

8   Freeman, *R.E. Lee*, vol. 2, 301–02. See also *Official Records*, vol. 12, pt. 2, 553–54 (Lee's report), 643–44 (Jackson's report); Allan, *Army of Northern Virginia*, 200.

9   Douglas, 136; Freeman, *Lee's Lieutenants*, vol. 2, 100–01.

CHAPTER 5

1   Henderson, vol. 2, 145; Allan, *Army of Northern Virginia*, 231–33; *Official Records*, vol. 12, pt. 2, 337, 360–61. Jackson in his report confirmed this view, writing, "Dispositions were promptly made to attack the enemy, based upon the idea that he would continue to press forward upon the turnpike towards Alexandria." See *Official Records*, vol. 12, pt. 2, 644; Ropes, 75–76.

2   Johnson and Buel, vol. 2, 510.

3   Ropes, 85–86.

CHAPTER 6

1   Johnson and Buel, vol. 2, 549–50.

2   *Official Records*, vol. 19, pt. 2, 600; Freeman, *R.E. Lee*, vol. 2, 358. At the same time, Generals Braxton Bragg and E. Kirby Smith were advancing into Kentucky, giving the impression of Confederate advances on all fronts.

3   *Official Records*, vol. 19, pt. 2, 590; Allan, *Army of Northern Virginia*, 323; Woodworth, 185.

4   Johnson and Buel, vol. 2, 687–88.

5   Ibid., 604–06; *Official Records*, vol. 19, pt. 2, 592; Freeman, *Lee's Lieutenants*, vol. 2, 160 n. 30; *R.E. Lee*, vol. 2, 362.

6   Allan, *Army of Northern Virginia*, 440–41; Freeman, *Lee's Lieutenants*, vol. 2, 715–23. Lee's decision to give battle must have come not when he went into Maryland, but shortly after his conversation with Walker. See *Official Records*, vol. 19, pt. 2, 592; Johnson and Buel, vol. 2, 604–05.

7   Freeman, *Lee's Lieutenants*, vol. 2, 721.

8   Dabney, 548–49.

9   Lee had marched about 53,000 men to Maryland. But only about 45,000, perhaps fewer, were still in the ranks on September 10. See Freeman, *R.E. Lee*, vol. 2, 359, 411; *Official Records*, vol. 19, pt. 2, 639. James Longstreet's estimate is a little higher, saying the army totaled 57,000 men, not counting artillery and cavalry, when it entered Maryland, but lost nearly 20,000 to straggling. See Johnson and Buel, vol. 2, 674; Henderson, vol. 2, 208.

10 Porter Alexander, *Fighting for the Confederacy*, 141. D.H. Hill was extremely sensitive about the lost order, and maintained that it helped Lee, since McClellan thought Longstreet's force was at Boonsboro, not Hagerstown, therefore making him more cautious. See *Southern Historical Society Papers*, vol. 13, 420–21. Lee was convinced the order permitted McClellan to move quickly against him, when without it he would not have done so.

11 *Official Records*, vol. 19, pt. 1, 951; pt. 2, 608; Freeman, *Lee's Lieutenants*, vol. 2, 196; *R.E. Lee*, vol. 2, 375.

CHAPTER 7

1   Lee's letter to Mrs. Jackson is in the one-volume reprint of Henderson's book, *Stonewall Jackson and the American Civil War* (New York: Longmans, Green and Co., 1936, 1937, 1943, 1949), 694–95. Dabney's version is in Dabney, 570.

2   Fuller, 169. Porter Alexander (*Fighting for the Confederacy*, 145–46) wrote that the battle "was the greatest military blunder that General Lee ever made."

3   Porter Alexander, *Fighting for the Confederacy*, 146.

4   *Southern Historical Society Papers*, vol. 8, 528; Freeman, *Lee's Lieutenants*, vol. 2, 209.

5   Farwell, 447.

6   Gordon, 86–87.
7   Johnson and Buel, vol. 2, 684.
8   Henderson, vol. 2, 259–60; Johnson and Buel, vol. 2, 679–80; *Official Records*, vol. 19, pt. 1, 151, 956–57; Freeman, *Lee's Lieutenants*, vol. 2, 242–43.
9   Freeman, *R. E. Lee*, vol. 2, 397.
10 Johnson and Buel, vol. 2, 661–62.
11 *Official Records*, vol. 19, pt. 1, 957–58; Johnson and Buel, vol. 2, 680.

CHAPTER 8

1   *Official Records*, vol. 19, pt. 1, 151, 820; Freeman, *R. E. Lee*, vol. 2, 405; Maurice, 154; Douglas, 179; Woodward, 194; Henderson, vol. 2, 263–67. Looking out on the Union north early on September 18, Jackson asked Longstreet's chief of artillery, Stephen D. Lee: "If I give you fifty guns, can you crush the Federal right?" Stephen Lee responded: "General, it cannot be done with fifty guns and the troops you have here." See ibid., 265.
2   Dabney, 595; Johnson and Buel, vol. 3, 71–72.
3   Dabney, 610; Freeman, *Lee's Lieutenants*, vol. 2, 343, 347, 393–94; Freeman, *R. E. Lee*, vol. 2, 467; *Official Records*, vol. 21, 553, 631–33, 645–46, 653–54, 676; Allan, *Army of Northern Virginia*, 478–79.
4   Cooke, 184; Freeman, *R. E. Lee*, vol. 2, 462.
5   Johnson and Buel, vol. 3, 79; Porter Alexander, *Fighting for the Confederacy*, 169.
6   Johnson and Buel, vol. 3, 98.
7   Freeman, *R. E. Lee*, vol. 2, 468.
8   Freeman, *Lee's Lieutenants*, vol. 2, 378–80; *Southern Historical Society Papers*, vol. 8, 187–88.
9   Freeman, *Lee's Lieutenants*, vol. 2, 385; *Official Records*, vol. 21, 142, 562; Longstreet, 316.

CHAPTER 9

1   Freeman, *R. E. Lee*, vol. 2, 477.
2   Johnson and Buel, vol. 3, 216–17, 239–40; Donald, 411–12.
3   Thomas, 272.
4   This map is reproduced in the *Official Records* atlas as plate CXVI.
5   Porter Alexander, *Fighting for the Confederacy*, 195.
6   Henderson, vol. 2, 417; Bigelow, 223.
7   *Southern Historical Society Papers*, vol. 34, 16–17; Freeman, *R. E. Lee*, vol. 2, 521; *Lee's Lieutenants*, vol. 2, 541; Marshall 163–70.
8   Henderson, vol. 2, 431–32 (Henderson's source was a personal letter from Jedediah Hotchkiss); Bigelow, 272.
9   Johnson and Buel, vol. 3, 198.
10 *Official Records*, vol. 25, pt. 1, 483; Bigelow, 311.
11 Henderson, vol. 2, 449; Freeman, *Lee's Lieutenants*, vol. 2, 564–65; *Southern Historical Society Papers*, vol. 6, 267.
12 Freeman, *R. E. Lee*, vol. 2, 533–35; Bigelow, 342; *Official Records*, vol. 25, pt. 2, 769.
13 Porter Alexander, *Military Memoirs*, 345.
14 Bigelow, 338.
15 The Federals, with 134,000 men at Chancellorsville and Fredericksburg, suffered 17,300 casualties. The Confederates, with about 60,000 troops, lost 12,700. See Hattaway and Jones, 384.
16 Dabney, 723; Henderson, vol. 2, 470; Bigelow, 439. For a full account of Jackson's death and burial, see Dabney, 707–35.
17 Johnson and Buel, vol. 3, 202.

CHAPTER 10

1   Freeman, *R. E. Lee*, vol. 3, 15.
2   Ibid., 34–36; Tucker, 25–26; Thomas, 289.
3   Doubleday, 83.
4   Johnson and Buel, vol. 3, 241 n., 265; David, 438–39; Tucker, 67–68; *Official Records*, vol. 27, pt. 1, 31, 34–35.

⁵ Tucker, 69; *Official Records*, vol. 27, pt. 1, 35.

⁶ *Southern Historical Society Papers*, vol. 4, 157; Tucker, 97–102; Freeman, *R.E. Lee*, vol. 3, 65; *Official Records*, vol. 27, pt. 2, 317, 607, 637.

CHAPTER 11

¹ Longstreet, 357; Freeman, *R.E. Lee*, vol. 3, 67.

² Porter Alexander, *Fighting for the Confederacy*, 232.

³ Freeman, *R.E. Lee*, vol. 3, 72, 75; *Lee's Lieutenants*, vol. 3, 90–99; Douglas, 247; *Southern Historical Society Papers*, vol. 26, 123–24; vol. 33, 144; Gordon, 155–56. A little later, Lee sent Colonel A.L. Long of his staff to reconnoiter the front of Cemetery Hill. Long found the position formidable, strongly occupied, and not easy to strike with artillery fire. He reported back that an attack would be hazardous. See *Southern Historical Society Papers*, vol. 4, 66.

⁴ Porter Alexander, *Fighting for the Confederacy*, 233.

⁵ *Official Records*, vol. 27, pt. 2, 308, 318.

⁶ *Southern Historical Society Papers*, vol. 4, 271ff.; vol. 5, 193, 274; Freeman, *R.E. Lee*, vol. 3, 79–80; Tucker, 211–15.

⁷ Long, 277; Pfanz, *Second Day*, 28–29.

⁸ *Annals of the War*, 439; Tucker, 237.

⁹ Johnson and Buel, vol. 3, 320–21; Pfanz, *Second Day*, 163–65. Hood apparently sent his own scouts out to Round Top, and they reached conclusions similar to those of Law's men.

¹⁰ Hood, 59; Freeman, *Lee's Lieutenants*, vol. 3, 117–22; *Official Records*, vol. 27, pt. 2, 375, 428–29.

¹¹ Johnson and Buel, vol. 3, 322; Porter Alexander, *Fighting for the Confederacy*, 237; Hood, 58–59; Tucker, 246–48.

¹² Pfanz, *Second Day*, 140–44. Meade censured Sickles's decision afterward, setting off a dispute that raged for decades after the war.

¹³ Pfanz, *Second Day*, 223.

¹⁴ Ibid., 212.

¹⁵ Tucker, 260.

¹⁶ Porter Alexander, *Military Memoirs*, 403.

¹⁷ Johnson and Buel, vol. 3, 342–43.

¹⁸ Porter Alexander, *Fighting for the Confederacy*, 251; *Military Memoirs*, 417–18, 426–28; Freeman, *R.E. Lee*, vol. 3, 152–53.

¹⁹ This message from Longstreet and the exchanges following between him and Alexander are from Marion Alexander Boggs's *Alexander Letters* (Boggs, 254–56). The quotes are slightly different from those appearing in Johnson and Buel, vol. 3, 362–64, and in Porter Alexander, *Fighting for the Confederacy*, 254–55, 258–59, and in *Military Memoirs*, 421–23. But, as they are drawn from Alexander's dispatch book, they are more accurate.

²⁰ Johnson and Buel, vol. 3, 363; Porter Alexander, *Fighting for the Confederacy*, 255.

²¹ Johnson and Buel, vol. 3, 364.

²² Ibid., 344–45.

²³ Doubleday, 193.

²⁴ Johnson and Buel, vol. 3, 387–90.

²⁵ Douglas, 212.

²⁶ Tucker, 372.

²⁷ Ibid., 374–75; Carol Reardon, "Pickett's Charge: The Convergence of History and Myth in the Southern Past," in Gallagher, 56–92.

²⁸ Fremantle, 213, 215; Johnson and Buel, vol. 3, 347.

²⁹ Johnson and Buel, vol. 3, 421.

³⁰ Ibid., 349.

CHAPTER 12

¹ *Official Records*, vol. 51, pt. 2, 752–53; vol. 29, pt. 2, 640; Freeman, *R.E. Lee*, vol. 3, 156–58; Thomas, 307–08.

² Long, 311; *Official Records*, vol. 51, pt. 2, 811; Freeman, *R.E. Lee*, vol. 3, 183; Johnson and Buel, vol. 4, 84.

3 Porter Alexander, *Fighting for the Confederacy*, 349.
4 *Official Records*, vol. 36, pt. 1, 133. Porter Alexander, *Military Memoirs*, 508–09, estimated about 14,000 Confederate casualties.
5 Freeman, *Lee's Lieutenants*, vol. 3, 396.
6 Freeman, *R.E. Lee*, vol. 3, 357, 359; *Southern Historical Society Papers*, vol. 14, 535; Porter Alexander, *Military Memoirs*, 532. Of course, Lee was wrong about Jackson: he tried always to avoid frontal attacks.
7 Johnson and Buel, vol. 4, 142.
8 William Swinton, *Campaigns of the Army of the Potomac* (New York: 1866), 487.

CHAPTER 13

1 Basil H. Liddell Hart, *Sherman: Soldier, Realist, American* (New York: Dodd, Mead, 1929), 356; William Tecumseh Sherman, *The Memoirs of General William T. Sherman* (Bloomington: Indiana University Press, 1977), 271.
2 Freeman, *R.E. Lee*, vol. 3, 496 n.
3 Porter Alexander, *Military Memoirs*, 577.
4 Johnson and Buel, vol. 4, 492 n.
5 Ibid., 493.
6 Gordon, 342.
7 *Official Records*, vol. 43, pt. 1, 582; Freeman, *Lee's Lieutenants*, vol. 3, 609.
8 Jubal A. Early, *An Autobiographical Sketch and Narrative of the War Between the States* (Philadelphia, 1912), 452; *Official Records*, vol. 43, pt. 2, 891; Freeman, *Lee's Lieutenants*, vol. 3, 612.
9 Johnson and Buel, vol. 4, 563.
10 Ibid., 553–54.
11 Ibid., 565.
12 Porter Alexander, *Military Memoirs*, 585–86.
13 *Official Records*, vol. 47, pt. 1, 1044; pt. 2, 1238; Freeman, *R.E. Lee*, vol. 4, 4.
14 *Official Records*, vol. 47, pt. 2, 1374; Freeman, *R.E. Lee*, vol. 4, 11.
15 Freeman, *R.E. Lee*, vol. 4, 47.
16 *Official Records*, vol. 46, pt. 3, 1378.

CHAPTER 14

1 Freeman, *Lee's Lieutenants*, vol. 3, 718.
2 Longstreet, 619.
3 Gordon, 438; Long, 421.
4 Long, 421; Freeman, *R.E. Lee*, vol. 4, 120.
5 C.C. Chesney, *Essays in Modern Military Biography* (New York: 1874), 127; Cooke, 461; Freeman, *R.E. Lee*, vol. 4, 121.
6 Longstreet, 625.
7 Porter Alexander, *Military Memoirs*, 604–05.
8 Ibid., 609; Longstreet, 628.
9 Quotations from the meeting at the McLean house and events afterward are drawn from Freeman, *R.E. Lee*, vol. 4, 125–55; *Lee's Lieutenants*, vol. 3, 733–52; *Official Records*, vol. 46, pt. 1, 1266; pt. 3, 664–65; Longstreet, 625–27; Porter Alexander, *Military Memoirs*, 606–14; *Fighting for the Confederacy*, 538–55; Johnson and Buel, vol. 4, 734–47.
10 Johnson and Buel, vol. 4, 745.

INDEX

Note to the reader: Bold page numbers indicate photos and maps.